THE JAPANESE LANGUAGE

Haruhiko Kindaichi

THE
JAPANESE
LANGUAGE

translated and annotated by UMEYO HIRANO

CHARLES E. TUTTLE COMPANY
Rutland · Vermont : Tokyo · Japan

Originally published in Japan as *Nippongo*
by Iwanami Shoten, Tokyo (1957).

Published by the Charles E. Tuttle Company, Inc.
of Rutland, Vermont & Tokyo, Japan
with editorial offices at
2-6 Suido 1-chome, Bunkyo-ku, Tokyo 112

© *1978 by Charles E. Tuttle Publishing Co., Inc.*

Library of Congress Catalog Card No. 77-93226
International Standard Book No. 0-8048-1579-8

First edition, 1978
First Tuttle Book edition, 1988
Seventh printing, 1998

Printed in Singapore

◆ PUBLISHER'S FOREWORD

No one would believe it now, but thirty years ago, the Japanese language was living on borrowed time. In the agonizing national reappraisal that followed defeat in World War II, even the most hallowed national institutions were subjected to keen scrutiny. The language itself was no exception.

Some people—and not just the Americans—blamed the war itself on the formality and complexity of the national idiom. At one time, the occupying authorities seriously considered replacing Japanese with English as the sole official language. And a renowned literary figure of the prewar period proposed the adoption of French.

It was in 1956, barely four years after the end of the occupation, that Haruhiko Kindaichi wrote his classic defense of the national language under the title of *Nippongo*. Rejecting the arguments of those who had predicted linguistic decline or degeneration, he pointed instead to the language's sturdy powers of assimilation. Far from collapsing under a tide of foreign words, Japanese was becoming bolder and more innovative.

Kindaichi was determined to explore all facets of his forbidding subject. To do so, he drew not only on the resources of the literature but also on Japan's numberless dialects and professional jargons, about which he is the acknowledged expert. No one can emerge from this book without a feeling for the richness and complexity of the language spoken today throughout the world by over 100 million Japanese in all fields of human endeavor.

◆ TABLE OF CONTENTS

7

◆ AUTHOR'S PREFACE

Nippongo (The Japanese Language), my earlier book, has been translated and is about to make its appearance before the English-reading public, thanks to the endeavor of Miss Umeyo Hirano. I feel happy about this, perhaps to the point of mild embarrassment, but at the same time I have a vague apprehension as I look back through my original *Nippongo* and find points that I should have revised or wonder if there may be other defects here and there which escaped my notice.

I have looked over Miss Hirano's translation and found that it is a painstaking work, for in my original, especially, there are several places that could easily have been misinterpreted. Up to the present, the Japanese people have not been so strict about errors in their own literary works, but with translations of Western writings into Japanese there has been a disposition that does not allow even a tiny error. I can see now that we should be more broadminded in the future, for not all translators can possibly bring to their works the care and tenacity that is exhibited in this volume.

What Miss Hirano has taken special pains about is the clarification of the notes for each of the sources of material I quoted from other people's works. In my original *Nippongo,* notes were removed one after another at the request of the publisher, who said they made the book hard to read. Some of these notes involved quotations from the lesser magazines, and I cannot begin to imagine how troublesome the search for their exact sources must have been. Indeed, without such diligent labor this translation would perhaps have been completed earlier.

One thing I noticed when I saw this translation was the system of roman letters used to transcribe Japanese words. It is the romanization developed by James Hepburn, who came to Japan in the early Meiji period, and has been used in this book because it is the system most generally used in Japan and abroad. Of course, since it cannot conform exactly to the phonemics of Japanese, there are in Part III, which deals with pronunciation, some descriptions that inevitably deviate somewhat from what I call the orthodox pronunciation. It should be pointed out, too, that though passages from Japanese classics have been romanized according to the same Hepburn system, these readings represent those used by contemporary Japanese when reading such works. The pronunciation prevailing at the time the various classical works were actually written was, of course, different.

There are also places in my original which, if translated simply as they are, would not be easily understood by people unfamiliar with Japanese. At Miss Hirano's request

I have either rewritten such places or given fuller explanations.

I would finally like to express my heartfelt thanks to Miss Hirano, who has exerted untiring efforts in translating my book, and also to the people of the Charles E. Tuttle Company, who made it possible for this book to see the light of day.

—HARUHIKO KINDAICHI

Tokyo, Japan

Note: Throughout the main text, all Japanese proper names are written in the traditional style: family name first, given name last.

◆ TRANSLATOR'S NOTE

This is an English translation of *Nippongo* (The Japanese Language) by Kindaichi Haruhiko, published by Iwanami Shoten in 1957.

When I first read it some years ago, I thought it very interesting and stimulating, for it explains the different aspects of the Japanese language which are intimately connected to the nature of the Japanese people and the country in which they live. For a foreign student of Japanese it will serve as a wonderful guide for solving some of the difficult problems and as a good introduction to Japanese studies. Several years later when I was at Columbia University teaching Japanese and Japanese literature, I realized the value of this book even more keenly, and it was then that I decided to translate it into English.

The book abounds in proper names, historical analogies, literary references, classical quotations, and, above all, book references. Since the book was originally written mainly for the Japanese reader, footnotes and annotations were not necessary. Foreign readers, however, would not be able to sufficiently understand and appreciate the book without them. Hence, the translator has added annotations, mostly in the form of footnotes and supplementary notes at the back, totaling several hundred items.

By its very nature as a work dealing mainly with words and characters, this book contains frequent insertions of romanized Japanese words and phrases. In such cases their English translations appear along with the words and phrases and after the quotations. All sources referred to in the text are listed by publisher and date of publication at the back of the book.

One of the interesting features of the book is the author's use of comparative examples from various languages of the world in discussing the characteristics of Japanese. I sincerely hope that this book will be of interest not only to the student of Japanese language and literature, but also to the general reader with an interest in Japan and the Japanese people.

Finally, I am deeply grateful to Father E. R. Skrzypczak of Sophia University for his valuable advice and to Professor David A. Dilworth of New York State University and Miss Sharon Woods for their assistance in the preparation of this book.

—Umeyo Hirano

THE JAPANESE LANGUAGE

◆ INTRODUCTION

The life of the Japanese language

Soon after World War II, Shiga Naoya wrote an article entitled "Japanese Language Problems" for the magazine *Kaizō* that shocked the Japanese people. The article began with the following words: "Japan has never experienced such hard times as the present. We are ceaselessly buffeted by an angry sea of difficulties." Shiga went on to argue that the Japanese language was the cause of the terrible war and of Japan's present sufferings. He concluded by saying, "Japan might as well, at this juncture, adopt French as her national language."[1]

At that time the Japanese were beginning to lose confidence in all things Japanese. Shiga was a person of stature, referred to as the God of Fiction. Once during the good old days, before Japan dashed into the doomed war, Shiga appeared in a newsreel, and a literary-mad youth blurted out spontaneously, "Hats off to Shiga Naoya!"

What Shiga said about adopting French was, of course, whimsical, but it nevertheless reflected a widespread feeling that the Japanese language had suddenly lost its vitality. There were even some people who had the illusion that in ten years' time the Japanese language would be prohibited in the elementary schools and parents would be listening with sad resignation to the fluent English of their children.

Now, thirty years after the war, the Japanese language is as vital as ever. The voices that advocated the adoption of French have disappeared, leaving only a subject of reminiscence. This is as it should be—the language of a whole people does not disappear so easily.

It was in the 16th century that the Spaniards came to the Philippine Islands. At the end of the 19th century, America displaced Spain as the dominant power there. Thus, until their acquisition of independence in 1932, the Filipinos were under Western control for a total of four hundred years. But after regaining their independence, they found no obstacles to adopting the Philippine language as their national language, for the Filipinos had not forgotten their language during those four hundred years of foreign rule.

There is a tribe of people called Lati in the mountainous region deep in the Yunnan province of China. It is said that they are a community of only four hundred people. The Lati language which these people speak is even purer than modern Japanese and does not seem to have been influenced by surrounding languages.[2]

There was no reason why the language of close to 100 million Japanese should disappear just because they were under the influence of the United States for a period of only five or ten years. It seems the Japanese and their language are bound to be inseparable for a long time to come. If so, we Japanese cannot help being greatly concerned about our language: What kind of language it is; whether it is a superior or an inferior language; what its strong points are; and how its weak points can be overcome.

I intend to discuss in this book "the nature of the Japanese language" in the terms stated above, or, to use a more ambitious expression, "the characteristics of the Japanese language."

Evaluation of the language

Various evaluations of the Japanese language have been made. The view of the poet Hagiwara Sakutarō (1886–1942) can be taken as a representative opinion:

> When Japanese is compared with other languages (especially Occidental languages), its conspicuous defects are, first, its lack of logicality and of precision of meaning, and second, its weakness in rhythmical quality and its monotony of auditory impression.[3]

However, if we turn this statement around, we can say as England's W. M. McGovern has said, "Japanese is flowing and melodious,"[4] and as Okazaki Yoshie, authority on Japanese literary arts, says, "Its simple construction permits it to embrace complicated flavors and relationships."[5]

But the most frequent criticisms of Japanese have been directed at its difficulty.

In 1942, at the beginning of World War II, when the Japanese people were in high spirits, the Japanese language spread east and west with its advancing army. Japanese was taught to foreigners in the scorching southern islands and in the frigid northern regions. *Kokugo Bunka Kōza,* Volume 6, entitled "The Japanese Language Expansion," was edited at that time. It was expected that Japanese would naturally be admired as an ideal language. However, Shimomura Hiroshi, who played a leading part in the overseas expansion of Japanese culture at the time, said the following at the beginning of the book:

> The Japanese language is making great advances abroad, following the expansion of the nation. Although this is the natural result of the advance of the Japanese nation, it is for that reason that I hope the Japanese language will become clearer and more accurate. I keenly feel that it is exceedingly disorderly at the present time. Indeed, Japanese speech and the characters that express it are extremely irregular and complicated. Recently at a university in Berlin, a course in Japanese was given for two academic years, but, by the time they had graduated, the students, who numbered thirty at first, had decreased to one-tenth that number. Likewise, it is said that at Helsinki University in Finland, the more than twenty students who enrolled for the Japanese course when it was first given had gradually decreased until not one was left at the end of the third year.[6]

We cannot say that Japanese is truly difficult just because it is difficult to teach to foreigners. In Europe, the Basque language is generally acknowledged to be difficult. It is the language of a small nation lying on the boundary between France and Spain. Legend has it that God, in punishing the Devil for the crime of tempting Eve, sent him away to the Basques with the command to master their language. After seven years, God, repentant for having dealt so severe a punishment, pardoned the Devil and called him back. The Devil rejoiced and immediately set out for home. The moment he crossed a certain bridge at the border, he completely forgot all of the Basque words which he had learned in seven years.[7]

The reason for the difficulty of the Basque language for neighboring peoples is that it is far removed from other European languages. The real difficulty of Basque, therefore, must be discounted. Likewise, we cannot say that Japanese is truly difficult if it is difficult only for foreigners.

The Japanese language, however, seems to be difficult not only for foreigners but also for the Japanese themselves. European children generally learn how to read and write their own language in two years in Italy, three years in Germany, and in Great Britain, where it takes longest, five years. In Japan, even after six years in elementary school and three years in junior high school, a pupil cannot adequately understand the newspaper. It is common knowledge that even after finishing senior high school, students cannot use the *kana* syllabaries* and *kanji* (Chinese characters) correctly when writing.

Kana: two syllabic alphabets. *Katakana* is angular, and *hiragana* is curviform.

After the war it was argued that one of the causes of Japan's defeat was the intricacy of the Japanese language. Commander Spruance, who took Japan's combined squadron by surprise in the Battle of Midway, is said to have acknowledged: "As Japanese is a language that lacks clarity, I thought confusion would surely arise in the transmission of instantaneous command, so I made a surprise attack."[8] An *Asahi* newspaper correspondent who collected data on the International Military Tribunal said: "Hearing the speeches in Japanese by Japan's defense counsel and those in foreign languages in the same setting, I was left with the disagreeable but distinct impression that Japanese is no match for foreign languages."

We have to recognize that Japanese is difficult, but we need not lament that we are burdened with a troublesome language. A language is something created. Present-day German and French both have a great many created elements.

Our predecessors have endeavored to reform the Japanese language. The establishment of many Japanese equivalents to foreign words at the beginning of the Meiji period (1868–1912) is a conspicuous example. Although this has, in some respects, led to difficulty in understanding Japanese, we have to recognize its merit in changing medieval Japanese into modern Japanese. When Ogata Tomio, a medical doctor, went to India and was asked by a professor of medicine at an Indian university, "In what language is medicine taught in Japan?" Ogata wondered what the professor was trying to say. He finally realized he was being asked, "Is medicine taught in English or in Japanese?"[9] We may think that this was a very odd question, but during the Meiji period such ideas were common among the Japanese themselves. Until Fukuzawa Yukichi's first speech in Japanese, it had been generally thought that one could not even make speeches in Japanese.[10] Today, however, Japanese can hold its own among present world civilizations. Ogata says: "People say again and again that Japanese is imperfect, but it is fortunate, at any rate, that science can be handled quite accurately in Japanese."

After the war, a series of language reform policies were put into practice, such as the establishment of the Tōyō Kanji* and the revision of the use of *kana*. These reforms were made possible through the efforts of the People's Federation of the Japanese Language Movement organized under Yamamoto Yūzō,[11] the major driving force, and the Ministry of Education's Japanese Language Section, the executive organ led by Kugimoto Hisaharu. All these reforms properly aimed at the simplification of Japanese. It is fitting that we, too, search out the areas where our language is deficient and devise possible means to correct them.

Characteristics of Japanese

Clear establishment of the nature of the Japanese language is essential to its improvement and will make for other benefits as well.

Soon after the war, San'yūtei Kashō, a *rakugo* storyteller, was run over by an American jeep and died. A Japanese

*The 1,850 *kanji* officially selected for daily use in 1946.

reported this to an American in English, translating word for word the Japanese *jidōsha ni butsukatte* as "by running into the car." That made the American stare in amazement and say, "Why would the man do such a stupid thing?" It is natural that he should ask such a question, for actually the jeep collided with Kashō, and not Kashō with the jeep. But in Japanese we use the same form, "Kashō ran into the jeep," to describe both situations. This shows how English can be misused due to ignorance of the peculiarities of Japanese expressions. Thus, it is also desirable for us to understand the characteristics of Japanese in order to correctly translate Japanese into other languages.

This knowledge of Japanese is also necessary in teaching Japanese to foreigners. Furthermore, one must not disregard the peculiarities of Japanese in applying educational theories written in foreign languages to Japanese schools.

Again, a firm grasp of the characteristics of Japanese is important in discussing the genealogy and history of Japanese. Since Yasuda Tokutarō's book *Man'yōshū no Nazo* (The Riddle of the Man'yōshū)[12] raised the question of the relationship between the Japanese language and the language of a small race of people called the Lepcha at the foot of the Himalayas, the problems of the outstanding characteristics and, especially, the lineage of Japanese, have been much discussed. The characteristics of the Tibeto-Burman languages, including the Lepcha language, are similar to Japanese in various aspects, and therefore cannot be disregarded when one discusses the lineage of Japanese. In present-day Japanese, there are the following two types of characteristics: (1) those transmitted from the ancestor language before it split into other languages, and (2) those formed under the influence of other languages after the separation of Japanese from the ancestor language and its establishment as the Japanese language. If there is a language whose inherited characteristics resemble those of the Japanese language, that language must belong to the same lineage. If this is so, through which aspects of Japanese will the character of the ancestral language be conveyed? Generally speaking, when a language changes with the times, the sound changes least, and grammar only slightly more. This is an established theory in linguistics. Thus, the aspect that retains the ancestor's traces longest is, first, the sound system, and second, the grammar. What, then, are the peculiarities of the Japanese sound system and grammar, and what languages do they resemble?

The significance of clarifying the nature of Japanese is not limited to these points. In cultural anthropology, speech is called "the vehicle of culture," and the words of a language in particular are called "the index of culture."[13] This shows that language can be looked upon as a reflection of culture and not simply as a tool for the transmission of thought. In other words, the clarification of the Japanese language—especially its vocabulary and the characteristics of its expressions—will surely be helpful in any reconsideration of the life and way of thinking of the Japanese people.

日本語

THE POSITION OF
JAPANESE

◆

PART

I

◆ 1. AN ISOLATED LANGUAGE

What are the characteristics of the Japanese language? In thinking about this question, I would like first of all to consider the language as a whole, as "a system of signs," without breaking it into components such as pronunciation or vocabulary. There are two kinds of characteristics: those found when comparing Japanese with other languages, and those found when looking at the construction of the Japanese language itself, as something apart from other languages.

Origin

The Japanese language has a unique position among the languages of civilized countries. That is, there is absolutely no other language of a similar nature. This characteristic catches our eye when we compare Japanese with the languages of the world.

In the middle of the Meiji period when Western linguistics was introduced to Japan, the lineage of Japanese became a subject of much discussion. The Japanese language was said to be related to almost every known language, including: the language of the Ryūkyū Islands (B. H. Chamberlain and others), Ainu (J. Batchelor), Korean (W. G. Aston, Kanazawa Shōzaburō, and others), Chinese (Matsumura Ninzō), Tibeto-Burman (C. K. Parker), Ural-Altaic (H. J. Klaproth and others), Altaic (G. L. Ramstedt, Fujioka Katsuji, Hattori Shirō), Uralian (Izui Hisanosuke), the Mon-Khmer languages (Matsumoto

Nobuhiro), and Malayo-Polynesian (V. H. Lablerton). There were even some who linked Japanese with the Indo-Germanic languages (Taguchi Ukichi), and with Greek (Kimura Takatarō). And, as mentioned above, Yasuda Tokutarō thought Japanese to be from the same linguistic family as the language of the Lepcha people in the Himalayas.

Hattori Shirō[1] says that no other language has been the subject of so many attempts to link it with other languages. This is particularly noteworthy, for it really signifies that Japanese cannot be conclusively linked with any particular language. In fact, of the many languages given above, the Ryūkyū language is the only one that has been proven scientifically to belong to the same family as Japanese. There are some, including Tōjō Misao, the foster parent of Japanese dialectology, who are of the opinion that the Ryūkyū language is so similar to Japanese that it is in fact a dialect of Japanese. Next to the Ryūkyū language comes Korean, but it hardly fills the bill. Shimmura Izuru's[a] theory, that a dialect akin to Japanese must have existed in ancient Korea, attracted considerable attention. His theory is based on a study of Korean place names and numerals that appear in the chapter entitled "Geography" in *Sangokushiki* (The History of the Three Kingdoms), but as there were few examples it is difficult to form a definite opinion. Though the view that Japanese belongs to the Altaic languages, including Korean, has the support of a number of prominent linguists and is most influential, it is still very far from being proved. Hence, we cannot ignore the theory advocated by Shiratori Kurakichi that Japanese is an isolated language.

Originality

In his book *Kokugo Kenkyūhō* (The Methods of Research into the Japanese Language),[3] Tokieda Motoki writes that once while he was lodging at an inn in Paris, his French landlady and a Spanish lodger were engaged in a conversation. He overheard them say that they could understand each other when one spoke Spanish and the other Italian, but not when one of them spoke French. In short, people who had nothing to do with philology were discussing problems like "The Relation between the Romance Languages" in daily conversation.

This is an interesting story. When a Japanese hears Korean or Chinese, he thinks how entirely different it is from Japanese. In Europe, however, the degree of difference between languages can generally be illustrated as follows: one person speaks Swedish, one Danish, and another Norwegian, and yet they all understand one another. The Japanese equivalent might be a conversation among three people, one speaking the Tōkyō dialect, one the Ōsaka dialect, and the third the Yamaguchi dialect. When one hears about Russian, Serbian, Czech, and Polish, he imagines that they are quite different languages, recalling the complicated colored maps of Europe. It is astonishing, however, to find that people from these countries can understand one another even when each uses his native tongue. For example "good evening" is *dobry vyecher'* in Russian, *dobry wieczór'* in Polish, *dobrý večer'* in Czech, and *dobra večer* in Serbo-Croatian. Indeed, if this is all the difference there is, it is not hard to believe that they can understand one another.

Hearing the term Indo-European comparative philology, most Japanese think of something terribly esoteric that a scholar studies up in his ivory tower, his face screwed up in a look of intense concentration. Although this notion is probably not true of Indo-European philology, which has its origins in very simple and common facts, it is, I think, a fair characterization of Japanese philology. When Western philology was introduced into Japan in the middle of the Meiji period, the lineage of the Japanese language became a subject of much discussion, and it was thought that failure to produce a conclusive answer would bring disgrace to Japanese scholarship. However, try as they would, Japanese philologists could not establish a clear-cut relationship between Japanese and any other language. It is now obvious that, unlike the European languages, Japanese cannot be easily linked with any family of languages, and it will only be after the continuous efforts of many scholars that the question of the origin of the Japanese language is answered, if it ever is. It is definitely not the type of problem that can be suddenly solved by the novel theory of some ambitious scholar. The Basque language mentioned above, the Caucasian language at the foot of the Caucasus, Burushaski in northwest India, the language spoken in the Andaman Islands in the Indian Ocean, Lati mentioned above, Ainu of Hokkaidō, and Gilyak, spoken in some parts of Sakhalin, have all been left behind in the course of world progress. Together with these languages, the Japanese language seems like a one-man party occupying a lonely corner of an assembly hall. Such an isolated condition is something very rare for the language of a civilized people.

Role of isolation

What influence does the isolation of their language have on the Japanese people? On the plus side, it was thought during World War II that the enemy, owing to language difficulties, would be hindered in gathering intelligence. After the war, however, it was found that this was not the case at all. From the standpoint of national defense, isolation does not seem to have been of much help.

There are a great many entries on the minus side. The fact that Japanese differs greatly from the languages of highly civilized countries like England, Germany, and France has put Japan at a disadvantage in various ways. It is well known how difficult it is for a Japanese to master the languages of these nations. Even though he studies English in high school eight hours each week for five years, he is barely able to read the labels on canned goods. Of course, foreigners who wish to learn Japanese and study Japanese culture are also confronted with tremendous obstacles. Some time ago there was a newspaper article about some foreign students from Southeast Asia who complained that although they had come all the way to Japan to study modern technology, they were frustrated by the difficulty of the Japanese language. Similarly, in the field of literature, it is a pity that the numerous outstanding Japanese works cannot be more widely appreciated by the people of other countries.

Recently, international conferences on physics and genetics were held in Japan. According to some Japanese scholars who attended, while they welcomed scholarly authorities from distant lands, as soon as technical discussions started, language immediately became such a barrier that they could not help feeling a little frustrated. Some years ago when the American film *The Moon Is Blue* was produced, separate sound recordings were made in German, French, and Italian while the film was still being made, so that the movie could be shown immediately in those countries. But the Japanese had to resort to subtitles, which marred the film's visual effect.[4]

According to engineer Seki Hideo, a translation machine was devised sometime ago in the United States. When an English sentence such as "I love you" is typed into the machine, sentences like *Ich liebe dich* or *Je t'aime* come out. But a great deal of time and money will be needed to make a machine that can translate into Japanese, because Japanese sentence structure is entirely different from that of European languages.[5]

◆ 2. CONTACT WITH OTHER LANGUAGES

Linguistic isolation

Another point we notice about Japanese when it is compared to other languages is that it has very little direct contact with them. In other words, the region where Japanese is spoken is completely different from the regions where other languages are spoken. To be more specific, very few Japanese people speak languages other than Japanese.

It is said that Queen Cleopatra of ancient Egypt used eight different languages to entertain state guests, and President Tito of Yugoslavia reportedly speaks seven languages. Japanese are struck with admiration when they hear such stories. In such small countries in Europe as Switzerland, it is very common to hear people speaking two or three different languages. Father W. A. Grotaas, a scholar in Eastern languages residing in Japan, says that during the annual national census in his homeland Belgium, there is an accompanying questionnaire asking what languages a person can speak. There are very few people in Japan who speak any language besides Japanese, perhaps one in ten or twenty thousand. This does not necessarily apply only to Japan. There must be exceedingly few people in the world who can speak Japanese in addition to other languages. They are chiefly those who live in Korea, Taiwan, Brazil, and Hawaii. In Japan, a person like Hattori Shirō, who can speak more than ten languages, is called a linguistic genius. Such a person is an exception among exceptions.

In brief, Japanese occupies a clearly defined linguistic region, and within that sphere functions in good order—a characteristic that should not be overlooked.

"Degeneration" of the language

Since Japanese functions with hardly any contact with other languages, one would expect it to possess special characteristics. Theoretically, one would suppose Japanese to receive little influence from and assert little influence on other languages. At present, many so-called intellectuals and cultured people take every opportunity to complain that Japanese has degenerated. They worry as if the Japanese people would perish unless urgent measures were taken. But their fears are, as they were from the start, quite unnecessary, for Japanese is not so easily influenced. Actually, a careful look reveals more instances of firmness than frailty.

For example, the word "Christmas" was introduced from English. The Japanese write it *kurisumasu* in *katakana* and use it that way. There are people who say that *kurisumasu* is a foreign word, but those very people pronounce it *ku-ri-su-ma-su*, inserting three *u*'s which are not in the English word at all. Far from speaking English, they are pronouncing a word changed to conform to Japanese standards of pronunciation. The power of assimilation exhibited here is astonishing. Linguist Shibata Takeshi hopes that Japanese will eventually change its sound system under the increased influence of Western words,[1] but his expectation seems unlikely to be realized.

According to American linguist Mario Pei, the natives

of Hawaii cannot pronounce the sound *s* or the consonants by themselves without attaching vowels to them. So when they want to say, "Christmas in December," they say *kekemapa kalikimaka*.[2] It is surprising to learn that *kekemapa* is an imitation of "December," and *kalikimaka* of "Christmas." However, an American would likely find little difference between the Japanese *kurisumasu* with three *u*'s and the Hawaiian *kalikimaka*.

Before the war, when there were a great many Japanese in Manchuria, it is said that when a wife of a Japanese official wanted to buy some vegetables from a Chinese grocer, she would say something like the following:

> *Nide tōfu to iiyande shōshō katai katai, meiyō?*
> Don't you have the thing that looks like *tōfu* (beancurd) but is a little harder? (She is asking for *konnyaku*, a starchy, jelly food. *Nide, iiyande, meiyō* are Japanized Chinese words.)

> *Nide chaga daikon naka tonneru yōde. Pūshin.*
> This radish is hard and fibrous and not good, so make it cheaper. (*Nide, chaga, yōde, pūshin* are Japanized Chinese.)[3]

If people carried on conversations like this one everywhere in Japan, both the Japanese and Chinese languages would go to ruin. Or if all the Japanese were like the Japanese in Hawaii, most of whom are able to use both Japanese and English, Japanese would surely be greatly influenced by English. But actually Japanese is not. In fact we can say that most languages of the world other than Japanese are in a far more unstable condition.

Ogata Tomio articulated the following point in a round-table discussion, and I think it is worth heeding.

> The disorderly state of languages is common all over the world. The United States is very much concerned about it, saying it envies England. But the English, too, say their language is in disorder. It's really a common problem everywhere.[4]

The Japanese language is said to be in disorder, but unlike many languages this state of disorderliness came from within. This problem will be discussed in the next chapter.

Influence from foreign languages

The Japanese language has had little contact with other languages because the people did not move after they had migrated to the Japanese islands and, until the last war, had not been invaded by other peoples. Consequently, it is quite natural that Japanese was not influenced by other languages. It should be noted that only in its contact with Chinese did Japanese receive a great influence—especially on its vocabulary. However, it should be kept in mind that this direct influence from Chinese occurred hundreds of years ago, and that there has been no such influence since.

We can divide the Japanese vocabulary which we use today into Yamato words; *jiongo* or Chinese character words; Western words; and the compounds of and words transformed from these words. Western words have been introduced chiefly from Europe since the 17th century and are commonly written in *katakana*. Chinese character words are those introduced directly or indirectly from China since the introduction of Chinese culture in ancient times, or are words contrived in Japan through imitation. Chinese character words are commonly written in *kanji* (Chinese characters). Yamato words are either words that existed before other word-types had entered Japan, or else words subsequently based on them. Chinese character words represent sixty to seventy percent of the total vocabulary, according to the *Dainihon Kokugo Jiten* (The Large Japanese Dictionary).[5] Hayashi Ōki, a Japanese linguist, says that if nouns and verbs appearing in the newspapers were statistically analyzed, more than forty percent would be Chinese character words[6]—a noteworthy figure. In this sense we may say that Japanese is a language with a great many words of foreign origin.

In this respect Japanese contrasts with Chinese, German, and French, which have few words of foreign origin. The following languages are said to be rich in words of foreign origin: English (from French and other languages), Korean (from Chinese), Vietnamese (Chinese), Thai (Indian), Persian (Arabian), and Turkish (Arabian and Iranian).

Why did Japanese adopt many foreign words? Umegaki Minoru, an authority on words of foreign origin, gives the following reasons:

(1) There was a propensity in the Japanese character to adopt foreign culture.

(2) The Japanese language has qualities that facilitate adopting foreign words. For example, the lack of inflection in nouns.

(3) When Japan adopted Chinese characters (for Japan did not possess its own writing system), Chinese terms naturally entered the language.

(4) As foreign culture was more advanced than Japanese culture, the people felt loan words superior to indigenous terms.

Chinese character words—merits and demerits

At any rate, Japanese was greatly influenced by Chinese in the past. As a result, a large number of Chinese character words and similar character words coined in Japan have entered the vocabulary. This phenomenon parallels the pervasive influence of ancient Chinese culture on the lives of the Japanese.

In what ways did Japanese change with the introduction of Chinese vocabulary?

In the first place, it became possible to express abstract ideas which had been hitherto inexpressible. "Loyalty" 忠, "filial piety" 孝, and "humanity and justice" 仁義 are representative examples. This was a thing to be grateful for.

In the second place, expressions which had once necessitated many Yamato words became short and crisp. For example, before the introduction of Chinese character words, the Japanese expression for eleven was *towo amari fitotu* (one more than ten) and for twelve it was *towo amari futatu* (two more than ten). These became *jūichi* and *jūni*.

When such words as *i* (stomach), *chō* (intestines), and *kakuran* (cholera) were first introduced, the Japanese translated them as: *monohami* (food container) for stomach; *kuso bukuro* (a bag for excrement) for intestines; and *kuchi yori shiri yori koku yamai* (a disease that breaks through mouth and bottom) for cholera. All these can be found in the Chinese-character dictionary of the Heian period (794–1160), *Ruiju Myōgishō*.[7] The Japanese translations of these words, however, failed to gain popular usage. For one thing, people felt that medical expressions should be foreign and important-looking. But more than that, it was probably because Yamato words were long and cumbersome.

This reasoning can also be applied to the great number of Chinese character words coined as translations for European words in the Meiji period. For instance, some poets referred to *tetsudō* (railroad) as *kurogane no michi* (a road of black iron) and *denshin* (telegram) as *harigane dayori* (communication through wire), each of which was quite a mouthful. In this respect, too, we are grateful for Chinese character words.

In the third place, the Chinese character word strongly influenced Japanese through its own characteristic sound system. Literary critic Kamei Katsuichirō (1907–66) says, quoting from Hagiwara Sakutarō's writings:

> Although the Yamato words are exceedingly elegant, they are too weak to express strong emotions like anger, distress, and jealousy. The Yamato words lack elements that express such accents, but a strong emphasis can be attained by using Chinese character words. Through the simplicity and strength of these words, we can express human emotions effectively.[8]

The Chinese character word has thus contributed to the development of the Japanese language. On the debit side, however, it has unfortunately encouraged the proliferation of homonyms and the creation of expressions that need to be seen in their written forms to be understood. Sweden's Bernhard Karlgren, a Chinese linguist, talks about the strange fact that since homonyms abound in Chinese, sometimes one cannot make himself understood orally and must write out the words. This is all the more true with Japanese. The following exchange is not a mere creation by a novelist, but a typical example of what happens every day in the life of a Japanese:

> Son: Father, to you a love affair is only a kind of *shūkō* (disgraceful conduct), isn't it?
> Father: *Shūkō?*
> Son: *Shū* as in *shūaku* (ugliness).[9]

Furthermore, Chinese character words entered Japan where Yamato words had already existed, so an enormous number of synonyms developed. Hayashi Ōki counts this richness a special feature of Japanese. Indeed, we have Yamato synonyms for Chinese character words—exceedingly formal words—such as *kyō* for *konnichi* (today), *asu* for *myōnichi* (tomorrow), and *asatte* for *myōgonichi* (day after tomorrow). This phenomenon has become a burden to the memory. Okamoto Chimatarō gives examples such as the above in his book *Nihongo no Hihanteki Kōsatsu* (A Critical Study of Japanese), and says, "Is this richness really something we can boast of, or something to regret because of the double and triple burdens it imposes on us? At any rate we hope they can be put in better order by reducing their number."[10]

It should also be noted that of the two, Yamato words and Chinese character words, the latter more frequently have favorable connotations and give pleasing impressions. Thus, a barber (*tokoya san*) is not satisfied if he is not called a *rihatsugyō* (hairdresser), and when we go to a department store and ask, "Where are the *omocha* (toys) sold?" the clerk might respond, "Do you mean the *gangu* (plaything) department?"

The following *senryū* (satirical verse)* illustrates the point:

Shitsunen to	It sounds better
ieba kikiyoi	To say "lapse of memory"
monowasure.	Rather than "forgetfulness."

There are many other similar verses:

Sakkaku to	It sounds better
ieba kikiyoi	To say "an erroneous perception"
kanchigai.	Rather than "a misunderstanding."

Such depreciation of Yamato words has been foolish.

Moreover, when the Chinese character words displaced Yamato words, it was not done thoroughly, so in some cases the sphere of influence is divided. On the whole, this has resulted in an asymmetric system. For example, in counting persons we say *hitori* (one person), *futari* (two persons), *sannin* (three persons), *yottari* or *yonin* (four persons), *gonin* (five persons). Likewise, in counting days we

*Seventeen-syllable form, the same as *haiku*.

say *ichinichi* (one day), *futsuka* (two days), and *mikka* (three days).* I think it would be better to reserve the Yamato words *hitori* and *futari* for special cases such as "bachelorhood" or "a young couple" respectively, and to use the Chinese character words for numerals in general.

Originally the *ren'yō* (continuative) form† of verbs of Yamato words could form nouns, but the introduction of Chinese character words nipped this development in the bud. Linguist Izui Hisanosuke says: "The noun form for the verb *kuu* (to eat) or *taberu* (to eat) is now usually *shokuji* and that for *yomu* (to read) is usually *tokusho* or *etsudoku*."

Several years ago, when I took part in the editing of NHK's *Nango Iikae Shū* (Anthology of Simplified Terms for Difficult Words), the chairman asked, "How can we say *insotsu* (to lead a party) in some other way?" I said, "*Tsurete aruku* will be all right, won't it?" "No, I mean the noun *insotsu*," he said. I was at a loss for an answer as it would not look right to say *tsurete aruki*‡ (taking along). It seems we cannot avoid retaining the word *insotsu* after all. *Insotsu-sha* (the person who leads a party of people), also seems to have no counterpart in Yamato words.

Chinese character words— what shall we do with them?

One of the fascinating things about Chinese character

Hitori, futari, yottari, futsuka, and *mikka* are Yamato words. *Sannin, yonin, gonin,* and *ichinichi* are Chinese character words.

†A form linked to verbs and adjectives, e.g., *sakichiru* (bloomingly fall), in which *saki* is the *ren'yō* form of *saku* (to bloom) and modifies *chiru* (to fall).

‡This is the *ren'yō* form of *tsurete-aruku* (to take along) and was used as a noun equivalent in ancient times.

words is that they offer the possibility of combining a number of word roots to form innumerable new words. Sports editors create baseball terms like *kaishō* (an outstanding victory), *rakushō* (an easy victory), *shinshō* (a narrow victory), *sampai* (a crushing defeat), and *sekihai* (a regrettable defeat). To describe the pitching, they have created such words as *kōkyū* (a good pitch), *akkyū* (a wild pitch), *kantō* (pitching the whole game), and *shittō* (a bad pitch). Recently such expressions as *zekkōkyū* (a great pitch) and *myōtō* (a fine pitch) have appeared. The remarkable thing is that people understand the meaning if they see the written characters. We combine *shōgakkō* (elementary school) and *chūgakkō* (middle school) and call this *shō-chūgakkō*, and when we want to express the plural of *kikan* (organs), we say *shokikan*. Such tricks as these are possible only with Chinese character words.

In short, Chinese character words have many good points, and it would be unwise policy to heedlessly decrease them. Then, what measures should we take?

The first thing that recommends itself is the borrowing of Western words without translating them one by one into Chinese character words. Many people of nationalistic persuasion would object to such a policy. However, although we say we are borrowing foreign words, we have always first Japanized the words thoroughly. When the Japanese say *rajio* for the English word "radio," the word they are using is something quite different from the original. It is no longer English or any other language; it is genuine Japanese.

Secondly, we must get rid of the idea that names of things should look important. You go to a library, for example. You are given a card called *etsuran-hyō* (a perusal slip) at the entrance. On it you write your name and the name of the book you want to read, and take it to the *etsuran-gakari* (perusal clerk). The books you borrowed are to be taken to the room called *etsuran-shitsu* (reading room), where you read. There may be some charm in the difficult word *etsuran*, but we can easily say *tokusho-shitsu* (reading room) for *etsuran-shitsu*. As *etsuran-gakari* refers to someone who does not actually do the reading himself, this name is awkward. It had better be changed to *kashidashi-gakari* (a lending clerk). *Etsuran-hyō* can be changed to *mōshikomi-hyō* (application slip) or it can simply be called *kādo* (card), for no other card is used in the library. If this can be done, there will be no need to use the difficult Chinese character word *etsuran*. Ridiculously enough, the use of Chinese character words up to now reveals the feeling in Japan that names should look difficult and important.

What we call *mugen-kidō* (endless track; a Chinese character word) in Japanese is *Raupenkette* in German, which, if translated literally, means *imomushi-gusari* (caterpillar chain; a Yamato word). The coiner of *mugen-kidō* will probably not be satisfied if we use the term *imomushi-gusari*. We do not expect to go so far, but we would like to coin new words with popular connotations in the same spirit. As Kuwabara Takeo[11] has said, it is better to call a thermometer a *netsu-hakari* (a measure for fever) than *ken'onki* (temperature-detecting instrument), for the former, composed of Yamato words, is more simple, homely, and easy to understand than the latter, which is composed of stiff Chinese characters which are difficult to comprehend unless you see them written. And, for the same reason, *tō-*

megane (literally, distance-viewing glasses) is a better term for binoculars than *sōgankyō*.

Thirdly, in order to avoid the disadvantages of Chinese character words, those composed of two characters should, after careful selection, be treated as words understandable on the same level as Yamato words. On the other hand, the formation of new words by combining two one-character words should be avoided as much as possible. In the library there is a catalogue called *kemmei mokuroku* (item-name catalogue). The word *kemmei* is hard to understand. Kanda Hideo, director of Ueno Library, says he wants to change it to *shudai-betsu mokuroku* (catalogue classified by subjects). I agree with him—that would be easier to understand.

The reason why character words are often hard to understand is that new words are formed by indiscriminately combining two one-character words. The word *shūkō* noted above is an example. Therefore, with the exception of words often used as prefixes and suffixes, we should avoid the creation of new words as much as possible. And even those which are used as prefixes and suffixes should be reduced. For example, the sound *sho*, as a prefix, stands for "many" 諸, "first" 初, and "the fact" 所. It is best to retain only the meaning "many" and stop using the other meanings. The word *shoshin* 所信 (one's belief) with the prefix *sho* 所 can be replaced by *shin-nen* 信念, and similarly, we can replace the word *shokan* 所感 (one's impression) with *kansō* 感想. *Shotaimen* 初対面 (the first meeting) and *shonanoka* 初七日 (the seventh day after a person's death) could be read *hatsu-taimen* and *hatsu-nanoka* respectively. If this is done, one will immediately understand upon hearing *sho* . . . that it is a plural of something. Thus, it will be very convenient. Even in this case, we should try as much as possible to put the prefix *sho* on the character words already in existence. Among the character words in Japanese, we find a large number of words that require three or four *kana* for transcription. No wonder there are so many words of the same sound. The proposals I have stated here—(1) to stop making new words by combining single-character words, (2) to retain only a few prefix-like words, and to attach these only to the already existing unmistakable character words —will be helpful in overcoming the difficulty.

The influence of Japanese on foreign languages

As stated above, the Japanese language has been greatly influenced by a foreign language, that is, Chinese. But the influence exerted on other languages by Japanese has been exceedingly slight—something rare in the language of a civilized country. H. G. Wells says: ". . . her secluded civilization has not contributed very largely to the general shaping of human destinies; she has received much, but she has given little."[12] The Japanese language, too, though it has received many loanwords from all over the world, has made few contributions to other languages.

According to Ichikawa Sanki, Japanese loanwords in European languages are "bonze," "inro," "fune," "rickshaw," "kimono," "soy," "bushido," "harakiri," "geisha," "Korea" (from Kōrai), "moxa," "tenno," "judo," and others, which are mostly names of social structures peculiar to Japan or of things related to the unique arts and customs of Japan. "Kimonoed" means to be dressed in a kimono—

thus, "kimono" can also be used as a verb. Perhaps these are the most common Japanese loanwords.

During the U.S. occupation of Japan a great many Japanese words were picked up by the Americans. In the new-words section of the *New Webster's Dictionary*, I note the addition of "nisei," "kamikaze," "zaibatsu," and "geta." They are all words related to Japanese culture.

It is the language of our northern neighbor, Ainu, that has been influenced most by the Japanese language, followed by the languages of our western and southern neighbors, namely, the indigenous inhabitants of Taiwan, the Koreans, and the Chinese.

Ainu essentially has strong verb inflection according to person. For example, different forms of verbs are used in the sentences "I catch a bear" and "He catches a bear." Japanese verbs do not make such changes. Thus, when first speaking Ainu, the Japanese used Ainu forms for person so poorly that it is said that part of the Ainu verb inflection has been lost.[13] Moreover it is said that Ainu is not only becoming Japanized but the entire language is perishing under the weight of Japanese. This is perhaps an example of the greatest influence Japanese has had on another language.

Both Korean and the language of the indigenous peoples of Taiwan have borrowed many Japanese cultural terms. Ogura Shimpei has listed examples of Yamato loanwords in his book, *Chōsengo Hōgen no Kenkyū* (A Study of Korean Dialects).[14] According to Ōkubo Tadatoshi, a linguistic psychologist, the Korean language is essentially wanting in vocabulary relating to love. Thus, a young couple whispering love under an acacia tree would have to resort to words of Japanese origin. Such a situation seems probable in a nation so long steeped in Confucianism. During the Korean War, it was rumored that the North Korean commands to charge were given in Japanese.

As for the influence of Japanese on Chinese, an article by Kuraishi Takeshirō called "Japanese Words that Became Chinese"[15] maintains that the largest number of Japanese loanwords pertain to economics (e.g., *nakagainin* [broker] and *torihiki* [transactions]). Next in number are words relating to law and lawsuits, such as *bengoshi* (lawyer) and *mōshitate* (declaration; testimony). They reveal the nature of the historical relationship between China and Japan. Besides these words, Wang Yun-wu's large dictionary gives the following as words introduced from Japanese: 相手 (the other party), 立場 (standpoint), 勝手 (convenience), 言葉 (speech), 手紙 (letter), and 場合 (occasion). What must be noted, however, is that these words have not been adopted into Chinese with the Japanese pronunciation. The word *nakagai-nin*, for example, has become *chung-mai-jen*, and *aite* has become *hsiang-shou*. That is to say, these Japanese-created Chinese character words are taken into Chinese but assigned Chinese pronunciation. Therefore, we must say that it is not the spoken Japanese language that they have adopted, but the written one.

Thus, there is hardly any real introduction of Japanese into the Chinese language. A rare example appears in Kuo Mo-jo's childhood reminiscences of how, during gymnastics in elementary school, the teacher commanded, *Kiotsuke, migimuke migi!* (Attention! Right turn!). This was a real adoption of Japanese. However, this practice existed for only a short period of time in a certain locality. Right after the Sino-Japanese War, China, in trying to become a modern state, invited constitutional scholars from Japan to help establish the first Chinese constitution. Sanetō Keishū, a student of Chinese literature, says that among the technical terms used on this occasion were *tetsuzuki* (procedure) and *torikeshi* (cancellation), which were pronounced as Yamato words.[16] Of this, too, nothing now remains. The influence of Japanese on Chinese was exceedingly slight.

ASPECTS OF SPEECH

日本語

◆

PART

II

◆ 1. REGIONAL DIFFERENCES

What are the characteristics of the Japanese language?
Although we simply call it "Japanese," it is in reality a
complex of a great many languages. English, German,
Dutch, Danish, and the like are called Germanic languages
as a group. The whole of the Japanese language is equal to
the whole Germanic language group, as it were.

Japanese is often said to be complicated and difficult.
One of the causes can be found in its nature as a language
group. Herein also lies the reason why Japanese is said to
be in a state of disorder. Formerly, people of Kyūshū
generally lived in Kyūshū and people of Ōu lived their
whole lives in Ōu. But now we hear dialects of other areas
everywhere. Moreover, in former days each person's use of
language depended, to a large extent, on his or her social
position and trade. Now that we are becoming socially
homogeneous, speech differences according to sex and
situation are also growing less distinct. It is no wonder
that Japanese is said to be in disorder.

Differences in dialects

Russia is a large country. Consequently, Russian is spoken
over an area extending 2,000 miles from north to south and
1,500 miles from east to west. Dialects there differ very
little. The daily conversations of the fishermen on the
northern seacoast can be understood, it is said, by the
farmers in the Ukraine, the southernmost area. This is
natural, since people who speak Russian can understand

Polish, Czech, and Serbo-Croatian, as mentioned above. It is as if a person in Siska, in the former Japanese domain of Sakhalin, and a person in Kaohsiung, Taiwan, could understand one another, each talking in his own native tongue.

The differences among dialects in Japan, however, are conspicuous. A place like Kagoshima is an entirely different world. The everyday conversations of people of Kagoshima prefecture cannot be understood even by the people of the neighboring prefecture of Kumamoto, not to mention those on Honshū and Shikoku. In the Kagoshima dialect sounds like *ki, ku, gi, gu, chi, tsu, bi, bu* all become a stop sound at the middle or end of a word. Thus, the sentences *Kuki ga aru* (There is a stem), *Kuchi ga aru* (There is a job), *Kutsu ga aru* (There are shoes), *Kugi ga aru* (There is a nail), and *Kubi ga aru* (There is a head) all become *Kugga ai*. Such sentences as *Kut no kug ga dete itōte naran* and *Kut ba kirareta node atarashii kut ba sagaite oru* become, in standard Japanese: *Kutsu no kugi ga dete itakute tamaranai* (The nails of my shoes poked through and are hurting me so much) and *Kubi o kirareta node atarashii kuchi o sagashite iru* (I was fired, so I am looking for a new job). It is no wonder that this dialect cannot be understood in other districts. A popular story relates that during the feudal ages the Satsuma clan purposely made the speech of its domain unintelligible to outsiders in order to guard against spies from the shogunate. At any rate, the Kagoshima dialect is so extraordinary that such a story does not seem unlikely. But there is an even more peculiar place, a fishing port called Makurazaki at the southern end of Satsuma peninsula in Kagoshima prefecture. Although I visited this port in winter, I saw irises and evening primroses already in bloom on the roadside and felt quite strange. This district is said to possess an especially peculiar dialect even within Kagoshima, the speech of a pure native being incomprehensible to people in other parts of the prefecture. A school teacher living there said that in former days when a person from Edo (Tōkyō) had to speak with a person of Makurazaki two interpreters were needed, one who could interpret both Edo and Kagoshima dialects and another who could speak the Makurazaki and Kagoshima dialects. To use a Chinese classical expression, it was a place which "necessitated a threefold interpretation."

A case like the above can be seen even within Tōkyō prefecture. The language of the residents of the island called Hachijōjima, south of Tōkyō, is altogether unintelligible to Tōkyō people. It cannot be understood even by those residing on islands of the same Izu island group. Moreover, on a tiny island called Kojima right near Hachijōjima, there is a village called Utsuki with only seventy-four people. It is perhaps the smallest village in all Japan. How strange it is that the dialect spoken on this island cannot be understood in nearby Hachijōjima!

Differences existing among Japanese dialects can be seen best in the accents of words. It is well-known that the accent of words like *aka* meaning "red" and "dirt," and *hashi* meaning "chopsticks" and "bridge" are quite the reverse in Tōkyō and in the Kyōto–Ōsaka district, *Aka* (red) and *aKA* (dirt) in the former, *aKA* and *Aka* in the latter. The dialects of Mito, Sendai, and Kumamoto and Kurume of Kyūshū make no distinctions at all in accents. In these places *aka* meaning "red" and "dirt" and *hashi* meaning "chopsticks" and "bridge" are all accented alike. That there are places like Tōkyō and Kyōto–Ōsaka districts where accents are distinguishable and that there are also districts with no distinguishable accents whatever shows how varied Japanese is.

The origin of dialects

Thus, marked differences exist among Japanese dialects. Why? The Basque language, which I have mentioned, is famous for its varied dialects. *Les Langues du monde* states that the results of investigations by a Lord Bonaparte showed that the Basque language was divided into three dialect groups and fifty dialects, and under them twenty-five subdivisions which again had fifty varieties and more than ten minor divisions.[1] We cannot tell how many dialects there were in all. In the East, reports have come frequently about one small island in the Pacific with many dialects which differ greatly from each other. Although Guadalcanal island, the scene of heavy fighting in World War II, is only about eighty by twenty-five miles in area, twenty Melanesian dialects are spoken there.[2] There is likewise a certain area in Australia with only a few thousand people but more than two hundred dialects.[3]

Generally speaking, divergences in dialects are conspicuous among primitive tribes which are small, closed societies. Even in Japan, when we watch children who are not yet attending school, we find that there is one society in every tiny block, and children living in one block cast menacing glances at the children from the next block as they pass by. This is a microcosm of primitive society. Thus, it is natural that differences arise among dialects.

Is, then, the large number of greatly differing Japanese dialects due to the primitive state of Japanese society? Perhaps, but there are also other, more cogent reasons. One of these is the antiquity of Japanese history which stretches back at least to the time of Christ, if not before. It was in the later half of the 15th century that the Russians overthrew the Kipchak-khan and established the Russian Empire. It was in the second half of the 18th century that the ancestors of the Americans established the United States on the American continent. Compared with Japanese history it seems that all this took place only a short time ago. And only thereafter did Russian and American English spread throughout the two countries. Thus, there was not enough time for these languages to split into different dialects.

Yet another cause for the appearance of so many different dialects in Japanese is the difference in the way of living in each locality. Coupled with the complexity of geographical features and the diversity in climate, there was great variety in the mode of living. In his account of travels in the United States, Yoshikawa Kōjirō, a scholar in Chinese literature, states that in his train journeys through the continent the yellow wheat fields stretched on endlessly, and when he entered a forest there was nothing but a dark forest no matter how far the train went. He was astonished by the immensity. Russia must also be the same. What a contrast, then, to the Japanese Ministry of Education's railroad song, *Ima wa yamanaka ima wa hama* . . . (Now we are in the mountains, now along the shore . . .), a description of scenes viewed from a train window. In Japan one finds, in rapid succession, farm villages, fishing villages, industrial cities, and mining towns, where people separate into even smaller groups in the course of making a living. Since speech is controlled by the mode of living, it is natural that different dialects should develop.

An investigation of Izu peninsula dialects revealed that the contrast between northern and southern or eastern and western Izu dialects was not so great as the contrast between the dialects spoken in fishing villages and farm villages. When Umegaki Minoru made a survey from the northern part of Wakayama prefecture to the Shima district of Mie prefecture, passing through the Kumanonada coast districts, he discovered that even in such widely scattered districts as Saigazaki of Wakayama city, Ōshima island across from Kushimoto, and the southern coast of Shima, there was a remarkable similarity in the speech of the fishing villages.

The standard language and the common language

Thus, one of the chief characteristics of Japanese is the great divergence among dialects. This brings about various inconveniences in the social life of the people. There are many dialectical expressions which cause misunderstandings among people of different districts, which the *kyōgen* (a Nō comedy) "Irumagawa" well illustrates. A Tōkyō man traveled to Saga on Kyūshū. Wanting to buy some cigarettes, he asked an old shop woman, "Do you have Shinsei?" She answered, "*Nai* (i.e., "there isn't any" in Tōkyō)." "Then how about Hikari?" the man said. "*Nai*," said the woman again. He gave up and returned to his lodgings, where he was told that *nai* meant "yes" in the local dialect.

A person from the Kansai district made the mistake of arranging to meet a person from Chiba prefecture on *shiasatte*. In Kansai, *shiasatte* generally means the day after *asatte* (*asatte* is the day after tomorrow), but in Chiba, Saitama, and Gumma prefectures, it means two days after *asatte*.

Japanese are not insensitive to the divergences between dialects. They devised a polished version of the Tōkyō dialect and made this the standard language to be taught at schools. The diffusion of this speech throughout Japan has met with great success. People who speak the standard language or the Tōkyō language exclusively are few, of course, but almost all the people of Japan can speak this common language with which they are able to make themselves understood by people of other districts. According to a survey made by Shibata Takeshi, even the Hachijōjima islanders, who formerly spoke such a strange dialect, could carry on conversations with people from Tōkyō, with the exception of one old woman.

This has not happened on small islands of the Pacific like Guadalcanal. When the German orientalist Gabelentz and the anthropologist Meyer traveled around the coast of Maclay in northeastern New Guinea, almost every village had its own dialect, and the people of villages six or eight miles apart could hardly understand one another. So it is said that they needed two to three interpreters on a single day's trip.[4]

Before World War II there was a school in Kanda, Tōkyō, for the Chinese residents in Japan called Nikka Gakuin. One day while I was teaching there, I saw two students talking in faltering English in the hallway during a break.

I learned that one was from Hupei province and the other from Fukien province. If they had spoken to each other in their own dialects they could not have understood each other, and since the two had no command of their country's standard language, they had to use English. It seems then that the spread of the standard language in Japan is a matter to be proud of.

The degree of difference in the Japanese dialects is probably equal to the differences between such European languages as English, German, Dutch, Danish, Swedish, and Norwegian. It is not so surprising, therefore, to hear of a European being able to use English, German, and Dutch. Most people along the borders of linguistic regions in Japan have long been accomplishing similar linguistic feats. That the Japanese have succeeded in establishing a modern state in the short period of time since the Meiji period illustrates the intelligence of the Japanese. The spread of the common language, too, is perhaps one of its manifestations.

◆ 2. OCCUPATIONAL DIFFERENCES

Military jargon

The differences existing within the Japanese language are largely regional and professional. One group famous for possessing a special jargon of its own was the old imperial army. The exclusive nature of armies is something international, and foreign armies also have special languages. A. M. Halpern, an American linguist who was once with the Civil Information and Education Section of the U.S. occupation forces, wrote in the magazine *Shisō no Kagaku* (The Science of Thought)[1] for January 1949 about the singularity of American soldiers' speech. Comparing it with Ōkubo Tadatoshi's article, "Japanese Soldiers' Language," in the same issue, I noted that American and Japanese soldiers' speech differed greatly owing to the large number of slang words used by the Americans to refer to women as merely physical objects. This seemed to me like an amusingly correct assessment.

The Japanese army used military terms formulated by the state, which abhorred words of foreign origin and used Chinese character words or their Japanese translations exclusively. New recruits had a hard time learning how to use terms like *henjōka* (lace boots)* and *bukkanjō* (a drying place).† At the Army Provisions Depot, *kyarameru* (caramel) was called *gunrōsei* (essence of army food), *sūpu* (soup) was *nōkanjū* (thick meat and vegetable soup), *raisukarē* (curried rice) was *karamiiri shirukake meshi* (rice with spicy

*Chinese reading of *amiage-gutsu*.　†Chinese reading of *monohoshiba*.

gravy), and *korokke* (croquettes) was *aburaage nikumanjū* (fried meatballs).[2]

Elements that are typical of military jargon can be found not only in vocabulary but also in grammar. The use of the *de-arimasu* style is, perhaps, most well known. In general, military expressions were conventional and lacked flexibility. The following account by Sakakura Atsuyoshi, a Japanese language scholar, conveys this characteristic very well.

> When I was a new conscript we once went on field exercises. I wanted to tell a superior private something about the target: *Itchō hodo saki ni ikken'ya ga mieru deshō?* (About one *chō* beyond you can see a solitary house, can't you?). But I could not express this in military language, no matter how hard I tried. I knew perfectly well that in military speech *itchō* was *yaku hyaku meitoru* (about 100 meters), *saki ni* was *zenpō* (ahead), *ikken'ya* was *dokuritsu kaoku* (an independent house). But I could not for the life of me express *mieru deshō* (you can see . . . can't you?) in *de-arimasu* style. *Miemasu ka* (Can you see?) could not be right, of course. *Miemashō* (You see, don't you?) would not likely be military speech. After thinking of this and that, I finally realized that expressions of familiarity, which require another's sympathetic response, simply could not be expressed in military jargon in the first place.[3]

The peculiarity of military terminology is due to the isolated nature of the military world. Similarly, there are many special terms maintained in Buddhist circles, and in gay society and the gambling world.

Official terminology

The following is a quotation from the writings of Japanese novelist Agawa Hiroyuki.

> Try and look up in the Tōkyō classified telephone book the numbers for a secondhand bookstore, a subway station, and an air-gun shop. Subway station (*chikatetsu*) will not be found in the index under *chi*, or under *den* (*densha*, electric car). You will have to look for it under the section *Teito Kōsokudo Kōtsū Eidan* (The Capital's Rapid Transit Traffic Organization) of the column *Tetsudō Kidōgyō* (Railroads and Tramways). Therefore, if one has left something behind in the subway train, the system is such that he cannot find the right telephone number quickly. It is the same with secondhand bookstore *(furuhon-ya)*, which cannot be found under the *fu* of *furu* or the *ho* of *hon-ya*. You will have to look under *koshoseki-shō* (old-book dealers). At present we don't say in our daily conversation, "Let's go into a *koshoseki-shō*," nor do we write in our diary even in literary style, "Today I dropped in at a *koshoseki-shō* in Kanda." Such a word, even as a synonym, is almost obsolete. As for "air-gun shop" *(kūkijū-ya)*, you will not find it under the *ku* of *kūkijū* or the *te* of *teppō* (gun). If you have time, please try look it up.[4]

There are many more terms of this type specially used by government offices. For example, what we ordinarily call *rintaku* (a bicycle taxi) is termed *sekkyaku-yō keisharyō* (light vehicles for customers), and what we ordinarily call *kuzuya* (a waste-paper dealer) is called *shigen kaishū-in* (resources recovery man).[5]

Railroad terms often come under attack, since they are in daily public use.

Fumikiri ichiji teishi.
Crossing temporarily closed—This makes one think: "What, is this crossing closed today?" (But the real meaning of this notice is: "Crossing! Stop for a moment before you proceed!")

Ishitsubutsu o sōsa itashimasu.
We shall search the carriage for lost articles—This makes one think: "*Ishitsu*? Why, you mean *wasure mono* (forgotten articles)."

Ori nori wa ohayaku negaimasu.
Please be quick in getting off and getting on—This makes one think: "Then we'll have to say *yokin no ire dashi* (the depositing and withdrawing of accounts), won't we?"*

Shūchakueki ni tōchaku no jikoku wa jūshichiji sanjippun de arimasu.
The time of arrival at the terminal station is 5:30 P.M.
—This makes one think: "It's enough to say, 'We'll arrive in Osaka at 5:30 P.M.,' isn't it?"

Kanamori Tokujirō says that each government office has

---

*It is customary to say *nori ori* (getting on and off) not *ori nori* (getting off and on). In banks, however, we say *dashi ire* (withdrawing and depositing), not *ire dashi* (depositing and withdrawing).

an individual character of its own. In the period before the war, when we saw the phrase *Ōmune tsugi no yōryō ni yoru* (In general according to the following outline) in an official document, we knew it was from military circles. If the phrase was *Shokan o motte keijō itashi-sōrō* (We respectfully submit this in writing), it was a diplomatic document under the jurisdiction of the Ministry of Foreign Affairs. If it was *Koko ni naninani an o setsumei itashimasuru kōei o yūsuru node arimasu* (Here I have the honor to explain the so-and-so draft), one could guess that it was most likely an address of the Minister of Finance at the Diet.[6]

Academic circles

It is often said that the language of scholars is too different from that of the public. It is true that a scholar should use precisely terms related to his special field of study, and for this reason technical terms are necessary. In comparison to Europe, however, scholarly terminology in Japan has gone to extremes.*

The philosopher Ikegami Kenzō says in an essay that a Japanese, on reading a scholarly German book, noted the part title "Erster Teil" (Part One). He thought that this expression was used only as an abstruse technical term. But when traveling in Germany, he entered a vaudeville theatre, and was surprised to be informed of the end of the "Erster Teil" during the intermission. This story reveals something about a Japanese scholar's attitude toward "technical terms."[7]

*This was especially true before World War II.

Among academic circles botanists do not use difficult Chinese characters but rather such Yamato words as *sumire* (violet), *tampopo* (dandelion), and *rengesō* (Chinese milk vetch). This practice is well received. However, I cannot quite approve of their using scientific terms understood only among Japanese botanical circles and not internationally.

The commonly used *kimpōge* (buttercup)—which I think excellent— was replaced by botanists with the bizarre *uma no ashigata* (literally, a horse's footprints). It is said that the cyclamen which decorates spring display windows and whose roots are used as pig food has the technical name *buta no manjū* (literally, a pig's bean bun).

Waga koi wa	My love
oiransō no	Is like the fragrance
ka no gotoshi	Of the phlox—
ame fureba nure	It becomes moist in the rain,
kaze fukeba chiru.	And scatters in the wind.

—KITAHARA HAKUSHŪ[8]

Oiransō (phlox; literally, courtesan plant), the plant mentioned in the poem, is not so listed in Makino Tomitarō's *Nippon Shokubutsu Zukan* (A Japanese Plant Book),[9] but is instead entered under some unimaginable name. Furthermore, according to Makino, the yellow flower that blooms on summer evenings and which we call *tsukimisō* (evening primrose; literally, moon-viewing plant) is incorrectly named. The real *tsukimisō* is a white flower.

In the academic world, the medical group is known for its use of the most troublesome words. This was especially true before the war. What ordinary people call *mizubōsō* (chicken-pox; literally, water smallpox) was called *suitō*. Since this is short, we can bear it, but for *otafuku kaze* (mumps; literally, plump-faced cold), the name used in the medical world was *kyūsei jikasen-en* (acute parotid gland inflammation), which was very troublesome. The popular term *mimikuso* (earwax) was called *teinei*, and *mushiba* (decayed tooth; literally, worm-eaten tooth) was called *ushi*. Furthermore, *kushami* (sneezing) was written 嚔噂, and we wondered how in the world this was pronounced. According to Shimose Kentarō, such unusual characters as 瘍, 瘤, 癰, 臕, 顛, 瘵 were used for names of diseases. Some of these names read like the Chinese book *Senjimon* (A Thousand-Character Classic).[10] Some examples are *gakan kinkyū* 牙関緊急, *kakukyū hanchō* 角弓反張, *shishi ketsurei* 四肢厥冷, and *donsan sōsō* 吞酸嘈囃.* Some looked like Buddhist names for the deceased engraved on gravestones; for example, *sentensei gyorinsen'yō kōhishō* 先天性魚鱗癬様紅皮症.[11]

Besides the above examples, there were many cases in which a technical term differed from one field to another. Uniformity has been established, but formerly the word meaning "constant" was *jōsū* 常数 in mathematics and physics, *kōsū* 恒数 in chemistry, *teisū* 定数 in engineering, and *fuhensū* 不変数 in economics. An American educational delegation took this up and said in its report that it was a manifestation of sectionalism. In astronomy, it was also well known that Tōkyō University used *wakusei*, while Kyōto University used *yūsei* for the same word—planet.

*These are all Chinese character words which have no meaning in Japanese. Yamato names of flowers and diseases have meanings such as "moon-viewing grass" and "plump-faced cold" that are easy to remember.

◆ 3. DIFFERENCES BY STATUS AND SEX

Upper and lower classes

It has often been pointed out that speech differences match people's stations in life. The ancient people of India were noted in this respect. According to Jespersen, the language generally called Sanskrit was spoken by gods, kings, princes, and Brahmans, but shopkeepers, minor officials, policemen, fishermen, and the majority of women spoke a different language called Prakrit.[1] Present-day Javanese is also well known for this. It is said that there are seven ranks, and the people of each rank speak a different dialect.[2]

In Japan it was in the middle ages (13th–16th centuries) that the differences in speech according to social levels were most intense, when nobles, warriors, priests, townsmen, and peasants all spoke different languages. This can be clearly understood when one listens with attention to the dialogue in a Kabuki drama. The following conversation in the *Tōkaidōchū Hizakurige* (Walking along the Tōkaidō)[3] shows how different the samurai's speech was from the townsman's:

Samurai: *Shite omitachi wa Edomono da na.* (Well, I see you are from Edo.)

Kitahachi: *Sayō de gozaimasu. Watakushidomo wa yazen no tomari de gomanohai ni toritsukarete ōkini nangi o itashimasu.* (Yes, sir. Last night at the inn we were attacked by a thief and now we are in great trouble.)

Samurai: *Hā, sore wa chikagoro kinodoku ja. Naruhodo*

gomanohai no sashita no wa itakarō. (Well, that is something to be pitied. It must hurt you, having been stung by the *gomanohai* flies.)

Kitahachi: *Iya, gomanohai to mōsu wa dorobō no koto de gozaimasu.* (No, sir. What we call *gomanohai* is a *dorobō.*)

Samurai: *Dorobō to wa nan ja.* (What's *dorobō?*)

Kitahachi: *Hai, dorobō to mōsu wa tōzoku no koto de gozaimasu.* (Well sir, *dorobō* means a thief.)

Samurai: *Hahā, nanika hito no mono o toriyoru tōzoku no koto o dorobō to yū ka.* (I see. Do you call one who steals something from others *dorobō?*)

Kitahachi: *Sayō de gozaimasu.* (Yes, we do.)

Samurai: *Sono mata dorobō o gomanohai to yū no ja na. Naruhodo geseta geseta.* (And you call this *dorobō* a *gomanohai,* don't you? I understand now.)

Superiors and inferiors

Differences in speech due to differences in social standing, as in the above example, are not conspicuous in European countries, although they do exist to some extent.

There was a scene near the end of the second act in the British movie *Romeo and Juliet* in which Juliet, seeing her nurse coming back after being sent to Romeo, implores Romeo's answer. According to the linguist, Izui Hisanosuke, there was a clear distinction in the use of honorific terms in the conversation between the two.[4]

Such differentiated expressions can be seen in Japan to a marked degree. In the examples of English usage below, you can hardly tell who is higher in rank:

A: I have sung too much and feel thirsty.
B: I'm sorry I did not bring some tea.

C: Don't you feel tired?
A: No, not a bit today. I think I have never had such a good time.

This is taken from Shioya Sakae's translation of *Hototogisu* (Cuckoo).[5] In the Japanese original, the high and low social standings of the three speakers can be seen quite clearly:

A (Namiko): *Amari utatte nandaka kawaite kita yo.*
B (Maid): *Ocha o motte mairimasen de.*

C (Takeo): *Kutabire wa shinai ka?*
A (Namiko): *Iie, chittomo kyō wa tsukaremasen no. Watakushi konna ni tanoshii koto wa hajimete.*

It is noteworthy that "A," a young girl like "B," lowers herself and uses polite words when talking to "C," but when talking to "B," her speech is so rough and blunt that it might even be taken for that of a man.

Before World War II there was a Shōchiku motion picture called *A Warm Current.* Sonoike Kinnaru praised the words of the mother in the story and said: "Her words spoken to her son are a little too polite for a parent. How well they reveal that she is his mother-in-law."

This problem is also related to the style of language used, which I shall discuss in the next chapter, "Differences by Situation" (p. 78).

Male-female distinctions

One of the peculiarities of the Japanese language is the difference in the language of men and women. If I may quote the example given by Nogami Toyoichirō in *Hon-yakuron* (On Translation),[6] the following conversation in English can be taken to be either between two men or between two women.

"You write uncommonly fast."

"You are mistaken. I write rather slowly."

"How many letters you must have occasion to write in the course of a year! Letters of business, too! How odious I should think them!"

"It is fortunate, then, that they fall to my lot instead of yours."

Now, if we translate this into Japanese, there will be the following differences when we consider the conversation to be between two men and then between two women:

Baka ni hayaku kakeru nē.

Iya, kore demo osoi hō da.

Yoppodo takusan no tegami o ichinenjū niwa kakun darō nē—bijinesu no tegami datte sa. Kangaetemo tamaranai nā.

*Tokoro ga, saiwai to kimi ga kakun ja nakute, boku ga kakun da kara nē.**

Zuibun hayaku okake ni naru no nē.

Chigau wa. Kore de atashi osoi hō yo.

*Between two men.

Donna ni takusan no otegami o ichinenjū niwa okaki ni narun deshō nē. Bijinesu no otegami datte, kangaetemo tamannai wa. Demo shiawase to anata ga okaki ni narun ja nakute, watashi ga kakun desu mono. *

The differences in expression between the above conversations are extremely clear.

Anata.	"Dear."
Nan dai?	"What is it?"
Ato wa ienai—	The rest she is too shy to say—
futari wa wakai.	The two are young.

—SATŌ HACHIRŌ[7]

It is a characteristic of Japanese that from such brief expressions as the above, one is able to guess that the speakers are a man and a woman, what their approximate ages are, and even what the relationship between the two is.†

Years ago when there were still many American soldiers stationed in Japan, we used to see an American, driving a jeep with a Japanese woman by his side. On seeing a Japanese car suddenly appear from a side street, the driver would say, *Dame nē, butsukaru wa yo!* (That's no good—you'll bump into me!).‡ We could guess with what kind of Japanese he was associating and from what kind of person he

---

*Between two women.

†*Anata* is a term used by a wife to call her husband. *Nan dai* is man's language. That the woman is too shy to answer shows they are newly-weds.

‡This is woman's language.

was learning Japanese; it was all very hilarious. But the American surely thought he was using proper Japanese. It would have been hard, indeed, to explain to him why it was funny.

According to Jespersen, it sounds womanish to use "so" when one means "very much," and "common" when one means "vulgar."[8] But it seems that there are very few differences in the expressions used by men and women in European languages in general.

In contrast, the languages of the American Indians are notable for the differences between the speech of men and women. It is said that among the Caribs of the Lesser Antilles in the eastern end of the Caribbean Sea, only the men speak Carib, while the women speak the same language as the Arawaks on the continent. It is as if the men spoke Japanese and the women Korean. There is a legend that the islands were formerly inhabited exclusively by an Arawak tribe and that the Caribs invaded them and killed all the men, sparing the women. This, they say, was the source of the anomaly.[9] The Arawak language must sound unspeakably bewitching to the men; if the boys by mistake should use Arawak, they would surely be jeered at and feel embarrassed.

There is a tribe in Greenland whose men use such consonants as p, t, and k, whereas women use the consonants m, n, and ng.[10] It is a wonder that they can understand each other.

The distinction between the speech of men and women in Japanese is not an old one. This is indicated by the fact that while the differences are strictly observed in the urban areas, they are little observed in most farming and fishing villages. In ancient times it seems that there were few such differences even in urban areas. In the 11th-century classic, *Genji Monogatari* (The Tale of Genji),[11] we hardly feel the difference between the speech of men and women. Omodaka Hisataka, an eminent scholar of Japanese literature, says that in the *Man'yōshū* anthology,[12] the expression *kimi* (you) was not used by a man toward a woman, or, if so used, done only in jest.[13] (In ancient Japanese, *kimi* was an appellation for men used by women.) During this period there seems to have been about as slight a gap between the speech of men and women as there is in modern English. The gap became more distinct after the middle ages, especially in the Edo period (1600–1867) when the unequal status of men and women was strictly enforced by law.

The difference between male and female expression is most remarkable in writing. I shall cite some letters from the *Gempei Seisuiki* (The Rise and Fall of the Genji and the Heike Clans).[14] The man's letter was written by Kumagai Naozane[15] to Taira no Atsumori's[16] father, Tsunemori, telling him he has sent Atsumori's head to him. The woman's letter is from Shunkan's daughter to her father, who has been exiled to the island of Kikaigashima.[17] The man's letter looks like Chinese, while the woman's is entirely in *hiragana*. The difference between the languages of the Caribbean men and women, then, cannot be considered unique.

A MAN'S LETTER

直実謹言上　不慮奉参会此君之間挿呉王得仍践

秦皇遇燕丹之嘉直欲決勝負刻　依拝容儀俄忘

怨敵之思忽抛武威之勇剰加守護奉共奉之処 ...

Naozane tsutsushinde gonjō su. Furyo ni kono kimi ni sankai shi tatematsuru no aida, Go-ō Kōsen o e, Shinkō Entan ni oo no kachoku o sashihasande shōbu o kessen to hossuru no kizami . . .

A WOMAN'S LETTER

そののちたよりなきみなしごとなりはて、おんゆく
へをもうけたまはるたよりもなし。みのありさま
をもしられまゐらせず、いぶせさのみつもれども、
よのなかかきくらしてはるるここちなくはべり。...

Sono nochi tayori naki minashigo to narihate, on-yukue o mo uketamawaru tayori mo nashi. Mi no arisama o mo shirare mairasezu, ibusesa nomi tsumoredomo, yononaka kakikurashite haruru kokochi naku haberi. . . .

Since the Meiji period the differences have gradually lessened, especially since the end of World War II. The following quotation is from a conversation in *Nigō* (The Mistress), a drama by Iizawa Tadasu. If we conceal the speakers' names, it is difficult to distinguish the sexes.

- A: *Anna hito ni tōhyō suru yatsu ga iru no ka nā. Watashi nara shinai nā.* (It's a wonder there is anyone who votes for that kind of fellow. I won't do it.)
- B: *Zuibun hidoi koto yū no nē.* (You really are hard on him.)
- A: *Datte hontō da mono. Shō ga nai darō.* (But it's true. I can't help it, can I?)

Actually, "A" is a woman called Fujiko, and "B" is a man called Haruo.

The tendency of female teachers in primary schools to call boys with *kun* attached to their names, such as "Aoki-kun" and "Inoue-kun," is an example of male and female speech coming closer together.* There are many people, however, who are adverse to this tendency. Naitō Arō, a French scholar, argued against the female teachers' use of *kun* in the editorial column of *Gengo Seikatsu*, No. 51.[18] When Ōtsuki Bookstore's *Kōza Nihongo* sent questionnaires to its readers, there were many approvals in principle for such new policies in Japanese language as the use of Tōyō Kanji and the adoption of Gendai Kanazukai (Standard Use of *Kana*),[19] but when it came to distinctions between male and female speech, a majority approved the preservation of the distinction. Even if attempts are made to abolish them, these speech differences will probably not disappear for some time.

---

*An honorific suffix to a boy's or young man's name, usually spoken by men, equal to *san* in the case of a woman's name, spoken by both men and women.

◆ 4. DIFFERENCES BY SITUATION

Literary style

The most characteristic feature of the Japanese language is the existence of two different styles of expression, according to the situation in which words are used. The colloquial style versus the literary style is one example. This can also be seen in other languages. What is noticeable with Japanese is the pronounced difference between the two.

The literary style in every language is built upon the framework of an older language system. The framework of the Japanese literary style was the Kyōto language of the Heian period. Many different kinds of literary arts flourished among the Kyōto people during the Heian period, and literary works were produced that served as models of poetry and prose for many generations, such as the *Kokinshū* anthology[1] and the *Genji Monogatari* (The Tale of Genji). Thus, the language of the Heian period was regarded as a model of literary style. What must be noted is that the all-important literary period was the 10th century—a very ancient time, indeed.

Chinese is representative of a language whose literary style is based on an ancient language. Karlgren says that the Chinese literary language is two thousand years old. On the other hand, a language such as English goes back to the 16th century at the earliest for its literary style.

The literary language of Japanese, having its basis so far in the past, is quite difficult for ordinary people to understand. At the beginning of the Shōwa period (1926–) when the present crown prince was born, a song in celebration of the occasion was composed, part of which went, *Hitsugi no miko wa aremashinu* (The heir to the throne was born). It was sung in primary schools. There was a girl, a third grader, in the household where I was then lodging, who sang it and then queried, "The crown prince was born, and isn't it strange to say he's dead?" I could not at first understand what she meant. But I realized that she took the expression *arema* of *aremashinu* (was born) to mean *aremā*, an exclamation of surprise, and had interpreted the phrase to mean *Aremā shinu!* (Alas, he died!). As I was wondering how to explain this correctly to her, the child's brother, a fifth grader who was there, said without hesitation, "Don't be silly. The literary expression is always the opposite of ordinary speech. That's true, isn't it?" And he looked back at me. In my opinion, this older boy had been dazzled by the literary phrases such as *natsu wa kinu*,* meaning "the summer has come," and *izaya yukan*,† meaning "let's go," and thinking he would not be tricked again, said this to his sister. He seemed to have missed the point.

Adults know better than this, but in the phrase *Ima koso iwae kono ashita* (Now on this morning we celebrate) of the ceremonial song for the 2,600th anniversary of the founding of the empire, there were many who mistook the word *iwae* for "celebrate" in the imperative mood (when actually it was in the *izenkei* or preterit form due to the particle *koso* before the verb).‡ I wonder how many of those who play

*The auxiliary suffix *nu* (or *nai*) is negative in colloquial Japanese.
†Similarly, in colloquial style, *yukan*, which is the same as *yukanu*, means "do not go."
‡Formerly, when *koso* came before a verb, the verb (here, *iwae*) took the *izenke* form, in many cases the same as *meireikei* or imperative form.

the card game *Hyakunin Isshu*[2] can say whether the word *nezamenu* of *ikuyo nezamenu Suma no sekimori* means "awakened" or "not awakened."* There are a great many people who just memorize the words without knowing their meanings. It is said that the natives of northwest Queensland can remember an almost unintelligible folk song which is so long that it takes five nights to finish.[3] Such a tendency can also be seen in Japanese folk songs.

If reading literary expressions is difficult, writing them is even more difficult. Takayama Chogyū,[4] the author of *Takiguchi Nyūdō*, wrote *Gojin wa subekaraku gendai o chōetsu sezarubekarazu* (We have to transcend the present at once), and was attacked by scholars of Chinese classics for his grammatical error.† Saitō Mokichi[5] used the honorific verb *osu* (to eat) in a poem about his own partaking of a meal, and he had a hard time justifying it. Furthermore, the compilers of the Imperial Rescript for Education wrote *ittan kankyū areba* instead of *ittan kankyū araba* (in case of an emergency).‡ Although they realized afterwards they had made a grammatical error, they had no way of correcting it, for "the emperor's words are final."

Persistence of literary expressions

This difficult literary language had a great influence on the daily language of ordinary people, giving them a great

*This means: "The guards of the barrier of Suma must have been awakened many nights (by the cry of the plovers)."
†When the adverb *subekaraku* modifies a verb, that verb must end in *subeshi,* not the double negative *sezaru bekarazu.*
‡In literary language, the form *areba* signifies actuality, and *araba* signifies conditional future. Here it should have been *araba.*

deal of trouble in its usage. Until the end of World War II, this literary style was used for all formal writings, such as imperial edicts, and all laws (including the constitution). Furthermore, they were written in a stiff and intricate style, with a mixture of Chinese character words, so the difficulty of understanding was doubled. Formal letters, too, were all in this literary style. The letters of ordinary people, too, were considered formal enough to write in *sōrōbun,* a form of literary expression. When we speak of the "Penal Regulations for Crimes" we expect them to be written in a style most familiar to ordinary people; however, the third article of this code was written as follows:

> *Kōshū no me ni furubeki basho ni oite tanseki ratei shi matawa dembu kobu o arawashi sono ta shūtai o nashitaru mono . . .*
> Persons who, in public places, strip themselves to the waist, or expose their buttocks or thighs, or perform other disgraceful acts . . .

> *Hōsha, senjō, hakuhi tō o yōsezu sonomama shokuyō ni kyōsubeki inshokubutsu ni fukugai o mōkezu tentō ni chinretsu shitaru mono . . .*
> Persons who do not put coverings on foods displayed in their shops which are to be eaten as they are without the need of cooking or washing or peeling off the skin . . .

On August 15, 1945, the emperor went on the air to announce the termination of the war. As the speech was given in difficult literary language, the meaning was not transmitted accurately to most people, and it is commonly known there were some who mistakenly thought a decisive battle would at last begin in Japan proper.

Through the Meiji period, even the newspapers were written in literary style. After the movement for the unification of written and spoken languages in the middle of the Meiji period, novels were written in colloquial style for the first time. We can hardly praise too highly the achievements of Futabatei Shimei,[6] Yamada Bimyō,[7] and Ozaki Kōyō,[8] who took the lead in this unification movement. Until then people had really been doing things the hard way.

The literary language lost its position with the termination of World War II, and this was a good thing. The draft for the amendments to the constitution published in April 1946 was a forerunner for legal texts written in colloquial style. The imperial edict for the convocation of the 90th imperial diet in May, the following year, was also written in colloquial style. A council for the improvement of official documents was established in October 1947, and in June 1948, *A Guide to Official Documents* was compiled. Thus, it was formally decided that official documents be written in colloquial style.

The literary style, however, has not entirely disappeared. Looking at the daily newspapers, we still find such headlines as *Yoshibayama yaburu* (Yoshibayama was defeated),* *Makuuchi tsui ni zenshōsha nashi* (There are no longer any wrestlers with perfect records in the *makuuchi* division),† and

*Yoshibayama is the name of a grand *sumō* champion. *Yaburu* is literary; its colloquial form is *yabureta*.
†*Zenshōsha wa nai* will be colloquial.

Wakanohana yūshō su (Wakanohana won the championship).* Titles of novels and movies are sometimes in the literary style: *Nozomi Naki ni Arazu* (There Is Still Hope), *Nogiku no Gotoki Kimi Nariki* (You Were Like the Wild Camomile), and *Nippon Kaku Tatakaeri* (Japan Fought Thus).

Lastly, regarding the colloquial style, we must not be misled by the term. This style by no means coincides perfectly with the language as it is spoken. *Kare wa kanarazu ya futatabi sugata o miseru koto wa arumai* (He will surely not make an appearance again) is an example of the so-called colloquial style, but in conversation we say: *Ano otoko wa kitto mō konai darō* (I'm sure that man will not come again).

The movement for the unification of written and spoken languages has not yet been completely successful.

Peculiarity of "desu" and "masu" forms

The most important stylistic distinction is not that between the literary and colloquial styles. This distinction can be found in many other languages, and occasions that require the use of literary style in Japanese are very limited. The distinction that most preoccupies the Japanese people is that between the "ordinary style" and the "polite style." In the round-table discussions on "How Foreigners Look at the Japanese Language" in the magazine *Gengo Seikatsu*, Brinkley, an Englishman living in Japan, said:

---

*Wakanohana was a grand *sumō* champion. *Yūshō su* is literary; its colloquial form is *yūshō shita.*

B: When I teach Japanese to Englishmen I say to them: "In order to learn perfect Japanese, you have to learn three languages."

A: And what are the three?

B: *Aru, arimasu,* and *gozaimasu.*[9]

In his book, *Conversational Japanese for Beginners,*[10] A. Rose-Innes, whenever he gives an example of a Japanese sentence, indicates whether it is in "common style," "polite style," or "extra polite style."

The fundamental differences between the three styles can be represented by *aru, arimasu,* and *gozaimasu,* as Brinkley has said. But that is not all. The expressions . . . *nasai* (please do so and so) and . . . *kudasai* (please do so and so) can be used only with the polite form represented by *desu* and *masu* although they take no suffix of *desu* or *masu.** They are not used with the "common style" or with the extra polite *gozaimasu* style. But . . . *nasaimase* (please do so and so) and . . . *kudasaimase* (please do so and so) belong to the extra polite form. Verbs such as *gozaru* (to be), *zonjiru* (to think), *mairu* (to go), and *mōsu* (to say) can be used only when *masu* is attached to them. Such nouns as *sakujitsu* (yesterday), *myōnichi* (tomorrow), and *kono tabi* (this time), and adverbs such as *ikaga* (how) are not used with the common form. The distinction between the three forms extends to interjections: *oi* (hey, say) and *un* (hmm!) gen-

---

*Desu is an auxiliary verb equal in meaning to the English verb "to be," which acts as a copula. *Desu* is attached to nouns and to the *rentaikei* or attributive form of verbs, adjectives, auxiliary verbs, and expresses politeness. *Masu* is an auxiliary verb attached to the *ren'yōkei* or continuative form of verbs to express politeness, as *yukimasu, arimasu.*

erally belong to the common form; *nē* (you see) and *ē* (oh
yes) belong to the polite form; and *moshi moshi* (I say) and
hai (yes) belong to the extra polite form.

Thus, the differences between the three stylistic forms
are far greater than we think. Father W. A. Grotaas says
that when he hears a young Japanese man talking to his
friend and when he hears him talking to his friend's
father, he feels as though the young man were using two
completely different languages.[11]

The distinction between the common form and the polite
form is essentially dependent upon the degree of respect
one feels toward the person one is talking to and how that
is expressed in words. This usage varies according to the
degree of familiarity between the conversants and according to the formality or nonformality of the occasion.

The distinctive usage of polite forms of speech, reflecting
respect for the person one is talking to, can be found in
European languages as well. In German, for example,
there is a distinction between the usage of *du* or *Sie,* meaning "you." According to Charles Bally, in former days
when the social class system was strictly observed, there
were four levels in addressing others. For "Do you understand?" they had *Versteht du?* (common form) and *Verstehen
Sie?* (honorific form). Besides these, there were the forms
Versteht ihr? and *Versteht Er?*[12]

The difference between the common form and the
honorific form in Japanese is a little different from that of
German. In German the forms of the words related to the
person addressed or to his action are changed, but not the
form of the things talked about. In German there is no
way of changing expressions like "The flowers have opened"

or "It has begun to rain," no matter how respectable the person addressed. In short, there is no change in the style of expression, but only in the form of honorific terms. In Japanese there are the common forms such as *Hana ga saku* (Flowers bloom) and *Ame ga furidashita* (It began to rain) in contrast to the polite forms *Hana ga sakimasu* and *Ame ga furidashimashita*. This is an altogether different dimension.

A somewhat similiar stylistic difference can be found in Korean, which makes us feel the resemblance of the two languages. In Korean the verb "to see" is *bonda* to one below you, *bone* to your equal, *bo'o* when you want to be polite, and *bomnida* when you want to be especially polite. According to Miyatake Masamichi, such differentiation can be seen in Javanese, too. Jespersen says it is also found in Burmese, but in general no such differentiation exists in European languages. Although it is a Far Eastern language, Chinese has no such differentiation.

"Desu" and "masu" forms in daily speech

The distinction between the common form and the polite form has brought some complexities into the daily speech of the Japanese. A bus conductor in the United States can just say, "Chicago Station next." In Japanese, however, it sounds incomplete if one says, *Nagoya Eki mae tsugi* (Nagoya Station next). You have to say, *Tsugi wa Nagoya Eki mae de gozaimasu*. As the sentence is long, the sound of the important place name *Nagoya Eki* is liable to become indistinct.

In English the single word "push" is sufficient on a door. In Japanese one would hesitate to write *ose* (the imperative form of "push"). Then you might ask if it is always right to use the polite form in Japan. This is not necessarily so. You pick up the receiver and answer the phone in a polite form, and if the other party happens to be your wife or a friend, you will feel a little embarrassed. Proper use of these forms is rather difficult.

It is noteworthy that this differentiation did not exist in Japan in ancient times. During the Heian period there was the verb *haberi*, which was somewhat similar to the present *masu*. Sakakura Atsuyoshi, however, has made it clear that this verb was never attached to the word that expressed the action of the person you were talking to or the action of a person who deserved respect. In brief, it was a word that expressed a feeling of modesty. The verb *sōrō** began to be used extensively in the Kamakura period (1185–1333), and this brought about the distinction between the common and the polite forms which we see today. The polite form of that period which still remains is the *sōrōbun* style used in letter writing.

The present *masu* developed from *mairasu*† and began to be used in the Muromachi period (1336–1568). Since this polite form is new, many dialects do not have it. However, in common speech the polite form has now become difficult to abolish. It is worth noticing that Miyagi Otoya, a typical champion of rationalism and a leading critic of the established ethics of modern Japan, advocates the preservation of the polite form in the following passage:

The most unpleasant thing in Japanese is the existence

*Same in meaning as the present *masu*.
†This originally meant "to present a thing respectfully to someone."

of "impolite words" rather than "polite words." The other day at Tōkyō Station I wanted to get on a train that was bound for Kyūshū, so I stopped a station employee with an arm band which said "passenger guard" and asked, *Ressha Aso wa nanji ni haitte kimashō ka?* (What time will the train Aso arrive?). *Kuji nijippun. Narabanakucha dame da yo* (9:20. You must get in line), he roared bluntly. That is the manner of an employee of the National Railways, which is a tourist business and is at present supposed to have been separated from the Ministry of Transportation. It may be natural after all, for the police to use such words as . . . *da** and . . . *nano ka*† in answer to one's polite . . . *deshō ka?* (Will it be . . .?). I beseech that something be done with the "impolite words."[13]

Toki Zemmarō, president of the Japanese Language Council, suggests that the *desu* and *masu* forms be considered as "social forms." Perhaps this is the final solution to the problem. More noteworthy is the fact that various good effects have resulted from the mixed usage of the common and polite forms in Japanese. I shall write about this on another occasion.

*An impolite form of *desu*.
†An impolite form of *desu ka* or *deshō ka* in asking questions.

PRONUNCIATION

日本語

◆

PART

III

◆ 1. THE SYLLABLE

Father W. A. Grotaas spent ten years in China engaged in Oriental studies and missionary work before coming to Japan. While he was living in a deserted village in Shansi province, the Japan-China incident occurred and Japanese soldiers began to enter the district. It was then that he first heard the Japanese language. Of course he did not understand Japanese, but he retains an impression of its rhythm. Japan being well known for its *kimono* and "Fujiyama," he had imagined Japanese to be a very elegant language. But upon actually hearing it, he found it an unrhythmical series of disconnected sounds like "pot, pot, pot, pot" that reminded him of a machine gun.

What Father Grotaas heard were syllables, the most distinct units in Japanese pronunciation.

Japanese speakers distinguish syllables from other phonetic units with comparative ease. For instance, when we pronounce the word *yamazakura* slowly and precisely, we get: *ya-ma-za-ku-ra*. In the absence of outside influences, we tend to give each unit the same length. Each unit is the rhythmic basis of Japanese verse. Taken individually, each is the smallest unit of sound in daily speech.

Distinct breaks between syllables

Languages other than Japanese also have syllables, but in some languages the breaks between syllables are not distinct. Phonologist Arisaka Hideyo (1908–52) writes in his *On'in-ron* (Phonology)[1] that French scholars differ in opinion as to where one syllable ends and the next begins. For instance, one scholar said the first *é* in *épée* constituted the first syllable and *pée* the second syllable. Another scholar said that the first syllable was the first forming of *p* until one closed his lips, and the second syllable began with opening the lips after *p*. And a third scholar said that to argue where the boundary lies between one syllable and another was like trying to determine where the bottom of a valley is between two mountains, and was childish and ridiculous.

Hearing these stories a Japanese might question the seriousness of these scholars. He would have no doubt that *épée* is *é* plus *pée*. We can attribute this assuredness (ill-founded or not) to the fact that breaks between syllables seem to be a peculiarity of the Japanese language.

This peculiarity may be related to the fact that the Japanese possess *kana* or words in which a syllable is the basic unit. The other day, I noticed as I passed that the station name "Shin Tarui" on the Tōkaidō Line was written in romanized style as "Shi n ta ru i," each unit set apart. This clearly shows what a syllable means to Japanese.

Japanese explain how a word, or part of a word, is pronounced by saying that it begins with a *shi* (as in *shiro*) or is pronounced with a *hi* (as in *hito*) and so forth, using the syllable as the easiest way of conveying the proper sound. This is probably due to the scarcity of syllable types and to the independent nature of the syllable.

Japanese poets, although never making great use of rhyme, have found alliteration based on the syllable much to their liking, as can be demonstrated by the following examples:

Nitsutsuji no niowan toki ni
sakurabana sakinan toki ni . . .
When the red azaleas bloom in splendor;
When the cherry blossoms are in bloom . . .

—TAKAHASHI MUSHIMARO[2]

Shinshū Shinano no shinsoba yori mo
watashi wa sonata no soba ga yoi.
Rather than have the new noodles *(soba)*
Of Shinshū, Shinano,
I prefer to be by your side *(soba)*.

The word game of capping verses played by children
(shiritori) is made possible through the nature of the Japanese syllable. Likewise, the children's riddle, "What is the
reverse of *tebukuro* (gloves)?" anticipates the answer
rokubute, a reversal of syllables—something unimaginable in
languages such as English.

Each syllable is a dot

Another characteristic of the Japanese syllable is its
brevity of pronunciation. The average person regards the
syllable as if it were a dot of next to no length. There is an
attempt to pronounce each syllable as briefly as possible.
Therefore, in imitating a long onomatopoetic sound, not
one but two or more syllables are used, as in *do-n* (bang) or
za-bu-n (splash).* This contrasts with the English "splash"
or "clack," each composed of only one syllable.

*Don is pronounced with two syllables, *do-n,* zabun with three syllables,
za-bu-n.

Generally speaking, there are very few one-syllable words in Japanese. When actually spoken, such words are very difficult to catch and make sense of. Once when I had to go to Tsu city in Mie prefecture, I had difficulty obtaining a ticket. At the ticket window I repeated "A ticket for Tsu" several times, but could not make myself understood until I had said, "A ticket for Tsu on the Sangū Line." A one-syllable station name like Tsu exists because people in the Kyōto–Ōsaka district pronounce a word of one syllable by prolonging the sound, making it a word of two syllables, thus, "Tsu-u." In a district like Kantō (the general Tōkyō area), speakers of the standard language, however, do not, and therein lies the diffculty. A one-syllable place name like Tsu would most likely not occur in an area like Kantō where the syllable is kept short. Tanabe Hisao, an authority on Oriental music, says that in Japanese two syllables make a rhythmical unit; this, too, is probably due to the shortness of the syllable.

End rhymes did not develop in Japanese poetry as in European and Chinese poetry, most likely for the same reason. The rhyme scheme of the following poem, taken from the *Kojiki* (Records of Ancient Matters), has been highly praised by Hatano Shirō, but I wonder if he has not gone astray here and tried to judge the poem by alien criteria.

Okitsudori	To the island
kamodoku shima ni	Where wild ducks flock,
waga ineshi	I took the girl
imo wa wasureji	And spent the night—
yorozuyo made ni.	I shall not forget it ever!

Rather than depending on just parts of syllables (the *i* in the above poem), Japanese poetry depends for its effect on the rhyming of whole syllables (the *ru* in the following poem).

Saka wa teru teru	The sun shines on the hill;*
Suzuka wa kumoru	It is cloudy at Suzuka;
ai no Tsuchiyama	And at Tsuchiyama in between,
ame ga furu.	It is raining.

If we are correct in contending that a series of syllables in Japanese is comparable to a row of dots, we would expect the speed with which the syllables are uttered to be very rapid. In fact, this contention is supported by statistics provided by Mario Pei, who has calculated the average number of syllables spoken per minute in a number of languages (as follows): 350 in French, 310 in Japanese, 220 in English, and not more than 50 in the languages spoken around the South Seas.[3] I think we can safely assume that Pei did not assign independent status to the Japanese syllabic nasal *(haneru-on)* and the syllabic stop *(tsumeru-on),* but merged them with the preceding syllable. If these two types of syllables had been included, the distance separating Japanese and English would be even greater. One might conclude from this that Japanese, producing so many syllables per minute, is a highly efficient language, but actually a number of considerations other than syllabic speed must be taken into account. One of these considerations is that several syllables are needed in Japanese to

---

*The hill refers to Matsuo-zaka.

produce a meaningful utterance, and to this we will address ourselves later.

The last point to be made about the syllable is its simple construction, but before we can go into this, we must take a look at the phoneme.

◆ 2. THE PHONEMES

The Japanese generally think that the syllable is the smallest unit of sound. Linguists, however, divide syllables into even smaller units called phonemes.

The Japanese word *sakura,* for example, when divided into syllables, is *sa-ku-ra,* but when divided into phonemes, is *s-a-k-u-r-a.* In general, each letter of the roman alphabet represents one phoneme. Kamei Takashi, who has by far the broadest scope among Japanese language scholars, holds that Europeans, influenced by the Roman alphabet, take the phoneme as the basic unit of pronunciation, while the syllable might actually be a more scientific choice.

This view is quite reasonable. For example, the word *kaki*, when divided into phonemes, is *k-a-k-i.* But the two *k*'s are not pronounced exactly alike, no matter how carefully one enunciates. However, for the purpose of the present discussion, I will take the phoneme to be the smallest unit of pronunciation. The American linguist W. F. Twaddel and the scholar Hattori Shirō both look at the phoneme as follows. The difference in sound between the two *k*'s in *kaki* is a difference only of context—one is before *a* and the other before *i*—but if they were in the same context, they would have the same sound.

There are three types of phonemes in Japanese:

(1) One type makes up a syllable by itself (and can unite with some other phoneme to make a syllable)
(2) One makes a syllable only by uniting with another phoneme

(3) One forms a syllable only when standing by itself

Of these, (1) is the vowel; (2) the consonant; and (3) is a special phoneme—something peculiar to Japanese. Included in the third group are the *haneru-on* (syllabic nasal) and the *tsumeru-on* (syllabic stop), and, depending on one's criteria, the prolongation of the vowel sound, the *hiku-on* (syllabic prolongation).

Vowels

There are five vowels: *a, i, u, e,* and *o*. The number is the same in Spanish and Latin. There are some languages like Arabian and Tagalog which have only three vowels. However, French has eleven and Korean nine. Japanese is one of the languages with few vowels. When a Japanese and a Korean study English together, the Korean's pronunciation is usually better, the number of vowels in Korean exceeding those in Japanese.

Among the Japanese vowels the most characteristic is *u*. Unlike the *u* in European languages and Chinese, it is not pronounced by protruding the lips. Although it cannot be seen from outside, the position of the tongue is also different —it is high and a little toward the front. It is represented phonetically by the phonetic symbol ɯ. It is a common characteristic of the Japanese to avoid using the lips while speaking. As will be discussed later, the consonants *v* and *f* are non-existent phonetically, although *f* is used in romanized Japanese; *p* and *w* are hardly ever used. Even sounds like *a* and *o* are pronounced with little lip movement. According to journalist Matsuo Kuninosuke, who lived in

Paris for more than twenty years, a French landlady said to him, "It's a wonder that the Japanese can speak so well. They hardly open their mouths."

My earlier statement that there are five Japanese vowels actually refers to present-day Tōkyō speech. It has been made clear by a number of scholars, starting with Hashimoto Shinkichi (1882–1945),[1] that there were eight vowels in ancient Japanese: *a, i, ï, u, e, ë, o,* and *ö.* At the beginning of the Heian period *i* and *ï, e* and *ë,* and *o* and *ö* fused to form the vowels we use today. The *ï, ë,* and *ö* of ancient Japanese are only said to be close to the current *i, e,* and *o;* their true values have yet to be established. This type of vowel system makes one think of the possible relationship of Japanese to the Altaic languages. In addition to ancient Japanese, some modern dialects are rich in vowels. The dialect spoken in Nagaoka in Niigata prefecture has seven vowels: *a, i, u, e, o, ε,* and *ɔ,* thus resembling Italian vowel formation. A dialect inside Nagoya city has the following eight vowels: *a, i, u, e, o, æ, y,* and *ϕ,* thus making it similar to German.

Of the present vowels, *a* is most frequently used, while *e* is least used. This order of frequency particularly applies to independent vowel syllables unaccompanied by consonants. In the card game *Hyakunin Isshu,* there are many poems that begin with *a,* a typical feature of Yamato words. As for the relative infrequency of the *e* sound, Ōno Susumu attributes this to its having developed from a diphthong, as well as the *ë, ï,* and *o.*[2] If this view is a correct one, the ancient Japanese vowels must have been *a, i, u,* and *ö,* very much like the primitive form of those in the Indonesian languages.[3]

Consonants

There are fourteen consonants in modern Tōkyō speech: *k, s, c, t, n, h, m, r, g,* ŋ, *z, d, b,* and *p.* Besides these, the vowels *i* and *u,* when followed by other vowels, become a variety of diphthong. We refer here to the syllables, romanized conventionally as *ya, yu, yo,* and *wa* but phonetically as *ĭa, ĭu, ĭo,* and *ŭa,* which were initially pointed out by Sakuma Kanae.[4]

Fourteen consonants is a small number for a language. Compared with the nine in Hawaiian and Ainu, it is larger, but among world languages, there is one language with forty-three consonants—Avar, one of the East Caucasian languages.[5]

What is noteworthy about Japanese consonants is that, first of all, there are few sounds that are modulated with the lips, as I have already stated. On the other hand, there are many sounds that are modulated in the back of the mouth, such as *k,* ɡ, ŋ, and *h.* Kindaichi Kyōsuke interprets this as the result of not only Oriental morality, which emphasized the suppression of emotions, but also strictures, especially for women, against moving the mouth.

In ancient Japanese, more sounds like *p* (and its development φ) and *ŭ* were used than at present. In the Edo period, however, the situation had changed, as expressed by the contemporary Japanese classical scholar, Kurosawa Okinamaro:[6] "Some people pronounce the sounds *ha, hi, fu, he, ho* with a flapping of the lips. . . . These are most vulgar sounds, and even at the present time people with any sensitivity would seldom use them in daily speech."

The sounds made at the back of the mouth are *k,* ɡ, ŋ,

and *h*, so they cannot be said to be many, as in the Hamito-Semitic languages.[7] Possession of the nasal sound, ŋ, is shared with the languages of southern China, Thailand, and Malaysia, and makes Japanese look very much like Southeast Asian languages. English has many sounds that are modulated by the teeth and the tip of the tongue. In Japanese, sounds which are articulated by the palate and at the back of the mouth, such as *k*, *g*, ŋ, and *h*, are used very frequently.

Mario Pei said of the Japanese language: ". . . the general acoustic effect of Japanese would be closer to that of Italian than to that of Chinese were it not for a certain guttural quality that distinguishes the tonality of most Far Eastern languages."[8] It is ironic that the names for the linguistic sciences are the most grating on the ears—*kokugogaku* (study of the Japanese language) and *gengogaku* (linguistics). In this respect Japanese is little different from Dutch, which, Mario Pei says, has many guttural sounds.

The pronunciation of Japanese is exceedingly indistinct when observed from the outside, for there are many consonant sounds that are pronounced at the back of the mouth. It is said that Japanese is an easy language for a ventriloquist, who must suppress the movement of the lips to the utmost. On the other hand, it must be a troublesome language for deaf mutes, who try to grasp what a person is saying by lip reading.

Another characteristic of Japanese is the scarcity of fricative consonants. There are only two genuine fricatives, the *s* and *h* sounds. The *z* consonant in the Tōkyō dialect, for instance, is actually *dz,* a kind of fricative-plosive. It is said that in the language of southern Australia there are no plosives; but English, on the other hand, is rich in plosives such as *s, z, f, θ, ð, v,* and *h.* In this respect, Japanese ranks a little above Hawaiian, Maori, and Andamanese, which, according to Friedrich Muller,[9] has an extremely primitive sound system. Moreover, scholars believe that in ancient Japanese the present *h* sound might have been *p* and the present *s* sound might have been *ts,* so possibly there were not any fricatives then.

Another characteristic is the existence of only one so-called liquid consonant. This is the Japanese *r,* which is generally neither *r* nor *l.* In an essay by Sugimura Sojinkan, a former journalist, appeared a story of a Japanese man in an English restaurant who ordered lamb meat but was brought ram meat. A male sheep is "ram," and a young sheep is "lamb," but in Japanese both "ram" and lamb" are pronounced *ramu.* Thus, the distinction in English is very difficult for Japanese. This tendency can also be seen in Korean and Ainu, and seems to be a fairly common characteristic of languages in the Far East and the islands of the Pacific.

In any discussion of Japanese consonants, the problem of *seion* (clear sound) and *dakuon* (unclear sound) deserves special attention. Phonetically speaking, the *seion* and *dakuon* have the same position and method of articulation, only the former is voiceless and the latter voiced. Those syllables with the consonants *g, z, d, b,* and *j* are *dakuon;* these have correlative voiceless consonants that are *seion: k, s* and *ts, t, h,* and *ch,* respectively. When written in *kana,* the *dakuon* is indicated by a mark on the *seion* letter, as is shown by the pair さ *sa* and ざ *za.* The consonants *n, m, r, y,* and *w* are voiced, but they are classed as *seion* because they have no correlative voiceless consonants. The vowel syllables *a, i, u, e,* and *o* are also treated as *seion.* In certain circumstances, such as when the composite elements of compounds are more fixed, Japanese unvoiced consonants tend to become voiced with consistency, as illustrated below.

VOICELESS	VOICED
kao (face)	*marugao* (a round face)
sake (liquor)	*amazake* (sweet liquor)
take (bamboo)	*aodake* (green bamboo)
tsuki (moon)	*mikazuki* (a new moon)
hana (flower)	*sakura-bana* (cherry blossoms)

The contrasting voiced and voiceless sounds are often not distinguished in daily speech. For instance, a person by the name 川田 will not care whether it is pronounced "Kawata" or "Kawada," and such an attitude often strikes the Europeans as strange. Some contrasts between the voiceless and the voiced sounds are now unsystematic, such as *h* and *b* in the above example, but in ancient times the contrast seems to have been an orderly one in which the position and method of articulation were the same in both, as illustrated below:

$$k\text{——}g \qquad t\text{——}d$$
$$s\text{——}z \qquad p\text{——}b$$

Relation between vowels and consonants

Lastly, as we look at the vowels and consonants comparatively, we find that Japanese is remarkably rich in vowels. Among European languages, Italian is known to possess many vowels, yet it has a word like *sdraiarsi* (to lie), with a cluster of consonants. In Russian, there are prepositions such as *v* (in), *k* (toward), and *s* (with), and greetings such as *zdravstvuytye*.

Hawaiian is known for its many vowels. Otto Jespersen gives the following example: *I kona hiki ana aku ilaila ua ho-okipa ia mai la oia me ke aloha pumehana loa.*[10] Japanese is not far behind. In the *Asahi* newspaper I once found the following slogan: *Tōei Awā—aita kuchi ga fusagaranu* (The Tōei Movie Company Hour—our mouths are wide open with astonishment). The expression *Tōei Awā* has many vowels indeed.

The proverb *Ao ŭa ai ĭori idete ai ĭori aosi* (Blue comes from indigo and yet it is darker than indigo; i.e., a disciple outshines his master) has a plethora of vowels. The expression *ai ŭo oiau u* (the cormorants that vie in chasing the sweetfish) is composed entirely of vowels.

Japanese is generally pleasant to the ear. As mentioned above, William M. McGovern remarked that Japanese is flowing and melodious. It is said that the American linguist, W. D. Whitney, also observed that Japanese is fluent and easy to pronounce. And recently Mario Pei has classed Japanese among languages that sound pleasant, together with Italian and Spanish.[11]

Some years ago Fujiwara Yoshie, Sunahara Michiko, and others of the Fujiwara Opera troupe performed the opera *Madame Butterfly* jointly with Americans at the City Opera House in New York. The Japanese sang in Japanese, and this pleased the public very much, and various newspapers, including those in New York and Los Angeles, commented on the beauty of the Japanese language.[12] What were the reasons for such a favorable reception? Perhaps one reason was simply that Japanese vowels and consonants do not sound strange to American ears. Another reason must have been the sheer volume of vowel sounds.

With regard to the total effect of a large number of vowel sounds, however, Jespersen made the following comments about Hawaiian.

> Can anyone be in doubt that even if such a language sound pleasantly and be full of music and harmony, the total impression is childlike and effeminate? You do not expect much vigour or energy in a people speaking such a language.[13]

What would Jespersen have said about Japanese? There is no objection to saying that Japanese lacks strength, but to link this directly with a nation's vitality is somewhat rash and not at all typical of Jespersen.

◆ 3. THE SOUND SYSTEM

Structure of the syllable

The structure of the Japanese syllable is characterized by extreme simplicity, as can be seen in the following list of structural types:

(1) Syllables of one vowel, e.g., *a, i, u*

(2) Syllables of two vowels, the first of which must be the semivowel *ĭ* or *ŭ*

(3) Syllables of one consonant plus one vowel, e.g., *ka, ki, ku*

(4) Syllables of one consonant plus two vowels. The first vowel must be the semivowel *ĭ*, e.g., *kĭa, kĭu, kĭo*

(5) Syllables of one special phoneme, i.e., the *haneru-on* (syllabic nasal),* *tsumeru-on* (syllabic stop),† and *hiku-on* (prolongation of the vowel)

According to the conditions in (3) and (4), there cannot be two consonant sounds in one syllable. That is, there is no word which begins with two or more consonant sounds. This was the characteristic cited by Fujioka Katsuji,[1] in his explanation of the lineage of Japanese, as an important factor shared with the Ural-Altaic languages.

Next, following the conditions in (1), (2), and (3), there is no syllable with a consonant after a vowel. The Japanese

---

*The nasal sound *n* expressed by the *katakana* ン as in *denwa* (デンワ telephone).

†The syllabic stop made by double consonants, as in *Nippon* (*Ni-p-po-n* ニッポン). It is expressed by the small *katakana* ッ.

word *san* (product) has two syllables *(sa-n),* and *katta* (won) has three syllables *(ka-t-ta).* They are different from the English "sun" and "cutter," although the pronunciation is somewhat alike. The nasal *n* in *san* and the syllabic stop in *katta* are independent syllables—different from *sa* (of *san*) and *ka* (of *katta*). Likewise, the Japanese *tai* (sea bream) and *kau* (to keep animals) are different from English "tie" and "cow" in that they are words of two syllables. In short, Japanese is a language of a typical open-syllable construction in which no dependent vowel or consonant follows the principal vowel. Among European languages, Italian is well-known as an open-syllable language, but sometimes a syllable may end in a consonant. Japanese surpasses Italian and competes in this respect with the Polynesian languages.

Furthermore, Japanese resembles Chinese and Korean in that a semivowel can come between a consonant and a vowel, as indicated in (4) above. This peculiarity is due to the agelong influence of the Chinese language. In the indigenous Japanese, therefore, each syllable was composed of either one vowel, or a semivowel plus one vowel, or one consonant plus one vowel. It had an astonishingly simple structure, unlike Korean, Chinese, Ainu, or Indonesian. Originally the Polynesian languages were the only languages known to possess such a structure. Later it was said that the Halmahera language also had such a simple structure. More recently the Chinese linguist Ma Hsueh-liang has reported that the Sani language of inner China has a similar structure.[2] At any rate, the simplicity of old Japanese was a rarity. This was one of the prominent arguments against any relationship between Japanese and the Altaic languages. Even if Japanese belonged to the Altaic languages, we would suspect its pronunciation had been influenced by the open-syllable system of the South Seas languages. Incidentally, the aforementioned Lepcha is not open-syllabled, and so has no connection with this matter.

Syllabic nasal and syllabic stop

Another feature of Japanese is the existence of the *haneru-on* (syllabic nasal), *tsumeru-on* (syllabic stop), and *hiku-on* (prolongation of the vowel). All these have very simple methods of articulation. The syllabic nasal is a sound uttered through the nose for the length of one syllable with the mouth in position to utter the next sound. The syllabic stop is a stop for the length of one syllable with the mouth in position to utter the next sound. The prolongation of the vowel is the prolongation of the previous syllable for the length of one syllable. Such sounds exist as phonemes in other languages but rarely as syllables.

Of these, the syllabic nasal has its counterpart in the Chinese Canton dialect and the aforementioned Sani. In the Canton dialect, "five" is pronounced ŋ, and in Sani "short" is *n*—both are similar to the Japanese *n* ン. On the other hand, we do not hear of any sounds similar to the Japanese syllabic stop. It apparently resembles the initial part of a long consonant in Italian and Hungarian, but the Japanese sound is counted as one syllable. It is extraordinary because we count as one syllable something we cannot hear at all. The Eastern aesthetic sense is said to emphasize the importance of blank space, but I suppose it would be stretching things a bit to connect the syllabic stop to this philosophy.

These special phonemes developed under the influence of Chinese, but they were not directly introduced from Chinese. In Chinese the nasal *n* and the double consonant stop did not originally exist as one phonetic unit. Therefore, when they were first introduced into Japanese they did not each constitute a single syllable. Let us look at the following *waka* poem, said to have been written by Dengyō Daishi (767–822).[3]

Anokutara	O the Buddhas
sammyaku sambodai no	Of unexcelled
hotoke tachi	Perfect Enlightenment!
waga tatsu soma ni	May you protect the wooded
*myōga arasetamae.**	mountains
	Where I stand!

Masaoka Shiki[4] praised this poem in his article "Nanatabi Utayomi ni Ataeru Sho" (The Seventh Writing to be Given to the Composers of Poems), saying he admired the courage of a person who could write such a hypermetric *waka* poem.†
However, the compliment was unnecessary. Dengyō Daishi lived just after the introduction of Chinese to Japan, and the *san*, *dai*, and *myō* in the poem were each composed of only one syllable then. Thus, there was probably no excessive number of syllables in the poem.

---

*From the *Shin-kokinshū* anthology.
†A *waka* is composed of 31 syllables, but this one has 36 by present ways of counting.

Paucity of syllable types

Viewing the syllable in this way, we naturally come to the conclusion that its structure is exceedingly simple. In addition to this, each syllable is usually pronounced evenly and with the same stress as all other syllables. This is due to the nature of Japanese accent, which will be discussed later. Here, then, are the reasons why Hagiwara Sakutarō stated that the Japanese rhythm is flat and unsatisfying.

Not only is the Japanese syllable simple in structure, but the types of vowels and consonants are few in number, as mentioned in the last chapter. Vowels and consonants total a little over twenty. The total number of possible syllables is 112. Even if we count the differences created by the two levels of accent, the high and low, the number only doubles. Mandarin Chinese, the official language of the People's Republic of China, has 411 syllable types, according to Ogaeri Yoshio, although Chinese usually is considered one of the less prolific languages. According to Umegaki Minoru, the number of syllabic types in English exceeds three thousand.[5] Arai Hakuseki (1658–1725)[6] touched upon a vital point, when, in the preface to his book *Tōga,* he wrote: "No languages have as few kinds of sounds as Japanese and no languages have as many kinds of sounds as the Occidental. Chinese is next in large quantity."

In short, the scarcity of syllable types is a great peculiarity of Japanese. This fact has had indirect influence on everyday speech.

The small number of syllables makes it possible for the Japanese in general to memorize all of them. This is facilitated by the *gojūon* (chart of fifty sounds of Japanese syllabary) and the poem *Iroha Uta* (syllabary song),* which are lists of syllables. Since they were based on the pronunciation of an ancient period, there are places where they do not correspond with the list of present-day syllables. Nonetheless, the creation of the *gojūon* and especially the *Iroha Uta*—a meaningful sentence using each syllable only once—was possible only in Japanese.

The existence of the *gojūon* and *Iroha Uta* means that the Japanese can memorize all the syllables. Therefore, even if a Japanese does not know how to express himself in *kanji*, he can write words in a certain order according to their sounds, or he can refer to a *hatsuon-biki jiten* (a dictionary in which words can be looked up according to pronunciation). In English, however, if one wants to look up the word "knife," for example, he has no way of doing it unless he knows that the word begins with the letter *k*.

Secondly, since there are few syllable types, it is easy for the general public to learn the syllabic orthography. I don't think that children anywhere can write the symbols for all the sounds of their native tongue as freely and early as Japanese children.

After World War II, when the Civil Information and Education Section of the occupation forces, with the cooperation of the Education Ministry, made an investigation of Japanese ability in reading and writing, they were surprised to find that there was hardly anyone who was

*The *Iroha Uta* is a poem using each of the 47 *hiragana* once, in alternating lines of seven and five syllables. It runs: *Iro wa nioedo/ chirinuru o/ waga yo tare zo/ tsune naran/ ui no okuyama/ kyō koete/ asaki yume miji/ ei mo sezu.* (Though flowers bloom, they soon fall; to everyone this world is transient. Crossing the mountains of life's vicissitudes today, we shall not have light dreams or be infatuated again.)

completely illiterate. This was probably due to the simplicity of Japanese syllables, for once a Japanese has learned
the 112 letters, he can write any expression correctly. This
is the strong point of Japanese, in contrast to English,
where the spelling of each word such as "dog" and "cat"
must be learned separately. In spite of this fact, after the
war a teaching experiment called *hitome yomi* (reading at a
glance) was conducted in some primary schools, in which a
word like *inu* (dog), for instance, was not separated into *i*
and *nu* but presented as a single unit. This was a waste of
time as Watabiki Masa of the Kuromon Primary School of
Taitō ward, Tōkyō, correctly observed.[7]

However, the lack of syllabic variety in Japanese has
produced many words that are pronounced alike or nearly
alike. The other day when I switched on the radio, I heard
the words: *shikai shikai shikai.* I wondered what it meant
and later learned that the correct form was *shika-ishi-kai
shikai* (chairmanship of the dentists' conference). Similarly,
if we compile a list of words in the dictionary that have the
same pronunciation, we will find that there are about thirty
words pronounced *kōshō.*

The existence of a great many words of similar sound has
made Japanese a language exceedingly difficult to understand orally. For example, the ordinary person long ago
gave up as hopeless the attempt to understand the spoken
passages in Kabuki and operas and the texts of *nagauta, koto-
uta,* and the like. If one hears "cher . . ." spoken in English,
one can immediately guess that it is either "cherry" or
"cherish." But *sa* . . . in Japanese, has the possibility of
developing into scores of words. Even if one hears as far as
saku . . . , he cannot be sure the word is *sakura,* for it could

be *saku* (to bloom) or *saku* (a fence) or *sakujitsu* (yesterday) or many other things. Even in the announcement of the parodies in a television quiz show called "Tonchi Kyō-shitsu," those who don't listen carefully often get lost. Some years ago when there was a celebration in honor of Hisamatsu Sen'ichi's sixty-first birthday, a former pupil recited a poem of his own composition in honor of the occasion, but almost no one present could understand the text.

In reaction to the great number of homonyms and near homonyms (which will be discussed later), there is an attempt to avoid the creation of more, which leads to individual words becoming excessively long. This is also related to the small number of syllable types.

The existence of many homonyms, on the other hand, has made Japanese a language in which puns can be made easily.

The following *haiku* is made up of puns on the names of insects:

Hiru kara wa	(*hiru*=leech, *ka*=mosquito, *ha-*
chito kage mo ari	*chi*=bee,* *tokage*=lizard, *ari*=
kumo no mine.	ant, *kumo*=spider, *nomi*=flea)

In the afternoon
There is some shade—
Clouds in the sky.

The *waka* below is made of puns on the names of provinces, something only Japanese can do.

*The character for *wa* can be pronounced *ha*. This with *chi* of *chito* makes *hachi*.

Yo wa uki to	(Hōki)*
itoikoshi mi no	(Higo)†
aki no tomo	(Aki, Noto)
aware mikawase	(Awa, Mikawa)
yamazato no tsuki.	(Sado,‡ Tsu, Ki)

This is a world of sorrows;
I, who have abandoned it,
And the moon, my autumn friend,
Face each other tonight
In this mountain village.

Also in Japanese are mnemonic devices used in memorizing such numerals as the following:

$\pi = 3.1415926535897932384$

Saishi ikoku ni muko sa, ko wa ku naku mi fusawashi.

A genius becomes a son-in-law in a foreign country; his child goes along without difficulty. (3=*san* or *sa;* 1=*ichi* or *i;* 4=*shi;* 1=*i;* 5=*go* or *ko;* 9=*ku;* 2=*ni;* 6=*muttsu* or *mu;* 5=*ko;* 3=*san* or *sa;* etc.)

$\sqrt{3} = 1.7320508075$

Hitonami ni ogore ya onago.

Girls, live in luxury like ordinary people. (1=*hitotsu* or *hito;* 7=*nanatsu* or *na;* 3=*mittsu* or *mi;* 2=*ni,* 0=*o;* 5=*go;* 0=*rei* or *re;* 8=*yattsu* or *ya;* 0=*o;* 7= *nanatsu* or *na;* 5=*go*).

*The *kana* "*wa uki*" can be pronounced *hōki.*
†The *kana* for *iko* of *itoikoshi* can be pronounced *hiko,* which is the voiceless sound of *higo* and can be accepted for it.
‡*Zato* of *yamazato* can be pronounced *sato,* and *to* variably becomes *do.*

◆ 4. FROM SYLLABLES TO WORDS

Laws uniting syllables

What features typify syllables in combination? Especially outstanding are the positions in which the syllabic nasal, the stop, and the prolongation of the vowel occur. But since the very existence of these syllables is unique in itself, there is no need to also take up their placement as a characteristic feature of syllabic combinations.

Compared with modern Japanese, ancient Japanese of the Nara (710–94) and pre-Nara periods had more striking characteristics. For example, since the time of classical Japanese scholar Moto-ori Norinaga (1730–1801), it has been established that in ancient Japanese voiced consonants and the *r* series (*ra, ri, ru, re, ro*) never came at the beginning of a word.

To the Japanese, as a result, words which begin with voiced consonants sound somewhat unrefined. And it is true that many Yamato words which begin with voiced consonants have unpleasant connotations. Take, for example, *gani** in contrast to *kani* (crab), *dobu* (gutter), *biri* (the last), *dani* (dog tick), *doro* (mud), *gomi* (rubbish), *geta* (clogs), and *buta* (pig). A recent radio commercial stated:

> *Tachimachi ni irojiro no bihada ni narimasu.*
> Your complexion will be fair and beautiful in no time at all.

*This means the same as *kani,* but is dialect. It is generally seen in compounds such as *isogani* (sand crab), *kogani* (small crab), etc. *Gani* sometimes refers to the poisonous part of crab meat.

One person, reacting to the voiced sounds of *bihada,* said she felt as if her skin would become rough instead of fair.

Ancient Japanese resembles Korean in that the *r* series in the syllabary does not come at the beginning of a word. Moreover, this characteristic of the language became one of the main justifications of the theory that the Japanese and Altaic languages, which share the same characteristic, had the same origin. However, in the Papuan languages of the South Seas, the consonants *r* and *l* also do not come at the beginning of a word.[1]

Although it has been stated above that ancient Japanese had eight vowels, there were certain restrictions on their usage. Arisaka Hideyo and Ikegami Teizō have informed us that *ö* and *o* did not appear together in the same word, and that *ö* seldom appeared with *a* or *u* in the same word.[2] This is an instance of vowel harmony, which can also be seen in Korean, the various Altaic, Ural, and Dravidian languages, and some branches of Munda.[3] Before this discovery, the supposed lack of vowel harmony in Japanese had been a weak point of the theory advocating a common origin for Japanese and the Altaic languages. There were scholars like Shiratori Kurakichi, a specialist in Oriental history, who had opposed the theory for this reason. Therefore, the discovery of vowel harmony in ancient Japanese had great significance.

Even in modern Japanese, there are many words with two or more identical vowels, as in *akasu* (to satiate), *okosu* (to raise up), *otosu* (to drop), *tsukusu* (to exhaust), and *orosu* (to lower). This phenomenon must be considered a remnant of the pattern of vowel harmony in ancient Japanese.

山田長政 when written in roman characters would be "Yamada Nagamasa," a succession of *a*'s, and 子供心 would be *kodomogokoro,* a succession of *o*'s. These words exemplify one of the features of the language—there are a great number of words containing several vowels of the same kind. A clever person might be able to compose a *haiku* or two using nothing but syllables with the same vowel.

It is also notable that modern Japanese syllables rarely change even when they come in succession. There is a phenomenon in which vowels become voiceless, but linguistically speaking, this is only a phonetic change. The French liaison and the changes in the vocal sound often seen in Korean hardly ever occur.

This unchangeable nature of the syllable is rather new. In ancient Japanese there was a tendency to avoid joining syllables composed only of vowels. For example, the present *araumi* (a rough sea) was *arumi* in ancient Japanese. In the middle ages (13th–16th centuries), the present *nembutsu o* (a prayer to Buddha Amida—used as an object) was *nembut wo,* which came to be pronounced *nembutto; ryōken o* (an intention—used as an object) was pronounced *ryōken no.* In short, what is called *renjō* (the formation of a new syllable when the final consonant of one word combines with the first vowel of the next) occurred when a syllable beginning with a vowel or vowels followed a syllabic nasal or a glottal stop. Now, however, no such changes occur.

Formerly, in combining two words to form a compound, the first syllable of the second word became voiced. This phenomenon has survived in reduced form to this day, but it has become unusual in new words. In particular, Chinese character words rarely become voiced in this manner. For example, the word that used to be pronounced *funjitsu* (lost or missing) is now *funshitsu,* and what was *tōbō* (eastern direction) is now *tōhō.*

In my opinion, the absence of *renjō* in modern Japanese is due to the greater importance attached to written characters, especially Chinese characters, rather than to the sound of individual words. When we see a word, we first think about the pronunciation of each character and try to read it as a whole, even if it is difficult to pronounce. Words like *gen'in* (cause) and *han'en* (a half circle) are very hard to pronounce.

The Japanese should pay more attention to the beauty of connected sounds rather than to the individual sound. We can learn from the French language in this respect. When we open a *hatsuon-biki* dictionary (in which words can be looked up according to pronunciation), we find initial listings like *ooo* and *oooo.* They certainly don't sound beautiful. The word *oóo* is the literary form of the word meaning "to cover," and *oo-oo* means "occasionally." Could there be any words in other countries with such ridiculous forms? The intentional form of the verb *iku* (to go) is *ikoo* (I will go), but how does one write the intentional form of *yoso-óu* (to dress)? If one writes *yoso-o-óo,* one somehow feels at first that there is one *o* too many, although later it sounds all right. Such connected sounds create a problem.

Pitch accent

Languages in which the relative pitch of syllables within each word is fixed are called languages of pitch accent, in contrast to languages of stress accent, such as English,

German, Italian, and Russian. In addition to Japanese, pitch accent can be found in Chinese (especially southern Chinese); the languages of Southeast Asia (such as Thai, Vietnamese, and Burmese); the Sudan languages of central Africa; the greater part of Bantu;[4] and the American Indian languages of Mixteco and Mazateco.[5] Although pitch accent is now evident in only a few European languages (such as Serbo-Croatian, Lithuanian, Swedish, and Norwegian), ancient Greek and Latin were pitch-accent languages.

The fact that Japanese has pitch accent, not stress accent, does not mean that there are no changes in stress in daily conversations. Changes in stress do occur in emotional speech, but the tonal relationship between syllables in individual words is maintained. In general, therefore, fluctuations in pitch are conspicuous in conversation. As Lafcadio Hearn (1850–1904)[6] once commented, Japanese is like a song. In writing the music to a Japanese song, there is no restriction as far as rhythm is concerned, but one must pay attention to the tone of each word in setting it to music, or the meaning may be misunderstood.

Once during the war I heard a song over the radio which went: *Uta de yamaji no* . . . (Singing a song as I walked along the mountain path . . .). I thought it was an unusually peaceful song for wartime. Then I discovered that it meant: "We will not stop fighting until we win. . . ." The words were set to music with the high pitch on the wrong syllables: *uTA de yaMAji no.** Naturally I had mistaken the meaning. Some time ago I read Mrs. Ichikawa Sanki's article in the

---

*The pitch should have been: *Uta de yaMAJI no.*

magazine *King* about her childhood recollections. She said that when she sang the railroad song, *Umi no anata ni usu-gasumu yama wa Kazusa ka Bōshū ka?* (The mountains beyond the sea covered with light mist, are they of Kazusa or of Bōshū?), she thought it was about a monster called Usu who lived on a mountain in Bōshū. The music to the song must have had the pitch: *Usu ga SUmu** (Usu lives).

What are the characteristics of Japanese pitch accent? First, it is composed of two levels, the high and the low:

HAshi ga (the chopsticks . . .)	high-low-low type
haSHI ga (the bridge . . .)	low-high-low type
haSHI GA (the edge . . .)	low-high-high type

Thus, there are fewer pitch levels in Japanese than in most other pitch-accent languages. According to Kenneth Pike, Sechuana and Mixteco have three levels of high, medium, and low, and Mazateco has four levels.[7] Japanese has the minimum number of levels. These tonal relationships never change. Although the referents "bridge" and "chopsticks" are reversed in the Kyōto dialect, the relationship of the two levels remains fixed and invariable.

Second, the change in pitch usually occurs when one syllable shifts to another; for example, take the phrase *HAshi ga* (the chopsticks . . .) of the Tōkyō dialect. The voice drops at the point where it shifts from *HA* to *shi*. In *haSHI ga* (the bridge . . .) the voice rises at the point where *ha* shifts to *SHI* and drops at the point where *SHI* shifts to *ga*. No pitch changes occur within a syllable.

*It should have been: *uSU-GASUmu* (to be slightly misty).

In contrast, take, for example, the Chinese word *erh shih erh* (twenty-two), which is a word of three syllables. The pitch shifts from high to low within the syllable *erh* itself, and rises from low to high within the syllable *shih*, and in the last syllable *erh* again drops from high to low. I agree with Father Grotaas when he said that Chinese sounds as if someone were singing, while Japanese sounds monotonous.

Third, the arrangements of pitches are quite limited. For example, in the Tōkyō dialect there are only four types of tone patterns in four-syllable words: *KAmakiri* (a mantis); *aSAgao* (a morning glory); *kaRAKAsa* (an umbrella); *moNOSASHI* (a foot rule).

According to I. C. Ward, an English linguist, the following pitch patterns are found in three-syllable words in the Ibo language of west Africa: *OSISI* (a stick); *NKEta* (a dog); *NkaTA* (a dialogue); *Nnene* (a bird); *nDEDE* (wine); *uDOdo* (a spider); *onoMA* (an orange); *otobo* (a hippopotamus).[8] Here we find every possible combination of pitches on two levels.

In contrast to the Ibo pitch, pitch in the Tōkyō dialect is found under the following conditions: (1) When the first syllable is high, the second syllable is always low. When the first syllable is low, the second syllable is always high. In short, the pitch of the first syllable is always different from the pitch of the second syllable. (2) The following never happens: the second syllable in the middle is low and the first and third high. That is, two high syllables never exist separately.

Such being the case, Japanese pitch patterns are extremely limited in number, which means that many words cannot be differentiated by tone. How nice it would be if we could differentiate by means of pitch patterns, such words as *kōgyō* 工業 (industry) from *kōgyō* 鉱業 (mining), and *shiritsu* 市立 (under municipal management) from *shiritsu* 私立 (of private enterprise). These and other terms have the same pitch patterns and make us feel accents have little value. We would be hard pressed to find other groups of three-syllable homonyms that can be distinguished by pitch, as in the following: *Oyama* (name of a place), *oYAma* (a male player of woman's parts), *oYAMA* (a sacred mountain); *Oka-shi* (Mr. Oka), *oKAshi* (a candy), *oKASHI* (a loan).

The language of the Mazateco tribe, living on the Pacific coast of Mexico, has pitch accents. Reading the examples of Mazateco speech which K. L. Pike, the American linguist, has given in his book, *Tone Languages*, I find that their language possesses marvelously complicated pitch accents, different patterns of which can represent the inflections of verbs. Take, for instance, the verb *site*:

si^{d-c} *te*$^{b-c}$	I spin, *or* I shall spin.
si^{a} *te*^{b}	He spins.
si^{d-c} *te*^{b}	He will spin.
si^{d} *te*^{b}	We all (including you) will spin.

(Pitch *a* is highest, pitch *d* is lowest, and pitches *b* and *c* are intermediate.)[9]

When we look at books like *French in Four Weeks*, we find an enormous table of verb conjugations at the end of the book, showing, for instance, the first person singular, present tense, indicative mood of *aimer,* or its second person plural, past tense, subjunctive mood. In the Mazateco language, person, tense, number, and conjugation are all done through changes in pitch. This is an example of the function of pitch developed to an extreme degree.

Since the language of the natives of Mazateco has such complicated distinctions of tone patterns, they are said to be able to communicate to a certain degree by whistling.[10] For instance, when the chief of the tribe whistles, one of his quick-witted men, listening to the ups and downs of his speech tone, will say, "He wants to drink," and will go to fetch some water; or he will say, "Now he wants a pineapple," and will go to get one.

In a dictionary called *Ruiju Myōgishō,* compiled by a Buddhist priest of the Shingon sect in the middle of the Heian period, the author has painstakingly given each word the accent of the then-current Kyōto speech. Although it may seem a little strange to speak of the Japanese accent of that time, the intelligentsia in those days knew about the four tones (*ssu sheng*) of Chinese and apparently had quite an accurate understanding of Japanese accents, too. Through this work, we are able to know quite accurately the Japanese pitch of the mid-Heian period. We find that there was greater variety in Japanese pitch patterns than at present, and that word pairs like *kami* (meaning "paper" or "hair") and *kura* (meaning "storehouse" or "saddle"), which today are exact homonyms, were differentiated by pitch. Pitch accents of that period must have been more effective in distinguishing between words than they are now.

As mentioned above, in present-day Japanese, especially the Tōkyō dialect, the pitch level of the first syllable always varies from that of the second syllable. If the first syllable of a word has a high pitch, the second syllable has a low one and vice versa. Moreover, high tones do not exist separately in two positions in one word. That is, we do not find patterns such as "high-low-high-low" or high-low-low-high." On this basis, we can say that Japanese pitch creates unity by denoting where a word begins and where it ends.

Take, for example, the sentence: *Niwa no sakura mo minna chitte shimatta* (The cherry blossoms in the garden have all fallen). The sentence with tone accents will be as follows: *niWA NO saKURA MO miNNA chiTTE shiMATTA.* Here the low-pitched syllables all indicate superbly the breaks between words. If I may use Arisaka Hideyo's expression, Japanese pitch accent exhibits "the faculty to control" far more than "the faculty to designate." The Japanese pitch, in short, works more to give unity to a word than to distinguish one word from another. In regard to this point, even though the Japanese accent is said to be a pitch accent, its function more nearly resembles that of the stress accent. We know that ancient Greek, too, had such an accent, but the general scarcity of this type of accent makes it worth noting. Some say that the Japanese pitch accent is approaching a stress one and this is true in the above sense.

Rhythm

Since there is pitch accent but no stress accent in Japanese, the sounding of each syllable tends to be the same in length. As linguist Jimbō Kaku early indicated, this point is a distinctive feature of Japanese, and although it is true even of daily conversation, it is especially notable in formal speech. (This can be readily understood if we listen to a professional storyteller's way of talking and the way the father instructs his son Yotarō what to say in various greetings in the *rakugo* story called "Praising a Cow.") It is exactly the same thing that the aforementioned W. A. Grotaas said he heard in China—namely, Japanese people's conversation that sounded like a machine gun.

For these reasons the rhythm of Japanese is very monotonous. According to the critic Tanigawa Tetsuzō, a European heard the names of such places as Yokohama and Nagasaki while still in his own country and thought what beautiful names they were. But when he came to Japan and actually heard them pronounced in very short syllables, he was disappointed by their simplicity.[11]

The Japanese, however, are devotedly attached to pronouncing each syllable with the same length. On the eve of World War II, when members of the Hitler Youth organization visited Japan, the poet Kitahara Hakushū composed a song called *Banzai Hittorā Yūgento!* (Hurrah for Hitler Jugend!). When Sawazaki Sadayuki of Tōkyō Music School sang the song, however, he separated the syllables in the German way. Hakushū's protest against this led to some difficulties.

Due to the strong tendency to keep each syllable the same length, the Japanese are exceedingly sensitive to the number of syllables in a word. There are many instances when we forget a word but remember the number of syllables it has. For example, we may forget a person's name but remember that it was composed of four syllables. Having forgotten the name of a prefecture, we will recall that it was a word of two syllables, like Gifu or Shiga.

In Japanese poetry, rhythms of seven-and-five syllable meter and five-and-seven syllable meter have developed, and this, too, must be due to the equal length of all the syllables. But why were odd-numbered meters, such as five or seven chosen? Since Japanese syllables are very short, like dots, there is a tendency for two syllables to form a unit. Thus, when composing a poem one combines the long unit of two syllables with the short unit of one syllable. The rhythm of the popular Japanese limerick, *dodoitsu,* must be seen as a manifestation of this tendency. It is not merely the rhythm of 3–4–4–3 syllables, but is a rhythm of 1–2–2–2–2–2–2–1 syllables—a combination of one-syllable and two-syllable units.

VOCABULARY

◆

PART

IV

◆ 1. SIZE AND CONSTRUCTION

Tanizaki Jun'ichirō (1886–1965), a distinguished novelist of modern Japan, made the following comment on the vocabulary of the Japanese language:

> One of the defects of our language is that it does not have many words. For example, we use the same term *mawaru* or *meguru* to express the spinning of the top, the turning of a water mill, or the revolving of the earth around the sun. . . . The small vocabulary of Japanese is proof that verbosity is not a national characteristic.[1]

The opinion that Japanese is a language with poor vocabulary applies only to the indigenous Yamato words. As explained in the first chapter, in addition to Yamato words, present-day Japanese includes both Chinese character words and Western words. Both types originally came from foreign countries, but the Japanese have made good use of them, pronouncing them according to the sound system and accents of the Yamato words and inscribing them in Japanese characters. Thus, we can say that they all belong to the "Japanese" language. A quick count of all these words will show that the Japanese vocabulary is not small. As a matter of fact, the dictionary *Daijiten,* published by Heibonsha, contains 700,000 words, and the *Dainihon Kokugo Jiten* has well over 200,000 words. Okamoto Chimatarō says:

In Japanese, Yamato words, Chinese character words, and sometimes Western words are mixed in confusion. We would like to somehow put them in better order so that we may be able to use words which are more straightforward, orderly, and easier to learn. It is not commendable to see Yamato words, Chinese character words, and Western words all overlapping and sometimes snarling at one another as they are at present.[2]

The larger the vocabulary, the more numerous the functions it will serve. However, we cannot simply say that the larger the vocabulary, the better. The Maoris of New Zealand are an underdeveloped people. In the Maori language, according to British ethnologist R. Taylor, "Everything has its name: their houses, canoes, weapons, and even garments have distinctive appellations given them. Their lands and roads are all named; so also the sea beaches round the islands, their horses, cows, and pigs, even their trees, rocks, and fountains."[3] This superabundance of proper names leads us to believe the Maori vocabulary must be large. Livingstone (1813–73), the Scottish explorer of the interior of southern Africa, says:

It is not the want, but the superabundance of names that misleads travellers, and the terms used are so multifarious that good scholars will at times scarcely know more than the subject of conversation.[4]

In short, it is not necessarily desirable to have a large vocabulary. Whether or not the vocabulary is usable and can express one's desires is the important point in deciding its merit. How can we judge the Japanese language from this point of view?

Are there comprehensive words?

Several comments have been made concerning the nature of the vocabulary system in Japanese. Yanagida Kunio (1875–1962), the distinguished folklorist, makes the following comments about modern Japanese:

> There is probably no one who has not encountered the following aspects of present-day Japanese: the meagerness of Japanese vocabulary—although there are words, they are one-sided; and the lack of variety in the vocabulary, due to the conventional rules governing sentence structure. Consequently, when we write a longer article, we cannot avoid writing one that fills us with disgust.[5]

How, then, is the vocabulary one-sided? In the first place, a vocabulary must include words that have exceedingly vague and comprehensive meanings in order to be a good system. Lucien Levy-Bruhl (1859–1939), the French sociologist, ethnologist, and researcher in primitive mentality, states the following in *How Natives Think*:

> The nearer the mentality of a given social group approaches the prelogical, the more do these image-concepts predominate. The language bears witness to this, for there is an almost total absence of generic

terms to correspond with general ideas, and at the same time an extraordinary abundance of specific terms, those denoting persons and things of whom or which a clear and precise image occurs to the mind as soon as they are mentioned.[6]

In this respect the Japanese language is by no means primitive. The philosopher Watsuji Tetsurō (1889–1960) argued that from ancient times Japan has possessed words denoting an exceedingly broad meaning, such as *koto* (the fact) and *mono* (the matter), and that therefore Japanese is a language favorable for philosophy and speculation.[7] In his *Nihongo no Gengo Rironteki Kenkyū* (The Theoretical Study of the Japanese Language),[8] Sakuma Kanae points to the existence of the particle *wa*, which expresses the topic, and the auxiliary verb *da*, which denotes the copula in logic, and says that at least in this respect, it does not hold true that Japanese is not so logical as European languages; in reality it may be the reverse. Thus, he praises Japanese, albeit with restraint.

The fact that the Japanese vocabulary is well equipped with words denoting abstract ideas is another indication of its systematic nature. I shall discuss such words in Chapter 7 (p. 202).

Is the vocabulary system well organized?

With regard to the one-sidedness of the vocabulary, I must point out that frequently words are lacking which represent an idea intermediate between an upper concept, i.e., a word denoting the most comprehensive meaning, and lower concept, i.e., a word denoting a very particular meaning. (For example, of the three words "animal," "dog," and "terrier," the first is the most comprehensive, the third the most particular, and the second intermediate between the two.) The shortage of adjectives, which Yanagida Kunio repeatedly complained about, also creates difficulties of this kind. For example, we do not have an adjective which means "sweet-smelling." We have the adjective *kōbashii*, but it can only be used for the smell of heated coarse tea. We also have the word *kusai*, but this can be used only for a bad smell. We do not possess a simple adjective which designates "giving off a smell," and this is inconvenient.

German is a very systematic language: from one adjective can be made its noun form, its antonym, the noun form of the antonym, and so forth. In this respect, Japanese is very unsystematic. Miyamoto Yōkichi, a critic of the Japanese language, made the following comparison, which points out that from one German word the rest of its forms can be regularly inferred, whereas in Japanese one must go to the trouble of learning each form separately.[9]

Arbeit	*rōdō, sagyō, shigoto* (labor or work)
Arbeitgeber	*yatoinushi* (employer)
(*geber*=one who gives)	
Arbeitnehmer	*shiyōnin, hiyōsha* (employee)
(*nehmer*=one who takes)	
Arbeiten	*hataraku, rōdō suru* (to work or labor)

| *Arbeiter* | *hataraku hito, rōdōsha, shokkō, kin-rōsha* (worker or laborer) |
| *Arbeitseinkommen* | *kinrō shotoku* (earned income) |

Among European languages, French, like German, is a fairly systematic language, but established opinion has it that English is not systematic due to its mixed usage of indigenous English words and words of Latin origin. Mario Pei indicates that there are many nouns and adjectives which have completely different forms, as in the following examples. (Those in the left column are words of Anglo-Saxon origin, and those in the right are from Latin.)

son——filial
sun——solar
house——domestic
sea——marine[10]

Are there contradictory words and phrases?

Some prefixes to indigenous English words and to words of Latin origin have the same form but different meanings. For instance, the prefix "in-" in original English means "within," but in words of Latin origin it means "opposite." Therefore, the word "inhabitable," for example, which commonly means "fit to live in," signifies "not fit to live in" in Shakespeare's plays.[11]

Among the Asian languages, Chinese, which has few foreign words, is a fairly systematic language. There are some words, however, which use the same characters but have opposite meanings, similar to the English words with the prefix "in-." For example, the Chinese word *lan chên* 乱臣 generally denotes "the subject who disturbs the country," and the phrase 乱臣賊子 (one who disturbs the country and harms his master and parents) in *The Book of Mencius* has precisely this meaning. However, surprisingly enough, the same 乱臣 can signify "a faithful subject who governs the country," as in the phrase 武王曰予有乱臣十人 (Emperor Wu says: "I have ten faithful subjects who govern the land"), which appears in the *Analects of Confucius*. It is a mistake to think that the word *li* 離 always means "to part from." The word *li yu* 離憂 (literally, freedom from distress) means "to meet with sadness."

Words similar to those above can frequently be found in Japanese. In the first example below, the word *saki* mean "before," but in the second it means "after."

Tsuite miru to kare wa saki ni kite ita.
When I arrived, he had already come.

Tsuite kara saki no koto wa mada kimete inai.
I have not yet decided what I shall do after I have arrived.

The second example can also begin with *Tsuite kara ato* . . .

In ancient Japanese the phrases *oboroge narazu* (literally, not vaguely) and *oboroge ni* (literally, vaguely) meant the same. That is, the negative here was regarded as inoperative. Whenever this word appeared in classical literature, commentators had a hard time deciding what it meant. Even now we have the word *tondemonai* (literally, the negative of *tonda*), which means the same as *tonda* (shocking).

As will be discussed later, many Japanese verbs have broad meanings. Consequently, often one verb is used to express things which ought to be expressed by different verbs, as in the following example:

A customer came to a photo studio and said, *Shashin o tori ni kimashita* (I came to pick up the pictures).

The photographer answered, *Dōzo kochira de shōshō omachi kudasai* (Please come in and wait for a while).

Ano, tori ni kitan desu ga (Well, I came to pick them up), said the customer.

Hā, chotto sutajio ga fusagatte orimashite (I see, but the studio is occupied just now).

Iya, konomae utsushita no o tori ni kitan desu (No, I came to pick up the pictures which were taken last time).

The misunderstanding in this case arises from the word *toru,* which means "to take" a picture or "to receive" a picture when it refers to a photograph. Although somewhat different from the above, the word *shiku* means "to sit on" when used in connection with *zabuton* (a cushion to sit on), but when used in connection with bedding, it means simply "to spread," as in *futon o shiku* (to spread the bedding).

Expressions which are contradictory in ways different from the above examples can be found in compounds and composite words. When we look up the word *kokubi* in a Japanese dictionary, it says "same as *kubi* (head)." Likewise, when we look for *kote,* it says, "same as *te* (hand)." We wonder why these words mean the same thing, with or without the prefix *ko* (small). In the entry in the dictionary we find the examples *kokubi o kashigeru* (to incline one's head) and *kote o kazasu* (to shade one's eyes with one's hand). In the sentence *Kumagai Naozane kote o kazashi,* the *kote* may be interpreted as *te,* for Naozane could not have had especially small hands. Viewed in context, however, the prefix *ko* actually modifies *kazasu,* and the whole phrase means "to slightly shade one's eyes with one's hand." This meaning should have been expressed with a phrase like *te o kokazasu* (to slightly shade) in the first place, instead of *kote o kazasu.* These phrases have given trouble to the many compilers of dictionaries. They are examples of illogical construction in Japanese set phrases.

A slightly different contrast is the words *senjitsu* (some days ago) and *sennen* (some years ago) as opposed to *sengetsu* (last month) and *senshū* (last week). The *sen* in the first two words indicates "some time ago," but the *sen* in the last two words means "the one just before." Again, the word *hoshōnin* is "one who guarantees" but *shiyōnin,* although it is a word made by combining elements in the same way, means "one employed *by* another." Consistency is lacking here. Likewise, *fujin-yō tebukuro* means "gloves used *by* women," but *konchū-yō pin* denotes "pins used *for* insects." The *yunomi* is "a cup for tea," but *sake-nomi* (a drinker) does not mean "a cup for wine." It is strange that *ichibai* (literally, one double) in *hito ichibai* (*ichibai* more than others) denotes *nibai* (literally, two doubles, but actually meaning "double"). It is also confusing for *sankaiki* (the third anniversary of a person's death) to come the year after *isshūki* (the first anniversary of a person's death). Matsuzaka Tadanori, a leader of the Japanese language movement, gives the following examples of inconsistencies in Chinese character words, each character of which can have an individual meaning, creating all the more confusion.

For instance, if we did not know the meaning of *kūshū* 空襲 (air raid) but knew the meaning of each character, is it not natural to decide that *kūshū* means "to merely scare someone by attacking with blank shots," for there are words like *kūhō* 空砲 (a blank shot)? I have picked up the following words from the headlines of a newspaper at hand:

仏印 *Futsu-In*——French Indochina
亡命 *bōmei*——flight from one's own country
改革 *kaikaku*——reformation
画伯 *gahaku*——a master painter
弟子 *deshi*——a pupil
滑稽 *kokkei*——something humorous

If someone, not knowing the meaning of the above words, forms a judgment on the basis of the meaning of each character,* it is most natural for him to think that *Futsu-In* is "a seal of a temple"; *bōmei* "to lose one's life"; *kaikaku* "a new substitute for leather"; *gahaku* "a count who paints pictures"; *deshi* "the son of one's younger brother"; and *kokkei* "practice in skating."[12]

Futsu, Buddha; *in,* seal; *bō,* lose, die; *mei,* life; *kai,* reform; *kaku,* leather; *ga,* painting; *haku* can be a count; *de (tei),* younger brother; *shi,* child; *ko (kotsu),* slide; *kei,* think.

◆ 2. CHARACTERISTICS OF WORDS

How words are separated

When we compare several Japanese grammar books, we find that scholars are not in agreement as to where to place breaks between the words. Take, for example, the phrase *ikasetakara* (since I made someone go). According to Matsushita Daizaburō's grammar, the whole phrase is to be taken as one word, but in Yamada Yoshio's book, the phrase is composed of two words, *ikaseta + kara*. In Tokieda Motoki's book, the phrase is composed of three words: *ikase + ta + kara*. In the grammar of the Ministry of Education (which follows Ōtsuki's and Hashimoto's grammars), the phrase is composed of four words: *ika + se + ta + kara*.

I once thought such differences in distinguishing words in accordance with theories were due to the vagueness of the term "word" in Japanese, but I discovered that this does not seem to be the case. I have come to realize instead that since the Edo period Japanese grammarians have applied the traditional way of looking at ancient Japanese grammar to contemporary literary expressions and to contemporary spoken Japanese. According to ancient Japanese grammar, the phrase mentioned above would surely be *ika + se + tare + ba*, for when we examine the accent marks attached to words in old documents, it is clear that ancient Japanese phrases had to be broken in this way.

It would be wrong to think, however, that this is also true of present-day spoken Japanese. This is clear when we write the phrase, separating it into its components. If a child were asked to write the phrase *ikasetakara,* he would

138

most likely break it into two parts: *ikaseta kara.* The relative pitch of this phrase would be *iKASETA kaRA,* which also indicates that the phrase is composed of two elements. In his essay, "Fuzokugo to Fuzoku Keishiki" (Subordinate Words and Subordinate Forms) in the *Gengo Kenkyū* (A Study of Language), No. 15,[1] Hattori Shirō suggested an intelligible way of breaking words and phrases that can be generally applied to the languages of the world. According to him, the *joshi,* or particles, in the Ministry of Education's grammar are independent words, with the exception of a few words like *na,* which indicates prohibition, and the few connective particles called *setsuzoku joshi,* such as *ba, te, dewa,* and *temo,* which are verb suffixes. No auxiliary verbs *(jodōshi)* are independent (with the exception of *da, rashii,* and *darō),* but are attached to the preceding verb. Thus, the above-mentioned phrase, *ikasetakara,* would undoubtedly break in two: *ikaseta kara.* I think this theory will help lessen the chaotic state of Japanese grammar. Of the different theories above, Yamada's coincides with this one of Hattori. Yamada's grammar, on the whole, was excellent, but he was unwise in also trying to apply his theory to the grammar of ancient Japanese.

If one takes these things into consideration, Japanese is definitely not "a language in which the breaks between words are not clear." There are in fact languages in which such breaks are less clear. The languages of the American Indians, which are said to be composite and synthetic, are perhaps typical examples. Chinese word breaks are also exceedingly indistinct. The word *Jih pên* 日本 (Japan) in Chinese, for example, is distinctly composed of two words on the basis of its accent, but on the basis of its meaning we are inclined to consider it as one word. When the Chinese come across the word *Jih pên*, they are probably aware of the original meaning of the word ("the origin 本 of the sun 日") and feel the same way as the Japanese do toward words such as *sugi no ki* 杉の木 (the tree by the name of *sugi* [cedar]).

Japanese words are long

Japanese words are characteristically long. The languages of southeast Asia, such as Chinese, Vietnamese, Thai, Burmese, and Tibetan, are called monosyllabic languages, and are known for their short words. Wang Li says that since there are many words of two syllables in Mandarin, it is not entirely appropriate to call Chinese a monosyllabic language.[2] Despite this, there are still a great number of one-syllable words in Chinese. Among the European languages, English is known to have many one-syllable words.[3]

On the other hand, languages known for their long words are those Polynesian languages extending from Hawaii to New Zealand. According to the mathematician Yoshioka Shūichirō, there is a New Zealand mountain top called *Taumatahakatangihangkoauauotamateapokaiwhenuakitanahatu*. This is truly astonishing. In Hawaii there was a girl, born in Honolulu around the year 1936, named *Kananinohoaokuuhonooopuukainananalohiloohinokeyauealaulanakakalani Judd*. Her name means "Judd, sweet-smelling and beautiful, of our home at Diamond Head, which makes heaven overlook with wide-open eyes."[4] As discussed in the last chapter, every syllable in the Polynesian languages has a simple structure consisting of one consonant plus one vowel. Consequently, words become very long, and, in the example above, even if "Judd" were omitted, the girl's name would still have forty syllables. If asked to sign her full name she would have quite a task.

The nature of Japanese syllables is akin to that of Polynesian ones; thus, Japanese words tend to be long. The ancient name for the Japanese nation was *Toyoashihara-no-chiihoaki-no-nagaihoaki-no-mizuho-no-kuni*. According to a legend, one of the ancestors of the Imperial family had the name *Amenikishikuninikishiamatsuhitakahikoho-no-ninigi-no-mikoto*. The Japanese can, it seems, compete with the Hawaiians in the length of their words. Even though we no longer have such lengthy personal names, there are still many railway stations on the Odakyū train line with long names, such as Sosigayaookura and Seizyoogakuenmae.* I have seen foreigners reading them with knitted eyebrows.

Naturally, the longer the words, the longer people's daily conversations and writings become. It is said that performing foreign plays translated into Japanese requires more than twice as much time as performances in the original language. Several years ago, when the Zenshinza troupe was energetically staging Shakespeare's plays, an actor such as Nakamura Shingorō would appear at the curtain just before the performance was to begin and make the following introductory remarks:

We shall speak very fast in the play we are about to

---

*These spellings show the romanization in use at the time this book was published in Japanese. Modern-day romanization is slightly easier to read.

perform—*The Merchant of Venice*. We must speak all the lines in the original Shakespeare, without omitting anything, and within a given time; thus, we must speak very quickly.

The NHK announcer Asanuma Hiroshi said that he doubted the worth of Japanese when he saw the war-crimes trial at Ichigaya. While Attorney Keenan was very slowly giving his address, first-rate Japanese interpreters, though speaking without a pause, were unable to keep pace with him.[5] In Arthur Waley's translation of *Genji Monogatari* (The Tale of Genji), a thirteen-syllable sentence, *Miya wa ootonogomorinikeri,* has been translated into a sentence of only five syllables: "The child is asleep."

Jespersen says in his *Language* that ancient languages, such as Sanskrit and Zend (ancient Persian), abound with very long words and that the further back we go, the greater the number of unduly long words. The English "had" is the same as the Gothic *habaidedeima.* Long and clumsy words, he says, should be considered signs of barbarism.[6]

Abundance of variable words

People often discuss the fact that there are many words in Japanese with no one set form. This is especially true of the written language. For example, the word *hito* (a person) can be written as 人 or ひと or ヒト. This is a marked peculiarity of Japanese that cannot be found in any other language. Karl Busse's poem "Beyond the Mountains" has been translated by the English-language scholar Ueda Bin (1874–1916)[7] as follows:

Yama no anata no sora tōku
saiwai sumu to hito no yū.
Aa ware hito to tome yukite
namida sashigumi kaerikinu.
Yama no anata ni nao tōku
saiwai sumu to hito no yū.

"Across the mountains, beyond the distant sky,
Happiness resides," say the people.
Alas! I went with someone to search,
And came back filled with tears.
"Across the mountains and far beyond,
Happiness resides," people still say.

In lines two and six *hito* (people) is written in Chinese characters: 人. But the *hito* in line three is written in *kana* (ひと) to show that two different people are involved. Such differentiation may be convenient when composing a literary work, but it is not so desirable in everyday life.

Before the end of the war, there were a number of people who wrote 他人 (*tanin*, other person) and printed ひと (*hito*, a person) in *kana* alongside the characters to show the reading. At the same time others wrote 女人 (*nyonin*, a woman) accompanied by the same *kana*, ひと. Neither was considered wrong. Since the end of the war, the notion that everyone should express the same word in the same form has become more popular, which is a good thing, but the variation of such word forms as the above has not yet disappeared. This is particularly a problem when words are written in a mixture of Chinese characters and *kana*. For example, the word *akiraka ni* (plainly) is currently written in four forms: 明きらかに, 明らかに, 明かに, and occasionally, 明に. We should soon establish uniformity in the manner of writing such words.

Apart from the written characters themselves, Japanese words have yet another form—many of them have more than two different pronunciations. For example, it is difficult to tell whether 朝飯 (breakfast) is *asameshi* or *asahan,* and whether 夕飯 (supper) is *yumeshi* or *yuhan.** The existence of two ways of reading a single Chinese character —the so-called *ondoku* (reading the *kanji* with a Japanized Chinese pronunciation) and *kundoku* (applying an original Japanese reading to the *kanji*)—leaves foreigners with a very odd feeling, particularly when reading a person's name. The proper name 南原繁 can be read either "Nambara Shigeru" or "Minamibara Shigeru," and 矢内原 can be read either "Yanaibara" or "Yauchibara." The reading of 吉田甲子吉 as "Yoshida Kanekichi" is unusual, but perhaps less exceptional than the reading of 松谷天光光 as "Matsutani Mitsuko." There is hardly anyone who can read this name properly.

The most diverse element in pronunciation, however, is the accent. Even among those words considered to have standardized accents, there are two kinds of pitch accents for words like *densha* (an electric car)—*DEnsha* and *deN-SHA*—and *eiga* (movies)—*Eiga* and *eIGA.* Less common words have greater variations. For example, *arika* (one's whereabouts) has three different accents: *Arika, aRIka,* and *aRIKA; atakamo* (just as) has four different accents:

---

*If you say *yuhan* for supper, your reading is *ondoku* for both characters. If you say *yumeshi,* the first character is *ondoku* but the second character *meshi* is *kundoku.*

Atakamo, aTAkamo, aTAKAmo, and *aTAKAMO.* In short, since these words are pronounced with every possible accent variation, it would seem that there are no fixed accent patterns at all.

Many homonyms and synonyms

Another peculiarity of the vocabulary in Japanese is the large number of homonyms. Even if we limit ourselves to words used only in the same context, there are such terms as *kōgyō* (manufacturing) and *kōgyō* (mining), the *seishigyō* of the paper industry and *seishigyō* of the silk-reeling industry, and others too numerous to mention.

The existence of many homonyms causes various misunderstandings in daily life. The recent distribution of *jun* 準 (semi-) home-grown rice disappointed the housewives who had rejoiced, thinking they would get *jun* 純 (genuine) home-grown rice. When the then Minister of Education, Takase Sōtarō, was asked at the Assembly by a member of the Diet: "What is your opinion on *kokuhō* 国法 (national law)?" he said sympathetically, "The recent fire at Hōryūji temple was most regrettable." The temple, preserved as a *kokuhō* 国宝 (a national treasure), had been partly burned not long before.

The following dialogue may look very artificial, but it is said that it actually happened and that "A" here is Ikeuchi Nobuyoshi.

> B: What business are you engaged in Tōkyō?
> A: I am publishing a magazine called *Nōgaku* 能楽 (Nō Plays).

B: What? *Nōgaku* 農学 (The Science of Agriculture)? That's fine. I would like my sons to read it, too. Its circulation must be large. *Nō* 農 (agriculture) is Japan's treasure.

A: Thank you. I am not a specialist in the field, but I would like to help this art develop and work with *nōgakushi* 能楽師 (Nō players).

B: Indeed! You don't look like one who has worked in *nō* (agriculture). It would be nice to work with the *nōgakushi* 農学士 (those holding degrees in agriculture).

A: Besides, the ones like the *hayashikata* (members of the orchestra) will gradually die out if left as they are. I want to make an effort to cultivate them, too.

B: The *hayashi* (forests) and *ta* (rice-fields) are indeed gradually decreasing. So more of your subscribers are in the countryside, I suppose.

A: Since there are few professional *gakushi* 楽師 (Nō players) in the countryside, naturally more people there read the magazine.

B: You're quite right. The young people in the rural areas have also become more educated nowadays. . . ."[8]

Hayashi Ōki regards the abundance of synonyms as characteristic of Japanese.[9] This abundance arises mostly from the existence of both Yamato words and Chinese character words for the same concept, and, similarly, of both spoken words and written words. The different synonyms for "many," such as *ōi, takusan, tasū,* and *amata,* may be found in other countries, too, but it must be a rarity for a language to possess such bilateral numerals as *ichi* and *hitotsu* for one, *ni* and *futatsu* for two, *san* and *mittsu* for three, *shi* and *yottsu* for four, and so forth. Japanese is, therefore, in this respect similar to English, which uses words of Anglo-Saxon and Latin origins. Mori Ōgai (1862–1922), the great novelist, playwright, and critic of the Meiji period, says that it is very easy to translate European writings into Japanese, for Japanese has a rich vocabulary. Japanese may be a language which can be easily manipulated by men of letters, but it is exceedingly difficult for foreigners to master. No doubt the language must also be difficult for Japanese children, too.

Distinctions between parts of speech

Lastly, the distinction between parts of speech of Japanese words is comparatively clear. Fundamentally speaking, verbs and nouns exist in extreme opposition to each other. In Semitic and Finno-Ugric languages, however, verbs and nouns are almost indistinguishable.[10] These elements do not seem to be very distinct in English, either. The word "but" is either a conjunction or an adverb, but there is a phrase, "but me no buts," meaning, "Don't say 'but, but.' " The first "but" is a verb, and the second a noun. In Chinese, the word *hsien* 賢 is essentially an adjective, meaning "wise," but in the *Analects of Confucius* is the expression 賢賢易色 (Respect the wise for being wise and substitute it for pleasures). The first 賢 is a verb, the second a noun. In the Malay language, too, they say that the same word may be used as a noun, an adjective, or a verb.[11]

One does not find such extreme cases in Japanese. During

the war, when the then Minister of Education, Hashida Kunihiko, said *kagaku suru* (to think scientifically), using the noun *kagaku* (science) as a verb, there was a loud protest, saying that no such verb existed. In Japanese, then, it is unthinkable to use a conjunction for a verb (as in the above example). Even the *kagaku suru* used by Hashida has the suffix *suru* (to do) attached to the noun. There is a group of words called *keiyō dōshi* (adjectival verb)—for example, *shizuka nari* (is quiet)—which often presents problems as to whether these words are nouns or adjectives. Actually, the distinction is very clear. The modifier *hijō ni* (very) can be placed before them, and the suffix *na* (which cannot be attached to a noun) can be placed after them; and from the standpoint of meaning, they are obviously adjectives, not nouns. In Europe there are many languages in which there is no clear-cut boundary between substantives and adjectives.[12] In the Orient, too, Korean does not clearly distinguish between adjectives and verbs.

The difference in opinion among Japanese scholars about the parts of speech is now a problem in the teaching of grammar, but if scholars were queried on this problem in, for instance, the English language, they would have even more varied opinions. The differences between the grammar taught in school and the grammar of Jespersen or C. C. Fries are far greater than the differences existing between the grammars of Ōtsuki, Yamada, Matsushita, Hashimoto, and Tokieda of Japan. At present the great variance in the theories in Japan is due to the different methods of separating words, and if this could be made uniform, probably all the theories would basically be alike in classifying the parts of speech.

◆ 3. THE CULTURAL INDEX

Nature of the vocabulary

The vocabulary system of a language is said to be the cultural index of the people. This is why the characteristics of the vocabulary of a language tend to excite a special interest.

A generation ago there flourished one after another theories linking characteristics of Japanese language to the Japanese mind. They asserted, for example, that the abundance of vowels in Japanese indicates that the Japanese are just and fair or that the lack of differentiation between singular and plural in Japanese indicates the lack of a numerical sense among the Japanese.

Such conclusions were mostly misapplications. The characteristics of the sound system or the forms of a language do not change so easily under the influence of different modes of culture. For example, in spite of the great differences between British and American national traits, there are hardly any differences at all between the sound systems and forms of the two languages. Sound systems and forms of languages are deeply rooted and quite invariable. Therefore, if peculiarities in the sound system and forms of a language show anything at all, they show the nature of the ancestral language or the nature of other languages which influenced that language to a large degree. On the other hand, vocabulary is easily influenced in various aspects by culture and life, and therefore clearly tells something about the characteristics of the people.

Various ways of differentiation

When we entered middle school and studied English for the first time, we were surprised at the narrow differentiation of domestic animals. The Japanese use the general term *ushi* to denote the bull or cow, and if we want to differentiate between them at all, we say *oushi* (male *ushi*), *meushi* (female *ushi*), *oya-ushi* (grown-up *ushi*), and *koushi* (young *ushi*), at the most. In English, however, a female *ushi* is a "cow," a male is an "ox" if it is castrated and a "bull" if it is not, and a young bull or cow is called a "calf." Every one of them is called by an entirely different name. When we learned that it is also the same for goats and sheep, we were amazed at the minuteness of differentiation in the language.

I have come to the realization, however, that perhaps we need not admire only English in this area. Although Japanese is less exact about the names of domestic animals, it is very particular in regard to the names of fish. For example, the roe of a herring is called *kazunoko*, while the roe of a salmon is called *sujiko* or *ikura*. Furthermore, the fish called *bora* (gray mullet) is called *subashiri* when it is very small, and as it grows larger is called *ina, bora,* and finally *todo*. Thus, Japanese is also quite detailed.

The reason why cattle are narrowly differentiated in England and other European countries is simply that these peoples have since early times raised cattle, drunk milk, eaten butter, and skinned the cattle to make shoes. Therefore, even in Japan, when we go to districts where cattle raising prospers, we see people readily making distinctions of this sort. In Hiroshima, for instance, a bull is called *kotoi,* a cow is called *oname,* and a calf is called *beko.*[1] Thus, people make detailed distinctions among things which have a great deal to do with their livelihood but only rough distinctions among things which do not. Consequently, we are able to know the broader aspects of a people's culture if we know what sorts of things their language differentiates in detail. Such things cannot be grasped through the clarification of a sound system or the phraseology of a language.

Before going further along these lines, I would like to call your attention again to the fact that Japanese comprises Yamato words, Chinese character words, and Western words or loanwords. Moreover, Shibuzawa Keizō has divided Japanese into primary and secondary words.[2] Words such as *yama* (mountain) and *hato* (a pigeon) are primary words, and words made by combining these primary words, such as *yamabato* (turtledove; literally, mountain pigeon) are secondary words. Furthermore, *yamabato-iro* (*yamabato*-color), if such a word exists, would be a tertiary word. When we classify words this way, we realize that things expressed by Yamato words have from ancient times been regarded as having more value than those things expressed by Chinese character words or loanwords. Among the Chinese character words and loanwords, there are some which have been coined or given new meanings in Japan. These words have not simply been imported and, therefore, have special value.

Words characteristic of a language

A vocabulary represents the life and culture of the people not merely through its exactness or vagueness of differentiation. According to linguist Kumazawa Ryū, one way of searching for the distinguishing traits of a people and their lives is to pick out the words in their vocabulary that cannot be translated into other languages.[3]

In his book *Eikoku Kokuminsei* (The National Traits of the English), Saitō Takeshi, a scholar in English literature, states that the word "gentleman" is a pride of the English, and, like "home" and "sports," is supposed to have a connotation that cannot be translated into any foreign language. They say that even in France, a country averse to foreign words, the Academy has decided to adopt "gentleman" as a loanword. Its Japanese translation is *shinshi*, which signifies an impeccable appearance but does not go further to indicate the perfection of a gentleman's personality. There is also the word *kunshi*, but this, too, falls short of describing the perfection of his common sense. There appears, after all, to be no exact counterpart of "gentleman" in Japanese.

According to Kumazawa, the German language has such untranslatable words as *Gemüt, Sehnsucht, Heimweh,* and *Biederkeit.* Similarly, there are words such as *esprit, gloire, bon mot,* and *frivolité* in French.

What, then, are some of the untranslatable words in Japanese? Strictly speaking, it is not correct to ask such a question in the first place. Each language has its own system of vocabulary, and the value of each word derives from its position in relation to all the other words in the language. Therefore, when we take an English word and its corresponding Japanese term, for example, their meanings can never be identical. Thus, theoretically, no words in Japanese can be translated.

Some very common words in Japanese require long explanations when they are translated into other languages. Such words can be said to be peculiar to Japanese. It is extremely important for us to pay attention to these words both when we teach the language to non-Japanese and when we ourselves learn foreign languages. Fortunately, a number of reports dealing with such words have been compiled by people in various fields of study.

We say "untranslatable," but it is only natural that the names of things that exist only in Japan be found only in Japanese. Among such words are *kadomatsu* (the New Year's decoration of pine branches at the entrance of a house), *shimekazari* (the sacred Shinto festoon composed of straw rope and paper), and foods such as *norimaki* (seasoned rice rolled in seaweed called *nori*) and *botamochi* (a rice cake covered with sweet bean paste). Such terms do not constitute real problems in translation. A characteristically Japanese word is one that is found only in the Japanese language, although the objects it indicates are also found in other countries.

Favorite words

Lastly, each country has its own favorite words. According to Sasaki Tatsu, a scholar of English, the Japanese are fond of using the word *kokugo* and, indeed, even primary school pupils are familiar with it.[4] Its English translation would be "the national language." This expression is said to be used in England only on special occasions. A book in which it appears is most likely to be a very difficult one written for specialists. The word *kokugo* is doubtless an expression of the Japanese psychology that makes a strict distinction between Japanese things and foreign things.

Fukuda Tsuneari says in *Nihon oyobi Nihonjin* (Japan and the Japanese): "To a Japanese, white people are white people before they are individuals like Mary or François. Similarly, we Japanese are Japanese before we are individuals like Tarō or Hanako."[5] The existence of words like *kokushi* (Japanese history), *hōgaku* (Japanese music), and *wafuku* (Japanese clothes) is one indication of our feeling that distinctions should be made between Japanese and foreign things.* The writing of foreign words in stiff *katakana* to distinguish them from other words as if they were objects of our enmity, is an expression of that same feeling.

Before the war, an exercise program on the radio began with: *Zenkoku no minasan, ohayō gozaimasu!* (People of the entire nation, good morning!). One story has it that a foreigner wondered why they used the term *zenkoku no* (of the whole country) every day. *Zenkoku* is surely one of our favorite words.

When General MacArthur came to Japan after the war and spoke on the radio to the American occupation officers and men, it was interesting that his first word was: "Boys!" Had it been a Japanese officer in command, what would he have said? Most likely he would have addressed them: *Chūyū musō no waga kokugun no shōhei ni tsugu* . . . (To the peerlessly loyal and brave officers and men of our nation's army . . .).

In short, the Japanese are very fond of the word *koku*

---

*The *koku* and *hō* mean "country"; when used as prefixes they mean "Japan." *Wa* is a name for Japan.

(country) and its compounds. This is probably similar to the fondness in the United States for using the word "world." The United States championship baseball playoff is referred to there as the World Series, but the Japanese, even assuming there were no better players in other countries and they were aware of it, would probably not call an all-Japan judo tournament a "world tournament."

In the chapters that follow, I will examine the special characteristics of the Japanese vocabulary.

◆ 4. NATURE

The weather

Kikuchi Kan (1888–1948), a prominent novelist, once wrote an essay in English called "Current Literature in Japan," in which he stated the following:

> There are over twenty names for rain. Rain is called by different names according to the season and the manner of its falling, and each name is rich in literary associations. *Harusame* means "spring rain," but in the Japanese word *harusame* there is an infinite wealth of poetry and vision.[1]

Indeed, there are a great many names pertaining to rain in Japanese: *shigure* (a late autumn or early winter shower), *samidare* (the long rain of early summer), *yūdachi* (a squall-like shower in summer, usually in the evening), *mizore* (sleet). Both *tsuyu* (the season of the long rain in summer from about the 10th of June to the 10th of July) and *samidare* refer to the same thing, but *samidare* indicates the rain itself, and *tsuyu* designates the period when *samidare* occurs. Consequently, we make the distinction between the two by saying *yanda* (has stopped) in relation to *samidare*, but *aketa* (is over) in relation to *tsuyu*. In his book *Fūdo to Bungaku* (Natural Features and Literature),[2] Terada Torahiko (1878–1935), a physicist and essayist, gives the following as examples of Japanese words that cannot be translated into other languages: *hana-gumori* (a hazy sky in the cherry-blossom

156

season; literally, flower cloudiness) and *inazuma* (lightning),*
in addition to *samidare* and *shigure*. For wind, there are
words like *kochi* (the easterly wind in spring), *nowaki* (the
strong wind that blows during stormy weather occurring
on about the 210th day after the opening of spring), and
kogarashi (the cold wind that blows from autumn to early
winter). As there were no original Chinese characters for
nagi 凪 (the calming of the waves) and *kogarashi* 凩, *kokuji*
(Japanese characters) were created especially for them.
In the coastal regions, people use many different names for
the winds, such as *narai* (a winter wind) and *inasa* (a southeast wind), according to the direction, strength, and season
in which they blow. All this is found in detail in the book
Fūikō Shiryō (The Data on Wind Directions).[3]

Thus, there are many words related to atmospheric
phenomena. Surely this is due to the fact that the Japanese
have lived in and adapted themselves to a land of enor-
mously changeable weather. It is widely known that the
Japanese talk first about the weather when exchanging
greetings. Commodore Perry, who came to Japan at the
end of the Edo period, criticized the inefficiency of the
Japanese officials who did this before beginning their discussions. That diaries printed in Japan always have a
column for notes about the weather is related to the same
practice.

Levy-Bruhl's statement that so exact a perspective on
weather can be seen frequently among uncivilized peoples
is disheartening to the Japanese. But it is true that, for

*Literally, "the husband of the rice." Lightning often occurs over the
paddy during the growing season, and it is believed that this ripens the
rice.

example, the Bawenda tribe of South Africa has a special name for every kind of rain and the North American Indians "have many expressions, which may almost be called scientific, for frequently recurring forms of the clouds."[4] Since weather is a major influence on the lives of such peoples, weather-related words have formed an extensive part of their vocabularies. Their daily conversations must have a poetic beauty.

The seasons

It is worth noting that weather differences are almost all expressed in connection with the seasons—a reflection of the remarkable transitions between seasons in Japan. In order to see how closely these transitions are related to the vocabulary, one should take a look at the *Saijiki*, the book that explains the season words of *haiku* verse. Indeed, the very existence of such a book is peculiar to Japan.

The special *haiku* phrases, such as *mizu nurumu* (the water has become less cold), *yama warō* (literally, the mountains laugh, a description of spring mountains in comparison with the desolate winter mountains), and *kaze hikaru* (the wind shines), are very characteristic of Japan. It is interesting that spring days are called *hinaga* 日永 (long days). The word *eijitsu* 永日 (long days), the inverse of *hinaga*, can also be found in Chinese. The Chinese term, however, originally referred to summer days. The following sentence appears in Po Chu-i's writings:[5] 竹院君閑銷永日 (The lord spends the long day leisurely in a bamboo garden). Here the word 永日 is said to refer to early summer. *Hinaga* in Japanese *waka* and *haiku*, however, refers to spring. The *haiku* book

Kokkei Sōdan (Humorous Idle Talks)[6] comments on long days, saying that the daytime is actually longer in summer than in spring, but that "in Japan it is generally accepted that the long days are the spring days, a strange idea."

But this explanation is too logical an attempt. Unlike winter days the spring day is slow to get dark; therefore, it feels long. Japanese poetical sentiment and the Japanese feeling for the seasons are fully manifested in this word. Such expressions as *mijikayo* (summer nights; literally, short nights), *yonaga* (autumn nights; literally, long nights), and *tanjitsu* (winter days; literally, short days) are all of great interest.

In *Tsurezure-gusa* (Essays in Idleness),[7] there is a famous passage admiring the natural objects of the four seasons that begins: *Orifushi no utsurikawaru koso* (The transitions of the seasons). It should be noted that the author, Kenkō, devotes his attention more to the transitions of the seasons than to the seasons themselves. Such phrases as *harumeku* (to become more like spring) and *akimeku* (to become more like autumn) are not found in either Chinese or English.

Thus, the Japanese attach importance to the natural phenomena that proclaim the passage from one season to another. *Hatsu-shimo* (the first frost of the year), *hatsu-yuki* (the first snow of the year), *hatsu-kaminari* (the first thunder of the year), and *hatsu-shigure* (the first late-autumn showers) are characteristically Japanese. Words dealing with food, such as *hashiri* (the first fish, vegetables, and so forth of the season), *shun* (the best season for certain foods), and *tabegoro* (the right time for eating certain foods) are said to be untranslatable.

Words relating to weather and seasons are gradually

disappearing, even in Japan. The following words have already become obsolete: *izayoi* (the 16th night of the lunar month), *imachi-no-tsuki* (the 18-day-old moon; literally, the sit-waiting moon), *tachimachi-no-tsuki* (the 17-day-old moon; literally, the stand-waiting moon), *satsuki-yami* (the dark nights during the rainy season), *ariake* (a daybreak with a wan morning moon), *akebono* (the break of dawn), *asaborake* (a dimly dawning day), and *shinonome* (the first hint of dawn). There was once a dispute in the newspaper over whether *hisame* (hailstorm) meant "hail" or "the winter rain," the original meaning of the word having been forgotten. The word *nowaki*, which originally indicated a typhoon occurring around the time of *nihyakutōka* (the 210th day after the first day of spring), was mistaken for *kogarashi* (the cold wintry wind) by the prominent novelist, Natsume Sōseki (1867–1916), and used for the title of his novel.[8]

Heavenly bodies

Japanese is not rich in names of heavenly bodies and is notably deficient in names of stars. Shimmura Izuru has noted in his book, *Namban Sarasa* (The Hand-patterned Cotton Prints from the South),[9] that this makes one wonder whether any attention was paid to heavenly bodies in Japan before the introduction of horoscopes and astrology from China; the names of stars used by the Japanese, such as *kinsei* (Venus), *kasei* (Mars), and *hokkyokusei* (the North Star) are mostly Chinese words. Original Japanese names for stars and constellations—like *subaru* (Pleiades), *akaboshi* (the morning star), and *yūzutsu* (the evening star)—are extremely few. The meagerness of such terms in Japanese offers a remarkable contrast with Chinese, Babylonian, Arabic, and Greek.

After Shimmura put forth this idea, quite a number of the names of stars used by Japanese farmers and fishermen were compiled by Nojiri Hōei and Uchida Takeshi, but these were all secondary words, such as *karasuki-boshi* (the three stars of the constellation of Orion; literally, the plow-shaped stars) and *oya-ninai-boshi* (literally, the parent-carrying star). Probably, the Japanese were preoccupied with many other things and did not feel the necessity of paying the stars much attention. Had *haiku* existed not in Japan but in a place like Egypt and had the *Saijiki* been edited there, the book would have, no doubt, been filled with the names of stars and constellations.

Topography

There are many words relating to nature which denote aspects of topography and flowing water. Yanagida Kunio writes in his *Chimei no Kenkyū* (A Study of Place Names) that it was foolish for geographers during the Meiji period to coin Chinese character words like *ryūiki* (a drainage area) and *bunsuirei* (a watershed) to describe the topography.[10] Unfortunately, people from the city who coined such words were unaware that from the very beginning Japanese has had an enormous number of words related to topography, such as *kawachi* (a small flat area in a valley), *tawa* (a depression on a mountain top), *hanawa* (a portion of a mountain which juts out), *yura* (land made level by water), *naru* (a flat place between mountains), *hoki* (a steep section of the mountain side), and *nozoki* (a border wasteland). It is natural that the Japanese use such words, for they live in a land of complicated topography and have been constantly subject to its constraints.

The Japanese, surrounded by water, have words such as *oki* (the offing) and *nada* (the rough open sea where navigation is difficult), which have no counterparts in Chinese. Consequently, they were forced to create such characters as 沖 *oki* or to appropriate characters with other meanings to use with words like *nada* 灘. The *kami* (upstream) and *shimo* (downstream) of a river also have no equivalents in Chinese; therefore, the character *ue* 上 (up) was appropriated for the former and the character *shita* 下 (down) for the latter. If Chinese characters had been invented in Japan, the basic index of a character dictionary would have been full of characters pertaining to seas and rivers; the character *oki* might have used *umi* 海 (sea) for its left-hand radical and *naka* 中 (middle) for its body; the character *nada* might have been created with *umi* as its left-hand radical and *nan* 難 (difficult) as its body. Perhaps the characters for "upstream" and "downstream" might have used "river" 川 as their left-hand radicals, with "up" 上 as the body of the former, and "down" 下 as the body of the latter. Japanese words like *e* 江 (an inlet), *se* 瀬 (shallows), *tsu* 津 (a harbor), and *su* 洲 (a sand bank) are all represented by characters with one-syllable readings.

Water

One representative basic word of the Japanese language is *mizu* 水 (water). Unlike the English "water," *mizu* has a very narrow meaning. It is unique in that it represents a thing in the natural world and does not include spittle, tears, sweat, and rain. Moreover, it indicates something cold, contrasting with *yu*, which means hot water. This can be illustrated in the following selection from *manzai* (a comic stage dialogue):

> A: Then I would like to ask you—what is *mizu* in English?
> B: Wōtā (water)!
> A: Excellent. What, then, is *yu*?
> B: (Somewhat hesitantly) Waitā (literally, boiled)!

An American who could not speak Japanese well came to a Japanese hotel and asked for some hot water to wash his face. He said in Japanese, *Atsui mizu o kudasai* (Give me some hot *mizu*), literally translating "hot water" into Japanese. The maid, who had always understood *mizu* to mean cold water, could not imagine what he meant.

Yu 湯 is a characteristically Japanese word. Hashimoto Shinkichi has said that it is typically Japanese to use the one-syllable word *yu* for "hot water." In modern Chinese the character 湯 is pronounced *tang* and means "soup." Hot water (Japanese *yu*) is either *kai shui* 開水 or *pai shui* 白水 in Chinese. Both in English and Chinese, therefore, *yu* is only a kind of *mizu* (water) and not, as in Japanese, something that exists in contrast to *mizu*. The attribute *nurui* (lukewarm) of *yu* is also a typically Japanese expression.

Koide Fumiko, head professor of Japanese at International Christian University, says it is very difficult to make American students understand the meaning of the Japanese word *nigoru*. *Nigoru* does not necessarily mean "muddy," whose meaning is more like *doro-mizu* (muddy water) in Japanese; therefore, *nigoru* must be expressed by two words in English: "not clear." This phenomenon is typical of Japan, where water is highly esteemed.

Another noticeable trait of Japanese concerning water is the number of words pertaining to moisture. There are words like *nureru* (to get wet with water), *shimeru* (to become damp), *shitoru* (to become moist), *uruou* (to be moistened, as of land), *sobotsu* (to become wet; sometimes used when speaking of a soft rain), and *hotobiru* (to be swollen with water). Such particularity based on the way a thing is moistened is typically Japanese. The profusion of onomatopoeic words in Japanese is well known; of these words, those related to moisture alone amount to a sizeable number: e.g., *shippori* (to be drenched with rain), *shittori* (to be softly moist), *jimejime* (to be sodden, as of the ground), *shimeyaka* (to be softly moistened, as by the quietly drizzling rain), *bishobisho* (to be soaking wet, also said of the drizzling rain), *gushogusho* (to be wet through), *bichabicha* (to be dripping wet, also said of splashing one's way through the water), and *jitojito* (to be damp). Koide says she has a difficult time making American students understand these words as well as expressions like *sugasugashii* (refreshing), *sappari* (to feel refreshed and relieved), and *sawayaka* (refreshing, also said of the bracing wind).

Similar to its lack of names for stars, Japanese has few indigenous terms for minerals. Two of the few Yamato words related to minerals are *suzu* (tin) and *namari* (lead). Even for such important minerals as *kin* (gold), *gin* (silver), *dō* (copper), and *tetsu* (iron), Chinese words have been used. There are Yamato words like *kogane* (gold; literally, yellow metal), *shirogane* (silver; literally, white metal), *akagane* (copper; literally, red metal), and *kurogane* (iron; literally, black metal), but they were probably translations of Chinese words. Most of the names of minerals which we learn in grammar school science class, such as *jitetsukō* (magnetic iron), *kōdōkō* (brass), *suishō* (crystal), and *hōkai-seki* (calcite), are Chinese character words. Apparently the Japanese first learned how to use minerals when they began to associate with the Chinese.

Vegetation

In contrast to its words for minerals, Japanese is rich in its vocabulary for vegetation. There are many names of trees expressed by primary words, such as *matsu* (pine), *sugi* (Japan cedar), *hi* (Japanese cypress), *kaya* (*Torreya nucifera*), *maki* (Chinese black pine), *momi* (fir), *tsuga* (hemlock-spruce), *kuri* (chestnut), *shii* (pasania), *kashi* (oak), *nara* (Japanese oak), *buna* (beech), *muku* (*Aphananthe aspera*), *kuwa* (mulberry), *kusu* (camphor), *hō* (*Magnolia hypoleuca*), *nashi* (pear), *tsuge* (box-tree), *kaki* (persimmon), and *kiri* (paulownia). Names of grasses—especially those with long leaves—are also numerous and include *take* (bamboo), *sasa* (bamboo grass), *shino* (small bamboo), *ashi* (reed), *ogi* (common reed), *kaya* (miscanthus), *susuki* (Japanese pampas grass), *komo* (water oat), *chi* (a species of reed), *suge* (sedge), *i* (rush), and *gama* (bulrush). All Japanese know these words even when they are not familiar with the actual vegetation to which they refer. This is only natural for a people born in a country rich in the variety of vegetation, who once lived in wooden houses and wore clothes made of vegetable fiber. Levy-Bruhl says that there are many names for plants in the language of the Maori tribe of New Zealand and that "they have distinctive names for the male and female of some trees" as well as different terms for "different stages of growth" of the same tree.[11] While the Chinese use only one word, *shu lin tzu* 樹林子, to represent a group of trees, Japanese makes a distinction in density, with *mori* 森 to signify a grove, and *hayashi* 林 to signify a forest. This might be expected in Japan, where vegetation is luxuriant.

It is intriguing that we have the word *saku* for the opening of a flower and *chiru* for its fall. The Japanese have applied the native reading *saku* (to bloom) to the Chinese character 咲. In Chinese, this character means "to laugh." Similarly, *chiru* has been applied to the character 散. In China, 散 is not commonly used in connection with flowers; the character 落 (to fall) is used instead. Where English "die" refers to both the animal and vegetable kingdoms, the Japanese word *kareru* refers only to the death of plants. It is hard to say whether the existence of the words *saku* and *chiru* is characteristically Japanese, but it has certainly enhanced *waka* and *haiku* literature.

Terada Torahiko, the physicist, says that the word *edaburi* (the way a tree branches) probably cannot be translated into Western languages,[12] and Tanigawa Tetsuzō has pointed to the beauty of the word *hanafubuki* (flowers falling in the wind like snowflakes).[13] Thus, Japanese abounds in words that reveal an appreciation of nature. The following words used in *haiku* are peculiar to Japanese: *shitamoe* (sprouts shooting from the ground), *wakakaede* (maples covered with new leaves), *natsukusa* (a luxuriant growth of summer grasses), *konoshita-yami* (darkness cast by dense trees), *hanano* (the fields covered with flowers in autumn), *kaerizaki* (the unseasonable blooming of flowers; also the second blooming of spring flowers in autumn), *kusa-momiji* (the tinged grasses in autumn), and *fuyu-kodachi* (the winter trees without leaves). Others include *yozakura* (the cherry blossoms viewed at night by torchlight; literally, night *sakura*), *hazakura* (the cherry trees with young buds, after the flowers are gone; literally, leaves *sakura*), and *osozakura* (the cherry blossoms opening late in season; literally, late *sakura*).

Animals

Japanese is especially meager in names for domestic animals. This is not surprising, for Japan is not a cattle-raising country. As already noted, English distinguishes cattle, sheep, goats, and the like; this tendency is widely seen from Europe to Asia. When we open a character dictionary to the section under the "horse" radical, we find numerous characters unknown to us with "horse" as the left-hand radical—all refer to various species of horses. It is said that there are more than five hundred Arabic words denoting various species of camels.[14] In the language of the Lapps, there are a great many terms distinguishing various kinds of reindeer according to age, from one to seven years.[15] When we look up the word *naku* (to cry) in a Japanese-English dictionary, we find a list of more than ten different English words for the cries of different domestic animals, such as cattle and sheep; in standard Japanese, however, there are only such words as *inanaku* and *hoeru,* for horses and dogs respectively. In the Lithuanian language, there are many words for the color gray, each of which is applied to a different domestic animal.[16] In Mongolian, the words referring to horse manure are differentiated on the basis of its age and dryness.[17]

Animal names that abound in Japanese are those of fish; this can be seen at once by opening to the listing for "fish" in the Chinese-character dictionary. There you will find an array of words, each with a note saying that its *kanji* was developed in Japan. Indeed, we see an enormous number of primary words which are names of fish; some of these are: *koi* (carp), *funa* (crucian carp), *tai* (sea bream), *sake* (salmon), *masu* (trout), *aji* (horse mackerel), *fugu* (globefish), *kochi* (flathead), and *hamo* (sea eel). Especially notable is the large number of fish, called *shusse-uo* (literally, the fish which rises in the world), whose names change according to the different stages in their growth. As already mentioned, *bora* (gray mullet) is called *subashiri, ina, bora,* and *todo* as it grows bigger. An extreme example of *shusse-uo* is the *buri* (yellow tail) found in the Sea of Kumano in Mie prefecture. As it grows, it changes its name from *sejiro* to *tsubasu, wakana, kateio, inada, warasa,* and, finally, *buri.*[18]

Japanese is also rich in names of birds and insects. This is due not so much to the fact that the Japanese have made use of these creatures as to their great variety and to people's familiarity with them. Just as European languages differentiate the cries of animals, Japanese differentiates between the cries of birds: *saezuru* for small birds, *tsugeru* (to inform) for chickens, *nanoru* (to call oneself) for cuckoos and skylarks, *tataku* (to tap) for water rails, and *kyō o yomu* (to read a sutra) for nightingales.

There are many names for insects that cry in autumn. For example, there are *kōrogi* (a cricket), *suzumushi* (a kind of cricket; literally, a bell-ringing insect), *matsumushi* (a kind of cricket), *kirigirisu* (a grasshopper), and *kutsuwa-mushi* (a very noisy species of cricket). When we look in a Japanese-German dictionary for *kōrogi* or *suzumushi* or *matsumushi,* the same German term appears. Kanetsune Kiyosuke, a critic of music, says in his writings that when he once climbed the Alps with some Germans, he heard a *suzumushi* chirping at the foot of the mountains. As he walked on he heard a *matsumushi*. When he told his companions about this, they were wide-eyed with wonder and admiration at his keen ear. Koizumi Yakumo says in his short essay, "Kusa Hibari" (A Small Cricket),[19] that the only people who appreciate autumn insects are the Greeks and the Japanese. This illustrates the preference of the Japanese people for nature.

◆ 5. HUMAN BIOLOGY AND EMOTIONS

The human body

When we turn from animals to the human body, the vocabulary of Japanese suddenly reveals its limitations. The Japanese are extraordinarily non-specific about the parts of the human body. An extreme example of this would be their practice of calling both the hand and the arm *te* and both the foot and the leg *ashi*. From any standpoint this is inconvenient. The differentiation between *te* (hand) and *ude* (arm) by the former Japanese army was quite unusual. Once an instructor, a graduate of a non-military school, wished to make the soldiers do some setting-up exercises, and ordered: "Raise your *te*!" Contrary to the instructor's expectations, not one person raised his arm. They all raised their fingers instead, bending them backward like those of the images of Sakyamuni Buddha.[1]

Similarly, the Japanese word *kubi* stands for both the head and the neck, and *shiri* stands for both the buttocks and the base of the spine. For *hige* (the growth of hair on a man's face), both Chinese and European languages use primary words like "beard," "moustache," and "whiskers," but Japanese uses secondary words—*ago-hige* (chin *hige* or beard), *kuchi-hige* (mouth *hige* or moustache), and *hō-hige* (cheek *hige* or whiskers). *Hana* (nose) and *chichi* (breasts) name both the organ and its secretions.

There are some words whose meanings have changed in time because it was not clear exactly which part of the body they indicated. For example, the word *tsura,* which is now

170

used in the sense of "face," formerly meant "cheek," as can be seen in the word *tsuragamachi* (cheekbones). The word *tsume* (fingernail) must have formerly been used to denote the tips of the fingers, since it is used in such words as *tsume-in* (thumb-print), *tsumasaki* (the tips of the toes), and *tsumaguru* (to roll something between the thumb and the fingers).

Some underdeveloped peoples make minute differentiations between the parts of the human body. The indigenous people of Australia have a name for every small portion of their bodies; were strangers to point and ask them the name for the arm, "one stranger would get the name for the upper arm, another for the lower arm, another for the right arm, another for the left arm, etc."[2]

According to Chiri Mashio's *Bunrui Ainugo Jiten* (Classified Ainu Dictionary),[3] Ainu is also very rich in such words relating to the human body. Different names, for example, are used for the inner and outer edges of the eyebrow. Therefore, in examining identical passages written in Ainu and Japanese, we notice that the Ainu words are short but the Japanese translations of them are exceedingly long. One such example is "the hollow between the upper edge of the thyroid cartilage and the hyoid bone." There is also a special name for the edge of the hand on the side of the little finger—the part with which the wrestler Rikidōzan used to give his karate punch. This word is said to be used to describe something long and slender, like a long face.

I recall reading in a book on anthropology that there is a word in Japanese, *wakiga* (underarm odor), which denotes a physical phenomenon which has no counterpart in any European language. According to the book, this phenomenon is inseparable from Europeans and consequently does not present them any special problem. The words *mochihada* (skin soft and white like *mochi* or rice cake) and *samehada* (goose skin) are said to be peculiar to Japanese, originating from the great attention we pay to the fine texture of the skin.

Internal organs

Japanese is even more deficient in words denoting internal organs. The Japanese took all the names for such things as stomach, intestine, lung, and heart from Chinese. *Kimo* (liver) is perhaps the only organ which has an original Japanese name. In German, words of this sort have become part of the everyday language. Ogata Tomio says that when his elder brother was in the department of pediatrics in a German graduate school, a mother once brought her child and talked about his *Magen* (stomach), *Darm* (intestines), and *Appetit* (appetite) in a manner which almost convinced him that she had studied medicine at school.[4]

According to Morris H. Swadesh, an American linguist who established a new form of linguistics called lexical statistics, there are basic words in the languages of the world which hardly change from language to language. Of the two hundred words which he selected as basic, three are names for internal organs: "guts," "heart," and "liver."[5] If a Japanese scholar had compiled such a list, he probably would not have included the names of internal organs. Yet it is not hard to conceive that such word-concepts would be common to many languages, including those of uncivilized peoples.

Before the war there was a magazine called *Kokugo Undō* (Japanese Language Movement) whose purpose was to renovate Japanese. The following story once appeared in the column called "A Side View of Japanese," edited by Miyata Kōichi, an English scholar. A Japanese in England once spat up something red. He telephoned a hospital and told them about it. The doctor, thinking that he was a tuberculosis patient, gave him an extremely thorough medical examination. When the doctors later discovered, however, that it was all a case of simple indigestion, they regarded it as an absurd mistake. Miyata concludes that the cause of this tragicomedy is attributable to the lack of a distinction in Japanese between "vomiting" from the stomach and "coughing" from the respiratory organs, both of which are expressed as *haku* in Japanese. This is another example of how general Japanese is with regard to physiology.

Injuries and diseases

Japanese is lax in describing external wounds. With the exception of *kizu* (an injury to the body, such as a cut or bruise) and *kega* (an injury to the body sustained accidentally), secondary words are used. This offers great contrast to both Chinese with words like *tzu* 疵 (mole), *shang* 傷 (wound), *i* 痍 (bruise), and *chuang* 創 (injury) and English, with its "wound," "cut," "bruise," and "scratch." It is said that the Abipones, one of the American Indian tribes, "have different words to indicate a wound caused by the teeth of man or animal, by a knife, a sword, or an arrow."[6] (It is well known that Japanese does not make minor differentiations between types of pain, so I shall omit giving examples here.)

Japanese is not very specific regarding the terms for diseases. The names of diseases which we use at present, such as *kekkaku* (tuberculosis), *rokumakuen* (pleurisy), *igan* (cancer of the stomach), and *ikataru* (catarrh of the stomach) are almost all Chinese character words or loanwords. The fact that there are hardly any Yamato words is probably an indication of the disregard the Japanese people have for the body.

Contrary to the scarcity of native names for wounds and diseases, Japanese has a great many terms relating to death. This illustrates not so much the placing of high value on life as the fact that Japan is a country known for suicide. The word *harakiri* is known as the first Japanese word to become famous all over the world.[7] *Harakiri* is further divided into *tsumebara* (*harakiri* forced upon someone) and *oibara* (*harakiri* done by subjects following their master). Mori Ōgai said about the term *shinjū* (lovers' suicide): "There are examples in the West but no term," which implies that it is untranslatable. Its synonym, *jōshi* (lovers' double suicide), is also a Chinese character word which originated in Japan. By the way, the word *senshi* (death in battle) when translated into English would be "to be killed in battle," using the passive form of a transitive verb. In Japanese, however, we say *senshi suru* (to do *senshi*—to die while fighting in battle). In short, it is expressed in the form of a verb in the active voice, as are the general term *shinu* (to die) and *tōshin suru* (to commit suicide by drowning)—something heroic and sad.

The senses

As with terms referring to the parts of the body, Japanese also classifies the senses roughly. Regarding taste, the Japanese use the common word *karai* to express the taste of both mustard and horseradish and the taste of salt water. Moreover, the Japanese say *katai* (hard) when they bite a piece of hard candy or chew a dried cuttlefish. The former is truly hard, but the cuttlefish is hard to bite off. In English the former would be "hard" and the latter, "tough."

Words relating to the senses of sight and hearing are also roughly classified. The words *miru* (to see) and *kiku* (to hear) are abstractions of their minute differentiations in other languages. Therefore, when we check the dictionary index for *miru* 見 (look), we see numerous words with the same pronunciation *miru,* such as 視 (to look intently), 覿 (to encounter), 観 (to observe), 覧 (to survey).

Differentiation of feelings

In contrast to the small number of words dealing with the senses, the Japanese vocabulary for feelings is extremely rich. S. A. Candau says that the Japanese word most difficult to understand is *ki* 気 (spirit, mind, soul).[8] Japanese has many words to denote subtle disturbances in one's mental state, such as *kigane o suru* (to feel constrained), *ki ga okenai* (to feel at home with), *kimazui* (to feel embarrassed), and *ki ga hikeru* (to feel shy of a person).

If we take up only those words related to anger, we have *okoru* (to be angered), *fungai suru* (to be enraged), *hara ga tatsu* (to get angry), *shaku ni sawaru* (to feel offended), and *mushakusha suru* (to be nervous and troubled), each of which is a little different in meaning from the other. There are also some with more delicate shades of meaning, such as *mukappara* (to fly into anger) and *chūppara* (to be offended at heart).

A great number of the Chinese character words formed early in Japan tend to express people's mental state as illustrated in the following examples: *shimpai* (uneasiness), *kenen* (anxiety), *munen* (resentment), *rippuku* (anger), *heiki* (composure), *honki* (seriousness), *daijōbu* (the feeling of security), *miren* (lingering affection or attachment), *zonbun* (to one's heart's content), *zongai* (contrary to one's expectations), *angai* (unexpectedly), *shaku* (provoking), *taigi* (troublesome), *kemmei* (eagerness), *kamben* (forgiveness), *tokushin* (conviction), *nattoku* (understanding, consent), *shōchi* (agreement), *yōjin* (caution), *ryōken* (notion), *shimbō* (patience), *enryo* (deference), *kakugo* (preparedness), and *tonjaku* (concern). Every one of these is a Chinese character word originating in Japan or an old Chinese character word which has come to indicate a specific narrow meaning.

Minami Hiroshi said that a great number of the Japanese words which express one's mental state represent negative feelings.[9] Words like *kōfuku* (happiness), *shiawase* (good fortune), *kōjin* (great happiness), or the like, are few in number and low in frequency of usage. On the other hand, their antonyms such as *hiai* (sorrow), *fukō* (unhappiness), *kurō* (hardships), and *nangi* (difficulty) are frequently used, as are adjectives like *kanashii* (sad), *aware na* (pitiful), *sabishii* (lonely), and *setsunai* (painful). This fact suggests to me that from ancient times there has been a tremendous number of adjectives with negative meanings such as *ajikinashi* (dreary), *asamashi* (lamentable), *wabishi* (comfortless), *kokorozukinashi* (disagreeable), *ainashi* (wearisome), and *warinashi* (exceedingly distressing).

In her book, *The Chrysanthemum and the Sword*, Ruth Benedict called the culture of Japan "a shame culture."[10] She says that the idea "not to disgrace oneself" is the basic principle that directs one's everyday conduct. There are many words in Japanese reflecting this idea—for example, *hazukashii* (to be ashamed of), *kimari ga warui* (to feel awkward), *mittomonai* (disgraceful), *terekusai* (embarrassing), *ma ga warui* or *batsu ga warui* (be embarrassed; find oneself in an awkward position), *kakkō ga tsukanai* (cannot save one's face), *hikkomi ga tsukanai* (cannot back out). In pure verb forms there are words like *tereru* (to feel embarrassed) and *hanikamu* (to be shy).

If we stop to think about it, it appears that in everyday life we feel far more shy or embarrassed about trifling matters than people of other countries. To illustrate my point, suppose that I meet someone toward whom I feel a little diffident in a dining room of a department store, and we exchange greetings in due form. First of all I apologize for not having been to see him for a long time and then I ask if his family is well. I rejoice upon hearing of their good health and ask him to definitely drop in at my house whenever he happens to be in the vicinity. All the while we repeatedly exchange bows. Finally I depart saying, "Excuse me for going first." After doing some shopping on the upper floors, I enter an elevator, whereupon I see the friend from whom I parted a while before. On such an occasion, the more solemn my salutation at parting has been, the more awkward I will feel. Moreover, if I buy some things in the bargain basement and happen to meet this friend again upon entering the men's room, even if we lightly say to each other, "We see each other often today, don't we?" I will be so embarrassed that I will even feel like cursing his existence. Once I told Father Grotaas this story, and he said that such feelings were not inconceivable to Europeans, but that there were no appropriate words for expressing them in European languages.

In addition to the words given above, there are some which are very difficult to explain to Americans and others, namely, *oshii* (to feel it hard to part with something) and *mottainai* (to feel that one's action, such as wasting money, is a sin against heaven). Since *oshii* is a very ordinary word to the Japanese, it seems strange that there are no equivalents in other countries. Apparently there is none in English. This is perhaps due to the differences in the life styles of the two countries.

Right after the war an American woman brought up the Japanese word *tsūkai* and said that the Japanese committed cruel acts because they possessed such a word. She meant, in short, that this word expressed one's delight at sufferings of other people, and therefore appropriately represented such a fondness among the Japanese. This is very scathing criticism. Doesn't it rather mean "the joy which one feels when a person who has been acting tyrannically exposes his powerlessness"? Thus, perhaps we can say that the *tsūkai* concept expresses resistance to unjust authority.

Value words

Another notable thing about the Chinese character

words originating in Japan is that many of them imply some
sense of evaluation. They consist of words like the following:
gyōsan (exaggerated), *shōshi* (absurd), *kyūkutsu* (cramped),
mendō (troublesome), *muda* (wasteful), *aikyō* (charming),
aisō (amiable), *fuben* (inconvenient), *kikai* (strange), *furachi*
(insolent), *toppi* (wild, extraordinary), *kennon* (dangerous),
jaken (wrong view), *ōhei* (arrogant), *richigi* (honest), and
wampaku (naughty). These words certainly indicate the
Japanese people's tendency to verbalize their various
emotional states.

The same tendency can be seen among adverbs, many of
which have subjective connotations. For example, the
expressions *sekkaku* (with much trouble) and *wazawaza*
(expressly) have the objective meaning, "by spending
one's labor." *Sekkaku* has the further implication of "fruit-
lessly," and *wazawaza* of "sympathy for a person's trouble."
The following are also adverbs with strong emotional
coloring: *tsui* (carelessly), *omowazu* (unintentionally), *ainiku*
(unluckily), *namajikka* (half-heartedly), *sazo* (surely, indeed),
sadameshi (presumably), and *dōse* (in any event).

It is also said that there are in general many words and
phrases which express a vague frame of mind. The following
are some of the typical ones, every one of which will cause
us a great deal of trouble when we attempt to explain it to
Americans and other foreigners.

Nantonaku ochitsukanai.
I feel restless *somehow or other.*

Sorosoro kaerō ya.
It's about time we were going home now.

Botsubotsu dekaketemiyō ka?
Let's be moving *slowly* now, shall we?

Sonouchi ni mata yatte kimasu.
I shall come again, *before long.*

Nandaka monotarinai.
I *somehow* feel as if something is lacking.

Dokoka pinto ga hazurete iru.
There is something off the point in this.

The expression *Chotto dōka to omou* (I kind of doubt the pro-
priety of the thing), which is said to have been invented by
Tokugawa Musei, a famous storyteller, is unique.

Body movement

Iwai Ryūsei, a linguist, has written an interesting article
called "A World Without Speech." Once while he was
teaching at a school for the blind and mute, he made the
children feel a model of a bird, explaining, "This is called a
bird, and it flies *(tobu)*." He reported that the children took
him to mean that a bird had something like wooden clogs
under its feet, and jumped and hopped about like a rabbit
or a grasshopper. As for the bird wearing clogs, we will
let it pass.* What is significant is that they thought birds
hopped. This error must have arisen from the fact that
both "flying" and "jumping" are expressed by *tobu*. Many
verbs including *tobu* have broad meanings, and in general

*The bird had a wooden base on which it stood.

those which have something to do with the changing of position are crudely classified. Therefore, when learning German, Japanese have a hard time differentiating between *gehen, fahren,* and *reiten.*

In like manner, the Japanese are also general in their differentiation of words related to speed. While English distinguishes speed as "fast," "rapid," "swift," "speedy," "fleet," and "quick," Japanese indiscriminately uses the one term *hayai* to represent a fast motion in different situations, such as walking, or riding a train, boat, or horse.

The words *nemuru* (to sleep) and *neru* (to go to bed) are sometimes just treated as one and expressed as *neru.* Could this confusion have arisen under the influence of children's speech?

As mentioned earlier, the English are proud of their word "gentleman." Both the Germans and French must possess words they are proud of. If we were to select words of this sort from Japanese, what would they be? I would like to propose the word *isoshimu* as one of the most qualified for this distinction. It means "to work with the feeling of happiness," and I think it is a representative term expressing Japanese diligence.

There are many words in Japan that deal with *rōdō* or labor. In the first place, the character for *dō* 働 (*hataraku,* if pronounced by itself) of *rōdō* deserves attention. The Japanese introduced *kanji* into their country from China and inscribed Yamato words using the *kanji* that had the closest meaning to them. When there were no *kanji* to express the meaning of some Yamato words, however, the people had to resort to using *kana* or to coining characters similar to the *kanji* of Chinese origin. These Japanese characters are the so-called *kokuji* or Japanese *kanji*. The most frequently used *kokuji* is the word *hataraku* (to work). Unlike the ordinary *kokuji,* this one has a *kanji* pronunciation of *dō*, thus being counted as one of the *kanji*. This illustrates what great importance people have attached to the word.

Similar to *hataraku* is the word *kasegu* (to work for one's living), to which the kanji 稼 has been assigned. It is said that this *kanji* did not originally have the meaning "to work for one's living." Therefore, this reading is a *kokkun* (a particular Japanese meaning illogically attached to *kanji*). It is interesting that both the *kanji* for *hataraku* and the reading *kasegu* originated in Japan.

Daily necessities

Among the words relating to food, Japanese has *yaku*, which is a general term covering the English "toast," "roast," "bake," and "fry." Boiling in water, on the other hand, is subdivided into verbs like *niru* (to boil food in water), *yuderu* (to boil food, mostly vegetables, in water), *fukasu* (to steam), and *wakasu* (to boil water). The word *taku* in particular denotes the boiling of rice by burning wood in the *kamado* (a cooking-stove made of brick or stone) —something expected of a rice-eating country.

It is often said that there are no equivalents in English for *shushoku* (staple food, mostly rice and wheat) and *fukushoku* (subsidiary food), but I am not sure if they can be called characteristic of the Japanese language. The English term "rice" is subdivided in Japanese into *kome* (raw rice) and *meshi* (cooked rice). When my classmates and I entered middle school and began to study English, we learned that "rice" in English meant *kome.* However, we objected, "Isn't it the 'rice' of 'curried rice,' which is cooked rice?" and were quite dissatisfied when we found out that both cooked rice and raw rice were referred to in English by one and the same word.

The Chinese word *tien* 田 designates both wet and dry rice fields. In Japanese, however, dry rice fields are called *hata* or *hatake,* each having a native *kanji,* and wet rice fields are simply called *ta* 田, a very important word. It is well known that *ta* is the word most frequently used in forming Japanese family names.

Contrary to the detailed distinctions made for rice in Japanese, *mugi* (wheat or barley) is very simply classified, as *ōmugi* (large *mugi* or barley) and *komugi* (small *mugi* or wheat), both secondary words. This contrasts with the English usage of primary words like "barley," "wheat," "oats," and "rye."

The Japanese word *abura* is a general term for both vegetable oil 油 and animal fat 脂, expressed by two different Chinese characters and by the two English words "oil" and "fat." This indicates that the Japanese have had little to do with either substance. Westerners would not so easily consider oil, fat, and grease as one.

Similarly, three different characters, *pi* 皮 (fur), *ko* 革 (hide), and *wei* 韋 (leather), are used for the Japanese word *kawa* (animal skin), but distinctions are seldom made, especially in regard to the last two. This must have resulted from the infrequent use of animal skins by the Japanese.

There are detailed differentiations in expressing the manner in which clothing is put on: *kiru* (to put on clothes), *hameru* (to fit into, as gloves or rings), *shimeru* (to tie or tighten, as a sash or a tie), *kakeru* (to spread on or over, as a shawl or a veil), *haku* (to wear something around the hips or on legs or feet, as trousers, stockings, shoes), and *maku* (to put a thing around, like a scarf around the neck). Westerners find it strange that the wearing of trousers and pants is expressed as *haku,* together with clogs and shoes. This, however, has something to do with the fastidiousness of the Japanese, who divide the human body into upper half and lower half, with the latter being considered impure. Ichikawa Sanki says that at the Westminster Abbey a curate once showed him the way by pointing with his leg.[11] (In Japan one never uses the foot or leg in this way, as it is considered very rude.) Ikejima Shimpei says that when he ordered two bottles of beer in a Paris café, a handsome waiter, putting one bottle between his legs and holding it there, took the cap off the other and poured it in that position—something which Japanese people would never do.[12]

The expressions *yuagari* (just after a bath) and *yuzame* (a chill after a bath) are characteristic of the bath-loving Japanese. They are untranslatable into either English or Chinese.

Moral and aesthetic consciousness

There are some characteristic words formed out of a distinctively Japanese moral consciousness. In her book, *The Chrysanthemum and the Sword,* Ruth Benedict pointed out the strong fondness of the Japanese for conduct appropriate to their station in life.[13] A woman who has married must no longer dress like a young unmarried woman. A housemaid must apply her makeup modestly so that she will not be mistaken for a young lady of the house. A *yoko-zuna,* a grand *sumō* champion, must look grand as befits his title. When he loses a fight twice or three times in a season's tournament, the spectators make a great fuss, for it is inappropriate to his status. In this respect, we can say that the Japanese enjoy social rigidity.

The adverb *sasuga ni* is a complimentary word used when a person in a certain station of life has done something appropriate to his station. It is a pet Japanese word. The *dake ni* (as may be expected) in an expression such as *Gakkō o dete iru dake ni* (or *dake atte*) *monowakari ga yoi* (He understands things, as may be expected of one who has graduated from school) also has a similar connotation. In contrast to these, there are adverbs such as *kuse ni* and *datera ni,* which imply reproach of a person's conduct as not suitable for his social standing; Takagi Masataka, a social psychologist, has included them among untranslatable expressions.[14]

Unlike the English word "gay," the words *hade* (gay or showy) and its opposite, *jimi* (plain), connote the appropriateness of clothing of a certain degree of gayness to one's age. Watanabe Shin'ichirō cites *toshigai mo nai* (something inappropriate to one's age) and *iitoshi o shite* (unbecoming to one's mature age) as peculiarly Japanese phrases that cannot be translated into European languages.[15]

The Japanese value honor highly and make light of their lives. This attitude has given rise to numerous synonyms, such as *homare* (honor), *hokori* (pride), *hitogiki* (reputation), *kikoe* (fame), *ukina* (the rumor of one's love affairs), *adana* (the rumor of one's amorousness). The words *taimen* (respectability) and *hyōban* (reputation) are Chinese character words which originated in Japan. Compound words like *meisho* 名所 (noted places) and *meikyoku* 名曲 (famous music) beginning with *mei* 名 (name; famous) are also peculiar to Japanese, as are the expressions *tsura-ate* (insinuating remarks), *tsurayogoshi* (a disgrace), *ikihaji* (living in dishonor), and *shinihaji* (shameful death).

Lastly, the Japanese think it desirable to hide one's own merits. A result of this unique valuation is the appearance of such words as *yukashii* (something graceful and engaging) and *okuyukashii* (something profound and appealing), which are difficult to translate into other languages. There is the custom of using the character 床 when we want to express *yukashii* in *kanji,* but this is due to the lack of a suitable word in Chinese characters. There is also the word *tashinamu,* which Shimmura Izuru gives as a characteristic Japanese word related to this idea. *Tashinamu* is a favorite word of the Japanese and means "to privately devote oneself to something, irrespective of whether there will be any result or not."[16]

There are some adjectives indicating praise and esteem of a person's personality and attitude which are peculiarly Japanese. *Kenage* and *isagiyoi* are examples of such. A Japanese-English dictionary gives "manly" and "brave" as translations for *kenage,* but there is a feeling of pathetic heroism implied which cannot be expressed by the English translations. *Isagiyoi* is a word used in praise for the courage one shows in reconciling oneself to one's loss.

Minami Hiroshi has pointed out in his *Nihonjin no Shinri* (The Psychology of the Japanese) that there are few words in Japanese that praise the act of not readily giving up.[17] The existence of the word *miren,* which criticizes one's reluctance to give up something, is characteristically Japanese.

Lastly, some distinctive words have been produced by the unique aesthetic sense of the Japanese resulting from their love of fine, subtle things. They are delicately suggestive; for example, *kime* (delicate texture), *koku* (good substance, as of fine wine), and *fūmi* (an elegant taste). There are also words which represent an ideal of beauty, such as *sabi* (antique-looking and elegant), *wabi* (quiet taste), *sui* (refined taste, gracefulness), *iki* (smartness, refined and romantic), *shibumi* (elegant simplicity), *fūryū* (romantic refinement). These are all said to be untranslatable.[18]

In Natsume Sōseki's *Bungakuron* (Comments on Literature), there is a story about his sojourn at a stately mansion in Scotland.[19] One day while he was strolling in an orchard with the owner, he saw a path beautifully overgrown with moss and felt as if he were back in Japan. Very much delighted, he praised it saying, "How nice—it looks as if it were ancient." Whereupon, the owner made a wry face and said, "No, it's so dirty-looking I intend to have my gardener scrape off all the mold in the near future." It is not possible for words like *sabi* and *wabi* to occur among people with such an outlook.

◆ 6. FAMILY AND SOCIETY

Kinship

It may seem as if there are many words representing human kinship in Japanese, but since Japan does not have a system of large families there are fewer kinship terms than in other Asian languages like Chinese and Mongolian. While Chinese has different names for "one's parent's elder brother," "one's parent's younger brother," "one's parent's elder sister," and "one's parent's younger sister," Japanese simply uses *oji* (uncle) and *oba* (aunt). According to Hattori Shirō, the distinctions between uncles, aunts, and cousins in Mongolian are no less complicated than in Chinese. For example, cousins are divided into (1) children of one's father's brothers, (2) children of one's father's sisters (or one's mother's brothers), and (3) children of one's mother's sisters, with each group being called by a different name. This distinction is related to the social system prohibiting the marriage of people with the same family name on the basis of a quasi-mathematical relationship:

(1)=family names are always the same—therefore, marriage is always impossible

(2)=family names are always different—therefore, marriage is always possible

(3)=family names are either the same or different—therefore, marriage possibility is variable[1]

People in Japan indiscriminately call old people, including their own grandfathers or grandmothers and even old beggar men and beggar women on the roadside, *ojiisan* (or *jijii*) or *obāsan* (or *babā*). This is marvelously broad-minded. In ancient times old beggar men and women were called *okina* and *ouna* respectively, but somehow confusion must have arisen in these terms from the use of children's language by adults. References by Japanese people to ancestors remoter than their grandparents are quite vague, unlike such references by Chinese people, who remember and observe the day that each of their great ancestors died.

The order of brothers and sisters, however, is rigidly fixed in Japanese. First comes *ani* (elder brother), then *ane* (elder sister), *otōto* (younger brother), and *imōto* (younger sister)—all basic words in the language. In this respect Japanese contrasts with European languages. In particular, words such as *oniisama* (or *niisan*), used in addressing one's elder brother, and *onēsama* (or *nēsan*), used in addressing one's elder sister, are Asian in that they possess a feeling both of respect and familiarity, which cannot be found in languages such as English. The existence of the word *sōryō*, a special name given to the eldest son, is reflective of the social system peculiar to Japan, where special esteem is accorded the eldest son. According to Kurata Ichirō's *Kokugo to Minzoku-gaku* (The Japanese Language and Folklore),[2] there are many localities where the eldest son alone is called *ani*, and the rest of the dependents, including the second and third sons, are all called *oji*. Formerly, it was customary to call the first, second, and third sons *tarō, jirō,* and *saburō*, respectively, and this custom still remains in some regions. In Hachijōjima, one of the Seven Isles of Izu, for instance, the first son is called *yakko* or *yarō,* and the second son, *jirō*. Similarly, the second, third, and fourth daughters are called *naka, tego, kusu,* and *jirō,* respectively.

Furthermore, the Japanese language, influenced by the family system, possesses primary words like *yome* (daughter-in-law), *muko* (son-in-law), and *shūto* (father-in-law), for which equivalents cannot be found in Western languages. After the war it was argued that the terms *totsugu* (a woman to be married into another's family) and *metoru* (to take a woman as wife) expressed inequality between men and women, and the phrases *yome ni yaru* (to give one's daughter away in marriage) and *yome o toru* (to get a wife for the son) plainly illustrated the idea that *onna sangai ni ie nashi* (a woman has no home of her own in the three realms, i.e., anywhere).

It is well known that the position of a woman changes with her age, and in some localities this is reflected in the vocabulary. Just as the fish *bora* is called by various terms as it grows—*subashiri, ina, bora,* and so on—a woman in some districts is called *aneko* when she is a young wife, *appa* when a mother, *onba* after becoming a grandmother, and *baba* after her grandson has married.

Social position and sex distinction

As stated in Kawashima Takeyoshi's *Nihon Shakai no Kazokuteki Kōsei* (The Family-like Formation of Japanese Society),[3] Japanese society is bound together by familial *oyabun-kobun* relationships such as the pseudo-parent-child relationship between landowner and tenant farmer, and between landlord and tenant; the master–house-servant relationship, such as that between master and houseboy or maid; the familial relationship in enterprises, such as that

between management and workers. The prestige and paren-
tal affection of those in a superior social position and the
loyalty and submission of those in an inferior one always
follow one about wherever one goes. Thus the difference in
social positions is rigidly distinguished in Japanese.

The many words used in connection with the imperial
household are especially notable for such distinctions. For
example, although in English one refers to the emperor
(kōtei) of Japan, in Japanese we do not use the word *kōtei*
to refer to our own emperor. Instead, we use *tennō* and it
would be more reasonable to use the romanized form of
this word in English. The words *kōshitsu* (imperial household), *kōgō* and *kōhi* (empress), *kōtaishi* (crown prince),
shinnō (an imperial prince), and *naishinnō* (an imperial
princess) are all Chinese character words that originated in
Japan. So are the words *kōka* (the marriage of an imperial
princess to a subject) and *rakuin* (an illegitimate child of a
man of rank). Taken all together, they clearly suggest the
characteristic Japanese trait of "respecting and honoring
people of noble birth," pointed out by Wakamori Tarō.[4]

Quite a number of the character words created in Japan
in ancient times reflect social status, such as *jōrō* (a noblewoman), *gerō* (a low official), *gesu* (one of low social standing), *genan* (a manservant), *gejo* (a maidservant), *kyūji* (an
office boy), *shosei* (a houseboy), *kazoku* (a peer), and *shibun*
(samurai status). There are also many common words relating to a person's social standing, such as *sujō* (lineage),
bunzai (one's social position or one's own place), *bungen*
(one's social position or limit). Ruth Benedict includes the
expression *kabun no* (more than one deserves) among the
favorite words of the Japanese.

There is, moreover, a strict order among the members of any group, and the word *bun* (one's standing or limit) has completely turned into a Yamato word, giving rise to a number of compounds with the suffix *-bun*, such as *oyabun* (the position of the chief who takes charge of his followers temporarily as a parent; literally, parent standing), *kobun* (someone whom the chief takes charge of temporarily as his child; literally, child standing), *anikibun* (a person whom one temporarily respects as his elder brother; literally, elder-brother standing), and *kyakubun* (a person who is treated as a guest; literally, guest standing). The words *shinzan* (a newcomer to one's service) and *kosan* (a person in one's service for a long time) as well as words with the suffix *-agari* (a person who was once . . .), such as *heitai-agari* (a person who was once a soldier) and *jochū-agari* (a woman who was once a maid), are very Japanese and their equivalents are not found in English.

The position translated as "wife" in English is called by different terms, depending on one's social status; for example: *tsuma* (wife), *fujin* (a term of respect designating another's wife), *kanai* (a term used by the husband to denote his wife), *sai* (same as *tsuma*), *saikun* (another's wife), *naigi* (a term of respect for another's wife), *nyōbō* (a term used by the husband to denote his wife, same as *tsuma* and *kanai*), *shufu* (the mistress of a house), *okusama* (a term of respect denoting another's wife, also used in addressing another's wife), *okugata* (the wife of a nobleman), *kisaki* (the wife of an emperor), *hi* (the wife of an imperial prince), *reikei* (a term of respect referring to another's wife), *reifujin* (a term of respect for a nobleman's wife; also used for another's wife), *daikoku* (the wife of a Buddhist priest), *okami* (or *okami-san*—another's wife), *kakā* (a term for one's wife, or another's wife, used among humbler classes), and *yamanokami* (one's wife, often implying a termagant wife). All indicate how strict is the distinction between the upper and lower strata of society. There are also terms like *kōgō* (an empress) and *urakata* (a nobleman's wife), which refer to the wives of only a limited number of people. These, together with such loanwords as *waifu* (wife), *madamu* (madam, another's wife), *furau* (German *frau,* one's wife or another's wife), and *betā-hāfu* (one's better half, one's wife), are used freely with an awareness of their delicate nuances of meaning.

It is the European languages, however, that rigidly separate human beings into male and female. Japanese is rather lax in this respect. Jespersen says that in Hungarian both "he" and "she" are expressed by the same word, a practice which strikes many Europeans as very strange. But the Japanese think it odd that people should make a fuss about such things. As a first step in learning French, we learn how to write the feminine form of nouns but in no Japanese grammar can such a thing be found. The English "actor" and "actress" both pass as *haiyū* in Japan. There is the word *joyū* (actress), but it is not necessary to use this term when referring to a woman of the screen or stage. English and other languages rigidly classify women into married and unmarried categories with Miss So-and-so or Mrs. So-and-so. The Japanese are magnanimous in this respect, too.

Kawamori Yoshizō says that in translating European novels, we are best in the description of nature and worst in love scenes because there are no love conversations in everyday Japanese.[5] In his *Pari no Hiru to Yoru* (Days and Nights in Paris)[6] Fujita Tsuguharu lists more than twenty different terms of endearment used by a wife to refer to her husband, a great number. Even more are used by her husband. Since a Japanese couple uses hardly any expressions besides each other's names and the terms *anata* (used by the wife) and *omae* (used by the husband), it must indeed be difficult to translate love conversations into Japanese.

Terms of respect

The complicated language of respect or *keigo* is related to the natural disposition of the Japanese to strictly observe different social standings. However, it is not characteristic of Japanese alone. Terms of respect can generally be found in the wide area from Korea, China, Vietnam, Thailand, Burma, and Tibet, to the Pacific islands. When compared with European languages, however, the terms of respect certainly constitute a characteristic feature of the Japanese language. Take, for example, first person pronouns. While English uses "I" to cover all situations, Japanese uses terms like *watakushi, boku, ore,* depending on the situation. For the second person there are also varieties like *anata, kimi,* and *omae.*

An Edo period *senryū* (satirical verse) cleverly manages to use different terms for the first person to convey its meaning:

Mizukara o	Abandoning his wife,
sutete wachiki o	The nobleman
gochōai.	Favors a courtesan.

The above verse literally means: "Abandoning *mizukara* (i.e., a first person pronoun for a nobleman or noblewoman), one favors *wachiki* (i.e., a first person pronoun used by a courtesan)."

There is also a *senryū* verse using the different pronouns for the second person to indicate the speakers:

Onore mā	The man's father,
onushi wa mā ni	His friends, and his wife
*omae mā.**	All say, "My!" in astonishment.

Verbs and adjectives also have honorific and nonhonorific forms, but since this is a problem of grammar, I shall not discuss it here. It should be noted that many words are limited in usage; that is, some words came to be used only in relation to people of a higher rank, and others only in relation to people of a lower rank, even though the words themselves do not possess any such distinctions.

In English the word "love" can express one's affection for any person, but the Japanese word *ai* (love) is used only for your friends or your equals or someone below you in standing. Some time ago I saw in a newly published Japanese dictionary the word *keiai* 敬愛 with the following definition: *uyamai aisuru koto* (to respect and love). According to traditional examples, however, no such Japanese phrase exists—*uyamau* (to respect) and *aisuru* (to love) cannot be practiced at the same time. The dictionary definition should have been *uyamai shitau koto*. Words like *shitau* (to long to

---

Onore, onushi, and *omae* are all second person pronouns. *Onore* was used for someone below one, *onushi* for one's equal, and *omae* for one's superior or senior. But these pronouns have different connotations now.

follow an admirable thing or person) and *kawaigaru* (to love someone below you or pet animals) are linked with the superior-inferior relationship of people. Similarly, *on* 恩 (a debt of gratitude) refers to something given to one from above for which one is thankful; therefore, we can say *oya no on* (*on* to one's parents), but we cannot say *ko no on* (*on* to one's children). The word *kanshin* (to be deeply impressed by something) also cannot be used toward someone of higher status, nor can the expression *gokurō sama* (thank you for the trouble).

Of the differences in social position, the most exacting is the difference between the emperor, his family, and *shimojimo*, or the rest of the people. Consequently, we see the strictest use of honorifics here. The visit of the emperor is called *gyōkō*, while that of the empress or the crown prince is called *gyōkei*. A poem composed by the emperor is called *gyosei*, but a poem by the empress is called *on-uta*. Thus, different words are used for even the same things. Formerly such differentiated usage relating to the emperor was very strict. Any mistake was considered a most serious blunder, and a radio announcer who made one would have suffered more than mere dismissal from office.

Once when the emperor of Manchukuo came to Japan, Prince Chichibu went to Haneda airport as a proxy for the emperor to welcome him. The NHK (The Japan Broadcasting Corporation) was to broadcast the description of the arrival, and the following directives were given to them by the government: Use the superlative honorifics in referring to the emperor; use high honorifics but not the superlative for Prince Chichibu; use honorifics which lie midway between the two for the emperor of Manchukuo.[7]

The idea of attaching great importance to the differences in people's ranks is linked to a way of thinking which highly values formalities and ceremonies. This, in turn, has produced such Japan-coined *kanji* words as *sahō* (etiquette), *gyōgi* (manners), *kōjō* (a verbal message), and *aisatsu* (greetings).

The great importance attached to the differences in social standing has given added significance to the idea of "proxy" and to many expressions for an act on behalf of some person of rank, as well as for an act done either by the person himself or directly to some person. The following words denoting the above ideas are all *kanji* words made in Japan: *myōdai* (a proxy), *daisan* (vicarious visit to a temple or shrine), *kōken* (guardianship), *sahai* (the management of land and house on behalf of the landlord), *daikan* (a local governor, originally a proxy of some office), *densō* (the intermediate act of transmitting a petition to the emperor),* *shinnin* (a personal imperial appointment), *shinten* (a confidential letter), *jikihi* (personally opening a letter),† *jikisan* (an immediate retainer), *jikihitsu* (one's own handwriting), *jikiso* (a direct petition to a feudal lord or *shōgun*), *osso* (an appeal to a government office higher than befits one's rank).

Social interaction

As Kawashima Takeyoshi has pointed out, Japanese society is made up of families or familial groups; conse-

---

*In the feudal ages, it usually meant the petitions from princes, temples, and shrines.
†*Shinten* and *jikihi* are used as directional words on the envelope.

quently, one's attitude toward his own group is very different from his attitude toward other groups.[8] The Chinese word *tanin* 他人, which had meant somebody other than oneself, came to be used in Japan to indicate "persons other than one's relations." Another word, *yoso* 余所, is a Japan-made *kanji* word which transmits a feeling of aloofness, the meaning of which cannot be fully conveyed by its English translation, "another place." The word *seken* 世間, also created in Japan, does not have the same nuance as its English translation "society," but goes further to suggest a realm where the individual is opposed and mocked. The following definition of *seken* by Kishida Kunio skillfully penetrates its meaning:

> First of all, what is *seken*? Of course, it does not have the same nuance as *shakai* (society). Rather, it expresses an outlook, controlled by mass psychology, which places importance particularly on morality, customs, and declarations of intention. Moreover, it has no ideal other than self-preservation, and following a rule which is so formal as to appear almost without feeling, it seems to designate a social body limited in area and time, which has an extremely conspicuous instinct that rejects the existence of all foreign elements.[9]

Hori Ichirō has asserted that there are very few people in the world who have a greater attachment to their native place than the Japanese.[10] The word *tabi* (travel) is distinctive in its implication of an unspeakable sadness. This feeling motivated the retitling of Hermann Hesse's novel *Peter*

Camenzind as *Kyōshū* (Homesickness) and of the movie *Summertime* as *Ryojō* (The Weariness of a Journey). They contain associations related to the concepts of *tanin* and *yoso*. It is said there is no equivalent for *natsukashii* (yearning for one's home, friends, etc.) in European languages.

The following *kanji* words created in Japan reflect the exclusive nature of Japanese society: *taken* (to be seen by others) in *taken o yurusanu* (not to be seen by others), *tagon* (telling something to others), and *tabun* (reaching others' ears). There are also expressions like *naibun* (not making a matter public), *naiyaku* (a private agreement), *naitei* (an informal decision), *naidan* (a personal talk), *naiji* (an unofficial announcement), and *naisai* (a private settlement).

Moreover, fellow members of a group are bound by so-called *giri* (a sense of obligation), a typically Japanese word. Father Candau says, "If we translate this word into French we have to use seventeen words.[11] Benedict, the author of *The Chrysanthemum and the Sword,* has translated *giri* as "something one does unwillingly to forestall apology to the world."[12] It is a painstaking translation.

One who repays his *giri* is praised as *girigatai* (having a strong sense of *giri*), but what does this mean in concrete terms? According to Wakamori Tarō, among simple village people *girigatai* includes going out to work or to a meeting, and exchanging presents properly.[13] A large number of character words created in Japan express the idea of mutual help. Words like *yakkai* (living in another's home as a dependent), *kaihō* (to look after a sick person), *kaishaku* (to assist a person in committing *harakiri*), *sōdan* (consultation), and *gōryoku* (cooperation) reflect the high value placed on friendly relations. Since those who help one another esteem warm feelings, words originating in Japan like *ninjō* (sympathy), *jōmi* (sentiment, warmth), *jikkon* (familiarity) have been produced, along with those related to friendly relations, such as *sanjō* (to pay one's respect to a person), *chakutō* (to arrive at a place), and *jisan* (to bring something, such as a gift, with one).

On the other hand, customary emphasis on the importance of exchanging presents has produced a surprising number of verbs related to the receiving and giving of things. There are, for example: *yaru* (to give a thing to a person, usually to someone below you), *kureru* (to let a person have something), *ataeru* (to give a thing such as a prize, medal, title, etc.), *ageru* (to give something to someone equal to or above you), *morau* (to receive), *kudasaru* (someone above you giving something to you), *itadaku* (to receive something from above), *sashiageru** (to give a thing to someone above you with respect), *tatematsuru*† (to respectfully present a thing to a person of high rank), *mitsugu* (to give financial aid), *megumu* (to aid the poor), *hodokosu* (to give to charity), *sazukeru* (to confer a title on a person), *yuzuru* (to bequeath), *watasu* (to deliver or hand over), *ukeru* (to receive), *kōmuru* (to receive a favor or damage), *osameru* (to dedicate or to pay). To these we can add native *kanji* words like *kishin* (to contribute to some fund), *kifu* (to donate money), *kenjō* (to respectfully present something to someone above you), and *shinjō* (to present a thing such as a book with the compliments of the author). Among nouns there are the following related to presents: *miyage* (some-

---

Kudasaru, itadaku, and *sashiageru* are polite forms.
†An extra-polite form.

thing one presents when visiting a friend), *hikidemono* (a present from the host to the guest at a party), *mimaihin* (a present to a sick person), *kokorozuke* (a tip), *sembetsu* (a farewell present), *kōden* (a monetary offering to a departed spirit). When we consult an English-Japanese dictionary for the definition of "present," we find the Japanese translation, *okurimono;* but it should be: "*okurimono* (a present given) or *tōraimono* (a present received)."

Likewise, it was inevitable that many words denoting gratitude have been produced, such as *mottainai* (be thankful, feeling you don't deserve such kindness), *arigatai* (be thankful), *sumanai* (feel thankful and sorry for having caused another trouble), and *katajikenai* (be very grateful). On the other hand, there is the word *meiwaku* (trouble, annoyance) which took on a special meaning after being introduced from China, particularly in the expression, *arigata meiwaku* (the kindness which is somewhat annoying to one), which is difficult to explain to foreigners.

When I read newspaper articles on baseball, I find different expressions used to explain the batters' hitting in relation to the pitcher. When batters produce a barrage of hits, they say, *Renzoku hitto o abiseru* (They pour a stream of continuous hits); when a batter hits a home run, *Hōmuran o mimau* (He sends a condolence of home runs); when he walks, *Shikyū o yokusuru* (He receives a favor of four balls); when he is struck out, *Sanshin o kissuru* (He suffers three strikes); when he hits back to the pitcher's mound, *Pitchā goro o teisuru* (He presents a grounder to the pitcher); and when he is struck by the pitch, *Deddo-bōru o kuu* (He suffers a dead ball). This attitude of feeling thankful or resentful after each turn at bat is very much in the Japanese vein.

◆ 7. ABSTRACT IDEAS

Spatial relations

Some years ago I went to Toyohashi from Tatsuno in Nagano prefecture by train on the Iida line. As we passed Iida we could see the beautiful scenery of the famous Ten-ryū River gorge below us. On one side, far above the ravine, rose a cliff, and on it a huge grotesque rock which looked as if it would fall down at any moment. A passenger muttered upon seeing it:

> *Anna ishi ga atama no ue kara ochite kitara osoroshii koto da.*
> How awful if that rock falls down from above our heads!

Those around agreed, but a faultfinder said:

> *Iya, atama no ue e ochite kitara darō.*
> No, you mean if it falls *on* our heads, don't you?

At this everyone burst into laughter.

This illustrates the fact that the Japanese word *ue* can mean both "on (in contact with)" and "above." Expressions dealing with spatial relationships in Japanese are quite generalized compared with English and therein lies the opportunity for the above faultfinding. In English there are three words, "on," "above," and "over," for the Japanese expression *no ue ni*.

Miyauchi Hideo, a scholar of English, relates the following anecdote:

202

Once I saw a Japanese woman suddenly say to an American who was with her, "Come here," as she walked briskly into an alleyway, taking him along. It is difficult to tell what she meant by "here" on the basis of the situation. She used this word because there is no equivalent in Japanese for "along."[1]

In English there are two distinctive ways of asking a person to come toward you: one when you stop and say it, and the other as you walk and say it. Apparently the Japanese once made this distinction in usage, for in *kyōgen* (a comic interlude in the Nō drama) a player says *Kō oide nasaremase* (Please come this way) when showing the way to someone.

As a first step in German grammar we learn that a strict distinction is made between the expressions "come in" and "go out," depending on whether the speaker is inside or outside. In view of such practices, expressions referring to spatial relationships in Japanese seem very generalized.

But there is another side to this. One day when I was in front of the main gate of Tōkyō University waiting for a bus bound for Tōkyō Station, two buses came along, one behind the other. On the first one, a municipal bus, was written: *Tōkyō eki yuki* (Bound for Tōkyō Station). On the second, a privately operated bus, was: *Tōkyō eki mae yuki* (Bound for Tōkyō Station Plaza [literally, the front of Tōkyō Station]). Upon seeing this, my companion remarked: "*Tōkyō eki mae yuki* is more accurate, isn't it?" He was certainly right. English and other languages cannot match the accuracy of Japanese in such cases. According to Wakabayashi Masao, there is no way of saying in English, *Tōkyō eki mae* or *Mitsukoshi mae*. Thus, it is impossible to avoid using "Tō-kyō Station" and "Mitsukoshi," terms which are inaccurate.[2]

In this respect one must take pride in Japanese, for its ease of expression. We find similarly convenient the pair of words *tate* and *yoko*, often defined respectively as "length" and "width," although no exact equivalents exist in English. (*Tate* actually means a vertical or front-back direction or length; *yoko*, horizontal or right-left direction or length.) We simply say that the area of a triangle is *tate* × *yoko* ÷ 2. At school, however, we are taught that the area of a triangle must be *teihen* (base) × *takasa* (height) ÷ 2. This is an example of Western influence, English having no expression for *tate* or *yoko*.

It also seems inconvenient to Japanese that English lacks an equivalent for *omote* (the right-side) and *ura* (the reverse side). The nearest pair in English is "front" *(mae)* and "back" *(ushiro)*, but they do not quite correspond to the Japanese terms. Consequently, in referring to the two sides of a coin or a stamp, different English word pairs have to be used in each case.* In baseball, one has to say "the first half of the first inning" for the Japanese *ikkai no omote* (the *omote* of the first inning).

Linguists call vowels such as *o* and *u* which are pronounced with the tongue placed in the back of the mouth *kōzetsu boin* (literally, back-tongue vowels), but from the Japanese point of view they are *oku no boin* (the *oku* vowels, or vowels in the back of the mouth). Since there is no word which corresponds to *oku* in English, these vowels have been

---

*In Japanese they are the *omote* and the *ura* of a coin, a stamp, etc.

called "back vowels," which in turn has been literally translated into Japanese as *kōzetsu boin*. The Japanese should have felt free to use the word *oku*.

Taking the above examples into consideration, it can be said that Japanese words which express differences in spatial relations are not inadequate. We should note that the words *omote, ura,* and *oku* not only denote spatial relationships, but can also imply value judgments. For example, *omote* can mean "formal" or "authentic," and *ura* just the opposite. *Oku* has the nuances of "secret," "incomprehensible," and "unattainable." The same can be said of *ue* (up) and *shita* (down), which have a variety of uses in value judgments.

Although I have sought comparative expressions for such pairs as *omote* and *ura,* and *tate* and *yoko* in English alone, other European languages also lack these expressions. Chinese, however, has had corresponding pairs from ancient times. This manner of viewing things would seem to indicate a general Oriental grasp of matters.

Colors

Minute distinctions are made in the names of the colors in modern Japanese. For instance, the following colors are types of blue: *ao* (blue), *ai* (indigo), *kon* (navy blue), *asagi* (light blue), *hanada* (light indigo), *mizuiro* (light blue), *sorairo* (sky blue), *ruriiro* (bright blue), and *seijiiro* (blue green). In addition to these, the Japanese freely adopted foreign loanwords such as *injigo* (indigo), *kobaruto* (cobalt), *raito burū* (light blue), and *perushan burū* (Persian blue). This reflects the keen Japanese sense of color and the Japanese tendency to love neutral colors.

Apparently there were not many names for colors in the past. *Aka* (red), *ao* (blue), *kuro* (black), and *shiro* (white) existed. *Aka* included both the color of clay and brown dogs, and *ao* included the modern colors blue and green. Furthermore, considering the existence of such old expressions as *aoni* (the blue-black earth) and *aouma no sechie* (literally, the court banquet of the blue-black horse),[3] the color *ao* seems to have referred to a number of colors. Satake Akihiro, a student of the *Man'yōshū,* believes that *aka* (red) is derived from the word *akarui* (bright), and *kuro* (black) from the word *kurai* (dark). *Shiro* (white), on the other hand, means *ichijirushii*, which is *ken* 顕 (clearness) and is contrasted to *ao* (blue), which refers to *baku* 漠 (vagueness).[4] If we draw inferences from the above, we see that the names of colors in ancient times belonged to two systems, the bright-dark and the clear-vague. The tendency to express things in a broad way can still be seen to a large degree in such expressions as *Kowakute massao na kao o shite iru* (He is so scared his face is actually blue, i.e., deadly pale), and *aoi tsukiyo no hamabe ni wa* (on the beach in the blue moonlight).[5] When the Japanese saw the title of the American motion picture *The Moon Is Blue,* which was released some years ago, they imagined lonely moonlight on a beach, but they were mistaken. *The Moon Is Blue* meant "something improbable," and therefore should have been translated by some phrase like *Misoka no Tsuki* (The Moon on the Thirtieth Night).[6]

Abstract ideas

There are two kinds of Chinese character words in Japan

dealing with abstract expressions: (1) those introduced from China, and (2) those created in Japan as translations of Western words imported during the introduction of Western culture from the early years of the Meiji period on. *Chūkō* (loyalty and filial piety) and *jingi* (benevolence and righteousness) are examples of the former, and *genshō* (phenomenon) and *kyakkan* (objectivity), said to have been created by Nishi Amane,[7] are examples of the latter.[8] Scientific essays can be written in Japanese because of the existence of such words, and in this respect Japanese is a civilized language, qualitatively different from the languages of primitive people. As mentioned above, these words have been adopted into and exerted influence on Korean and Chinese.

We must note, however, that there are fewer words with abstract meanings in Japanese—or at least fewer words habitually used—than in Western languages. For example, there are no words distinguishing between "possibility" and "probability." Japanese is still lacking clarity and accuracy in this respect.

Sometimes several different terms have been used for a single abstract Western term because the Western term is used in different fields. This has unexpectedly brought about detailed distinctions in translating. For example, Ikegami Kenzō points out that the following words are used to translate the word "subject": *shukan* (subjectivity), *shudai* (theme), *shugo* (subject), and *shutai* (the main constituent).[9] This has led to complexity on the one hand, but has contributed to making minute distinctions between vague ideas on the other. The distinction between the *shugo* (subject) and *shudai* (theme) in grammar theories is a typical example.[10]

SENTENCE
CONSTRUCTION

日本語

PART

V

◆ 1. FORM AND LENGTH

Sentence form

The Japanese sentence is quite a definite unit. When pupils write compositions in grammar school, they say that while even sixth graders cannot properly punctuate within the sentence, most second graders can put the period in the right place.

Take, for example, the English expression "It is pleasant." If there were no period after this sentence, you could not tell whether the expression stops at this point or is followed by a phrase such as "to take a walk." Moreover, you still could not predict if a phrase like "on a fine day" might follow the second phrase or not. Japanese is very clear in this respect. If someone says, *Sore wa suteki da* (That is splendid), we can tell the sentence has come to an end because there are fixed words and word forms at the end of a sentence.

In Japanese orthography, it is not customary to change the form of the initial character of a sentence. Moreover, some kinds of writings—such as letters up to the end of the war—had no punctuation marks. Yet we could pretty well guess where the sentences ended. This is due, in part, to the mixed usage of Chinese character words and *kana,* and, in part, to the fixed words, phrases, and word forms appearing at the end of a sentence.

Men of letters often express dissatisfaction at the clear-cut endings of Japanese sentences. If one writes about something in the past, every sentence ends in . . . *ta.* Satō Haruo, a poet and novelist, said that this sounded like the beginning

of the folk song *Rappa-bushi** or someone stammering. Once
one concerns oneself with it, the thought is definitely oppres-
sive. It is pleasant, however, to have a clear and definite end
to a sentence—a strong point, at least in a sentence in which
one wants to convey the meaning correctly. Furthermore,
doesn't a sentence ending with regular sounds or words
have a kind of formal beauty?

In Akutagawa Ryūnosuke's[1] famous short story *Rokunomiya no Himegimi* (Lady Rokunomiya), the uniform ending
of all the sentences, both long and short, in . . . *ta*, as seen
in the following quotation, gives one a feeling of balanced
beauty such as that in the "Rokudan," a piece in *koto* music
in which both the long and short melodies all end uniformly
in the keynote of the minor scale.

> *Shikashi himegimi wa itsunomanika, yogoto ni otoko to au
> yō ni natta. Otoko wa uba no kotoba dōri yasashii kokoro no
> mochinushi datta. Kao katachi mo sasuga ni miyabite ita.
> Sonoue himegimi no utsukushisa ni, nanimo-kamo wasurete
> iru koto wa, hotondo tare no me nimo akiraka datta. Himegimi
> mo mochiron kono otoko ni, warui kokoro wa motanakatta.
> Toki niwa tanomoshii to omou koto mo atta. Ga, chō tori no
> kichō o tateta kage ni, tōdai no hi o mabushigari nagara, otoko
> to futari mutsubiau toki nimo, ureshii towa ichiya mo
> omowanakatta.*

However, the young lady, before she realized it, began
to meet the man night after night. He was kind-

---

*One of the popular songs sung around Meiji 38 and 39 (1906–7). It
began with the well-known refrain, *toko-tot-tot-tō*.

hearted, as her nurse had told her, and, as might be expected, his features were also elegant. Moreover, it was plain to everyone that he was beside himself with joy at the young lady's beauty. She, too, of course, had no bad feelings toward him, and there were even times when she placed great trust in him. Even when the two exchanged sweet words, shunning the light of the oil lamp behind the curtained screens of butterfly and bird paintings, however, there was not one night when she felt happy.

Sentence endings

Sentence endings are thus extremely clear-cut. The Japanese, however, rather than utilizing this characteristic, have found more than they could handle. They dislike the sentence that ends so distinctly, for it looks stiff, formal, and brusque—or, in more modern terms, dry.

The telephone rings and a woman answers: *Hai, hai, Watanabe de gozaimasu keredomo* . . . (Yes, yes, this is Watanabe but . . .). Foreigners often ask us the meaning of *keredomo.* It does not have much meaning. The woman merely avoided being stiff and formal, or perhaps it would be better to say that she omitted some expressions that might have followed, such as "What can I do for you?" It is clear, at any rate, that she kept the sentence from ending at the point where it should have, thus completing it halfway through. Such expressions are frequently heard, especially among women. There are even some expressions which have become so stereotyped that there is no feeling of omission, as may be seen in the following examples:

Chotto matte.
Please wait. (*Kudasai* must be added to make a complete sentence.)

Atashi kirai.
I don't like it. (*Desu* must be added to make a complete sentence.)

Datte moenain desu mono.
But it doesn't burn. (Originally, this *mono* was *mono o*, meaning "in spite of." There should be some words following.)

Kore chōdai.
Give me this. (*Chōdai sasete kudasai* is the full form.)

Expressions like the above have been in existence from ancient times. It is truly ridiculous that in modern Japanese there is no distinction, for example, between the *shūshi* (conclusive) form and the *rentai* (attributive) form of a verb, both ending in *suru*. Up to the Heian period, there was a definite distinction: the conclusive form ended in *su* and the attributive form ended in *suru*. Toward the end of the Heian period, however, people began to feel that a sentence ending in the conclusive form was too cut-and-dried, and they used the attributive form instead, giving the impression that the sentence was both ending and yet not ending. This way of terminating a sentence became fashionable.

Nanigoto no	I don't know
owashimasu ka wa	What there is here,

shiranedomo	But my tears fall
katajikenasa ni	From thankfulness.
*namida koboruru.**	—SAIGYŌ HŌSHI[2]

This poem looks quite antiquated now, but it must have been extremely fresh and up-to-date at the time it was composed. In the present verb conjugation the conclusive form and the attributive form are the same because the usage of the latter for the former has become very natural.

When we compare the speech of women today with that of men, we find that women use the auxiliary *da* less than men.†

Hontō da yo.	*Honto yo.*
It's true.	It's true.
Sō da nē.	*Sō nē.*
Yes, it is.	Yes, it is.

The sentences on the left are spoken by men, and those on the right by women. Why do women avoid using *da*? It is not quite correct to say that they "avoid using the auxiliary *da*," for actually the auxiliary *da* has inflectional changes and women only avoid the conclusive form. This auxiliary is the only word whose attributive form is different from the conclusive one. Since *da* at the end of a sentence gives one the feeling that the sentence has come to a definite close, women avoid it.

*This ending is also in the attributive form, which ought to take a noun after it.
†*Da* is an auxiliary verb which expresses a decision. It is also used as an interjection. Its attributive form is *na*, and conclusive form is *da*.

The following passage appears in the chapter "The Changes of Seasons" in the *Tsurezure-gusa* (Essays in Idleness).

Tori no koe nado mo kotonohoka ni haru-mekite, nodoyakanaru hikage ni kakine no shitakusa moe-izuru koro yori, yaya haru fukaku kasumi watarite hana mo yōyō keshikidatsu hodo koso are, orishimo ame kaze uchi-tsuzukite, kokoro awatadashiku chiri-suginu.

The singing of birds is especially springlike, and from the time when the grasses beneath the fence begin to sprout in the gentle sunshine, it becomes misty with the advance of spring and flowers begin to bloom. Then rain and wind follow each other, suddenly disturbing our thoughts.[3]

The conclusive form, *chiri-suginu,* is used at the end of the sentence. Therefore, it looks as if the whole sentence ends here, and in fact when we read Japanese textbooks which quote this passage, we see that most of them have put a period here. When we read on in the original, however, we discover the following:

Aoba ni nari-yuku made yorozu ni tada kokoro o nomi zo nayamasu.
Until the green leaves are out, we only worry ourselves with myriad things.

The word *made* (until) in the phrase *aoba ni nari-yuku made* is connected with the word *yori* (from) in the previous phrase, *moe-izuru koro yori* (from the time they begin to bud). In short, Kenkō is saying here:

> *Moe-izuru koro yori aoba ni nari-yuku made, yorozu ni tada kokoro o nomi zo nayamasu.*
>
> From the time they begin to bud until the time they turn into green leaves, we only worry ourselves with myriad things.

Thus, the phrase *yaya haru fukaku kasumi watarite . . . kokoro awatadashiku chiri-suginu* forms a very large parenthesis, and the punctuation after *nu* of *chiri-suginu* is not a period but a comma. The Japanese have also used the conclusive form of a word in such places where a sentence has not actually ended.

The practice of writing such sentences which can be understood either as conclusive or continuative has continued up to the present. Do the slashes in the following *haiku* and *uta* indicate a full stop or not? There is surely some charm in this ambiguity.

Kamakura ya	O Kamakura!
mihotoke naredo	Though a Buddha,
Shakamuni wa	Sakyamuni
binan ni owasu/	Is handsome—
natsukodachi kana.	The summer grove.*
	—YOSANO AKIKO[4]

---

*This poem refers to the great image of the Buddha in Kamakura. Sakyamuni *(Shakamuni)* is the Buddha who founded Buddhism.

Hirugao no   It's already dry,
hana ni kawaku ya/ On the bindweed flower—
tōriame.   The passing rain.

                    —MASAOKA SHIKI

Sentence length

The Japanese felt uneasy about a sentence coming to a definite conclusion and admired a sentence that looked as if it would end but went on for several pages. In the *Makura no Sōshi* (A Pillow Book),[5] there is a story of a dog called Okinamaru which vividly depicts the dog's appearance, the behavior of the people around it, and Sei Shōnagon's feelings—especially her affection toward the dog. The sentence endings here are extraordinary. For example, there is a passage in which Sei Shōnagon was very much upset upon hearing her maid report to her: "The dog was such a bother that two stewards beat him to death." But that evening the wretched-looking dog came tottering along, covered with wounds. Sei Shōnagon was delighted to see him still alive and called his name, but he didn't wag his tail as he once had. She was very sorry, believing that something was ailing him and thought of giving him something to eat. The story is written as follows:

> *Kurete mono nado kuwase nado suredo, (inu wa) kuwaneba, "Okinamaru niwa araji," to ii-nashite, yaminuru yokuasa, (watakushi wa) miya no ogushi-age ni mairite ochōzu mairase, onkagami mochite, ommae ni saburō ni, atari chikaki hashira no moto ni inu no uzukumari ikereba, (watakushi wa) futo arishi koto omoi idete. . . .*

In the evening when we gave him something to eat, (the dog) did not eat, so we said, "It's not Okinamaru." Thus, the day passed, and the next morning when (I) went into the Princess's presence in order to dress her hair, give her water to wash with, and hold her mirror, I happened to see a dog crouching under a nearby pillar. It suddenly made me recall what had passed. . . .

Thus the sentence goes on and on without coming to an end. The sentence up to *yaminuru* and the rest of it beginning with *yokuasa* are accounts separated by the interval of one night. The sentence should end after *yaminuru*, but it does not. The writer may have purposely done this to give a special effect, but it cannot be considered an example of normal writing.

A long sentence is effective in creating tension in the reader. The transition of a story from one incident to another, taking unexpected turns, can certainly be deemed interesting. Miyazawa Kenji's[6] famous poem is another example of this interesting form.

Ame nimo makezu
kaze nimo makezu
yuki nimo natsu no atsusa nimo makenu
jōbu na karada o mochi . . .

By rain undaunted,
By wind undaunted,
By snow undaunted,
By the summer heat undaunted,
With healthy body . . .

The poet goes on to write about thirty lines before he comes to the final *watashi wa naritai* (so would I like to become), revealing for the first time that all this has been his desire.

At any rate, the Japanese are afraid of making a break in a sentence—a tendency not limited to literary works. Long sentences are even used in ordinary writings written for easy comprehension. Matsusaka Tadanori comments:

> The longest sentences are perhaps used in the texts of lawcourt decisions and other legal documents. In addition, long sentences are generally used in government documents. Officials seem to think that short sentences lack dignity, a frame of mind similar to that of the judges who wear gowns in order to enhance their dignity.[7]

The written indictment for the "Chatterly Case,"[8] composed of an extremely long single sentence, was much discussed at the time. The indictment for the "Teigin Case,"[9] too, had only one sentence of over a hundred lines with fifteen characters to a line. Ōkubo Tadatoshi has quoted as an example of a long sentence the statement of the counselor Fuse Tatsuji, who objected to the obliteration of the right to keep silent.

> *Tanaka saikōsai chōkan mo, Satō kenji sōchō mo, Ei-Bei no keiso tetsuzuki niwa, hikokunin ga mizukara shōnindai ni tatte sensei no ue mokuhi-ken o kōshi shi-enai kyōjutsu gimu ga aru noni, Nihon no keiso niwa hikokunin o shōnindai ni tataseru kitei ga nai genjō ni oite, mokuhi-ken bakari hoshō suru koto ga higōri da to hinan shite, mokuhi-ken no massatsu o kyōchō shite*

*iru ga, Nihon no keiso nimo bengonin no tachiai suru kōkai
hōtei ni oite, hikokunin o shōnindai ni tataseru yō na seido o
mōkeru koto niwa, watakushi mo sansei suru ga, hikokunin o
shōnindai ni tatasete, mokuhi-ken o seigen suru yō na seido o
shuchō shinaide bengonin no tachiai shinai keisatsu kenji no
himitsu torishirabe-shitsu de, jihaku o kyōyō suru gōmon bōei no
mokuhi-ken o massatsu shiyō to suru shuchō wa zettai ni futō de
aru.*

Both Chief Justice Tanaka of the Supreme Court and
Public Prosecutor-General Saito emphasize the obliteration of the right of silence, saying that it is un-
reasonable to guarantee only this right under present
circumstances when there is no provision for making
the defendant take the witness stand, while in the
British and American judicial procedures, the defendant, after taking the witness stand himself and taking an
oath, cannot use the right of silence, but has the obligation to testify and while I support the framing of a
system for making the defendant take the witness stand
in court where his counsel is present, their insistence on
formulating a system for making the defendant take
the witness stand, limiting his right of silence, and
obliterating the right of silence that protects the defendant from the torture compelling him to confess in
a secret examining room of the prosecution is absolutely
unjust.[10]

The Japanese have valued long sentences not only in
written articles but in speeches as well. The lines in the
Kabuki play *Uirō-uri* (Uirō-medicine Seller)[11] are typical

examples. Such a way of speaking was considered polite. The speeches of each of the thieves in the Kabuki play *Shiranami Gonin-otoko*[12] are also long. More recently, we have the speech of a principal played by Ryū Chishū in *Carmen Goes Home,* the first technicolor film made in Japan. His address at an athletic meeting goes on and on saying, ". . . and at the same time, . . . and at the same time. . . ." It depicts the Japanese way of speaking on such an occasion very well.

In the length of its sentence, Japanese forms a striking contrast with Chinese, in which sentences of even literary works are exceedingly short. For example:

> *—Tao Hua Yuan Chi—*
> *Tsin Tai-yuan chung,*
> *Wu-ling jen,*
> *Pu yu wei yeh.*
> *Yuan hsi hsing,*
> *Wang lu chih yuan chin.*
> *Hu feng tao hua lin.*
> *Chia an shu pai pu,*
> *Chung wu tsa shu.*
> *Fang tsao hsien mei.*
> *Lo ying pin fen.*
> *Yu jen shen i chih.*

> —A Utopia—
> In the period of Tai-yuan of Tsin dynasty,
> There was a man of Wu-ling
> Who made a living by fishing.
> Once he walked along a river valley,

And forgot how far he had come.
Suddenly he saw a grove of peach trees in blossom.
For several hundred feet along the banks,
There were no other trees but peach trees.
The fragrant grasses were bright and beautiful.
The petals of the peach blossoms fell and scattered.
The fisherman was greatly intrigued.

—TAO YUAN-MING[13]

German is known for its comparatively long sentences, and in Kant's writings there is a single sentence running for more than three pages. Japanese is similar to German in this respect but it must be noted that in German, no matter how long a sentence may be, the meaning of the sentence is said to be explicit. This is due to the fact that in German sentence construction the principal clause ends, and a relative pronoun comes next which connects the principal clause following. In short, it resembles a group of sentences containing subjects and predicates, placed one after another.

When one writes a long Japanese sentence, the predicate verb comes far behind the subject, which appears in the beginning. The many tiny clauses in between give listeners and readers a difficult time understanding the principal idea of any conversation. We must therefore make an effort to write short sentences in Japanese.

◆ 2. SENTENCE TYPES

Japanese sentences were formerly classified as declarative, interrogative, imperative, and exclamatory. Most middle school grammar textbooks up until the end of the war used this classification, which was an adaptation of the old-fashioned system used in European grammars unrelated to the nature of Japanese sentences. In languages like English, there are rules that require the omission of the subject in an imperative sentence, and the interchange of positions of the subject and the predicate verb in an interrogative sentence. In Japanese, however, the "subject" is very vague, and not used in many cases. The order of the constructive elements of a sentence, moreover, is so stable that it would not be unduly influenced by a mere change of sentence type. Therefore, Japanese sentences should have been classified on an entirely different basis.

What, then, is the proper classification for Japanese sentences? Thanks to the studies made by a great number of scholars since the days of Matsushita Daizaburō, grammars consistent with the nature of the Japanese language have gradually developed. At present the foremost among them is a grammar by Haga Yasushi, according to which all sentences can be divided into the following classes:

(1) The declarative sentence—one that expresses the speaker's feeling about the contents to be expressed.
GENERALIZATION BY DECISION
Ame ga furu. (The rain falls.)
Hana wa utsukushii. (Flowers are beautiful.)

223

DOUBT

> *Ame ga furu ka shira.* (I wonder if it will rain.)
> *Kimi wa gakusei ka?* (Are you a student?)

SUPPOSITION + EMOTION

> *Ame ga furu darō nā!* (Oh it will rain!)

DETERMINATION

> *Zehi atte miyō.* (I will see him by all means.)
> *Nido to kaumai.* (I'll not buy it again.)

DECISION + EMOTION

> *Ame!* (Rain!)
> *Ame da!* (It's rain!)

EMOTION

> *Ara!* (Oh!)

(2) The transmissive sentence—one that expresses the speaker's feeling of transmission to another.

COMMAND

> *Yuke!* (Go!)

INVITATION

> *Kampai!* (Your health!)

ADDRESS

> *Ojōsan!* (Young lady!)

RESPONSE

> *Hai.* (Yes.)

(3) The declarative + transmissive sentence—one that expresses both the speaker's attitude toward the contents to be expressed and his feeling of transmission to another.

DECISION + ANNOUNCEMENT

> *Ame ga furu yo.* (It will rain.)

DECISION +EMOTION +ANNOUNCEMENT

Ame ga furu wa yo. (Oh, it will rain.)

SUPPOSITION +PROPOSAL

Ame ga furu darō ne? (It will rain, won't it?)

DOUBT +PROPOSAL

Ame? (Rain?)

It should be noted that sentences of "address" and sentences of "emotion" are different although they look alike. Suppose that you notice a young lady coming toward you and you exclaim, *Ojōsan!* (The young lady!). You can add the auxiliary verb *da* to this sentence: *Ojōsan da!* (It's the young lady!). On the other hand, when addressing her, you say just, *Ojōsan!* (Young lady!). Therefore, we must distinguish between the *Ojōsan!* of address and that of exclamation, both of which have the same form.

Numbers (1) and (3) above are regular sentences in that both imply the attitude of the speaker toward the contents to be expressed. Most of the sentences we use can be classified under these two headings. Those classified under (2) are special kinds of sentences and most are short.

Significative words and phrases at the ends of sentences

The above classification of sentences represents the characteristics of Japanese sentence construction. To begin with, words which express the fundamental nature of a sentence come at the very end of a sentence as a rule. This characteristic is illustrated by the expressions *ka shira* (I wonder if) in *Ame ga furu ka shira* (I wonder if it will rain), and *darō nā* (Oh. . . will) in *Ame ga furu darō nā!* (Oh, it will rain!), and derives from the existence of the iron rule in Japanese according to which the principal word comes last when two words or phrases are combined. I shall discuss this further in the next chapter.

The second characteristic of Japanese sentence construction is the frequent usage of words that express the subjective view of the speaker or the writer, such as *ka shira, darō, nā, yo, wa,* and *nē.* This point is related to the first characteristic given above.

Kita Fumio, author of *Shinario to Kōgo Hyōgen* (Scenario and Colloquial Expressions)[1] calls such words and phrases (namely, *nē, yo, nā, wa*)* *hyōi goku* (significative words and phrases), and gives similar examples from English: "I say," "I think," "I see," "I mean," "I tell you," "I am afraid," "I am sure," "you see," "you think," "you know." However, in comparison with the Japanese *nē, nā, yo, wa, sa,* their English counterparts are used far less and, from an etymological viewpoint, all came from words like "I" or "you," or words expressing action like "say," "see." In short, they form a remarkable contrast to such Japanese expressions as *nē* and *nā,* whose origins are unknown but can be surmised to come from interjections.

The following dialogue is found in Ozaki Kōyō's novel, *Konjiki Yasha* (A Golden Demon). The daughter here is O-miya.

---

*These (except *nā*) are all particles placed at the end of a clause, expressing different meanings: *nē* is used to call a person's attention to something, or express a friendly feeling; *yo* is used to emphasize or announce something, or call someone; *nā* is an exclamation of admiration; *wa* expresses emotion.

Mother: *Mā, okiki* YO. *Sore wa* NĒ . . .
Daughter: *Okkasan, ii* WA—*watashi ii no.*
Mother: *Yok'a nai* YO.
Daughter: *Yok'a nakuttemo ii* WA.
Mother: *Are, mā. Nan da* NĒ.

The words in small capitals are all significative words, which are all words that directly express the feelings and intentions of the speaker. But what happens if they are translated into English? Arthur Lloyd's translation of this part in his English version of *Konjiki Yasha* reads:

"My dear child, listen to me. I think . . ."
"I don't want to listen to you. . . . I don't care for anything."
"What foolishness is this? There is nothing to weep about. I will talk it all over with your father when I go home. . . ."

It should be noted that not a single word with emotional meaning has been used in this translation.

Why are there so many sentences with significative words and phrases in Japanese? In his book *Kokugo to Kokuminsei* (The Japanese Language and Japanese Traits),[2] Kikuzawa Sueo gives examples of *waka* and *haiku* that end in the particles *kana* and *kamo,* and says that they represent the emotional nature of the Japanese language.* That is true, but this practice is also influenced by the idea of letting

---

*Both *kana* and *kamo* are particles attached at the end of a sentence to express emotions.

sentences end in ambiguity as described above. If one says, *yok'a nai* (that's not good) or *yok'a nakuttemo ii* (I don't care if it's not good), it sounds assertive and harsh. If *yo* or *wa* are added, however, (as in the quotation from the *Konjiki Yasha* above), the emotional import can be softened. It is akin to the custom of wearing *tabi*, or Japanese socks, to prevent one's individual toes from being seen, which would be unrefined.

The subject and the topic words

The third characteristic of Japanese sentence construction is the indistinctness of the so-called "subject." Take, for instance, the Japanese sentence: *Haru ga kuru.* In English this would be: Spring comes. The *haru ga* is quite different in nature from the English "spring." The English "spring" is *haru* but not *haru ga*. The *ga* of *haru ga* belongs to "comes" and not to "spring." "Spring comes" can be expressed in Japanese as: *Haru, sore ga kuru* (Spring—it comes). There is a gap between *haru* and *sore ga kuru*. Therefore, the English grammar says: "A sentence is made up of a subject and a predicate." The Japanese *haru ga* is completely dependent on *kuru* (comes). The whole of *haru ga kuru* is one, with an additional tone of announcement. The person who discovered this difference between Japanese and English was Mikami Akira, author of *Gendai Gohō Josetsu* (An Introduction to Modern Japanese Syntax)[3] who decided that English grammar is based on "the dual system of the subject and the predicate," while the Japanese grammar is based on "the single system of the predicate."

As Mikami notes, the subject in Japanese is actually the

subjective complement and is on an equal footing with an objective complement or nouns accompanied by case particles. This can be shown in the following way.

Japanese:

$$\left.\begin{array}{l} K\bar{o}\ ga\ (\text{A}) \\ Otsu\ ni\ (\text{to B}) \\ Hei\ o\ (\text{C—object}) \end{array}\right\} \quad sh\bar{o}kai\ suru\ (\text{introduces})$$

English and Chinese:

$$\begin{array}{ll} K\bar{o}\text{—}Sore\ ga \quad sh\bar{o}kai\ suru \\ (\text{A}) \quad (\text{He}) \quad (\text{introduces}) \end{array} \left\{\begin{array}{l} Otsu\ ni\ (\text{to B}) \\ \\ Hei\ o\ (\text{C—object}) \end{array}\right.$$

Thus, the existence or nonexistence of the subject in Japanese has nothing to do with the classification of the sentences. It is said that in English there is no subject in an imperative sentence, but in Japanese a definite subjective complement appears in an imperative sentence: *Ore wa ayamaranu, omae ga ayamare* (I will not apologize; you apologize); *Hayaku mi ga nare, kaki no tane* (Persimmon seeds, let your fruit grow quickly).

The Japanese system of expression in which the subject is absorbed into the predicate is perhaps an exception among the languages of the world. Korean, like Japanese, has a particle which denotes the subjective case and this leads us to believe that Korean must also be a language with a single system of the predicate. In addition, Burmese has been reported to have a particle for the subjective case and I wonder if it, too, might belong to this same type. I have heard of no other cases.

While the subject in the Japanese language is thus very indistinct, the Japanese sentence is divided into *daimoku-go* (topic words) and *jojutsu-go* (descriptive words). The existence of such a division is the fourth characteristic of Japanese sentences.

Sakuma Kanae divides sentences under (1) and (3) in the list on pages 223–25 into two types, the *shinasadame-bun* (prescriptive sentence) and *monogatari-bun* (narrative sentence).[4] The former is a sentence that gives a topic and makes a description based on it; it generally applies to the noun sentence in Vandryes's grammar.[5] The latter is a sentence that only gives a description without the topic. This is equal to the verb sentence in Vandryes. The following are examples:

> Prescriptive sentences (a):
> *Are wa Fuji da.* (That is Mt. Fuji.)
> *Fuji wa Nihon Arupusu yori mo takai.* (Mt. Fuji is higher than the Japan Alps.)
> *Fuji wa Shizuoka, Yamanashi no ken-zakai ni aru.* (Mt. Fuji lies on the boundary of Shizuoka and Yamanashi prefectures.)
>
> Narrative sentences (b):
> *Fuji ga mieru.* (Mt. Fuji can be seen.)
> *Fuji ga kumo ni kakureta.* (Mt. Fuji has disappeared behind the clouds.)

In (a) *are* (that) and *Fuji* are topics of the description, and *Fuji da* (is Mt. Fuji) and *Nihon Arupusu yori mo takai* (is higher than the Japan Alps) are their explanations. The *Fuji ga mieru* in (b) is different from the sentences in (a) in that it is not divided into the two parts, the topic and the description. However, a question like the following may arise: "Isn't the topic the whole scene in which Mt. Fuji can be seen?" But if it were so, the topic for *Are wa Fuji da* (That is Mt. Fuji) would be *are ga Fuji de aru jijitsu* (the fact that that is Mt. Fuji). Furthermore, we cannot understand it as the omission of a phrase like *are wa* at the beginning of the sentence *Fuji ga mieru,* for *Are wa Fuji ga mieru* does not make sense as a sentence. In short, sentences belonging to (b) are altogether different from those belonging to (a), since they do not have topics as those in (a).

According to Vandryes, these two distinctive classes of sentence are found in all countries. He even says that there may be languages in which nouns and verbs are indistinguishable, but there are probably no languages which do not distinguish between noun sentences and verb sentences. In European languages, however, this distinction does not so clearly appear in form, but in Japanese this distinction is very clear, because of the existence of the particle called *wa*. Sakuma considers the existence of this clear-cut distinction between the prescriptive sentence and the narrative sentence as a strong point of the Japanese language. According to him absurdities arise in the formal logic developed in the West since this distinction is not clear in the European languages. Suppose there is the sentence, *Uma ga hashiru* (A horse runs). Europeans consider this to be an expression of judgment and carry on an argument by altering the statement to: *Uma wa hashiru mono nari* (A horse is something that runs).

In Japanese, however, there is a very clear distinction

between the prescriptive sentences (a) and the narrative sentences (b) given above. In (a) the particle *wa* is used, but in (b) it is not. Of the two, only those sentences belonging to (a) express judgment. Sakuma says that, due to this basic characteristic, Japanese can be considered more logical than various European languages.[6] Perhaps we could say that, had the mother tongue of Aristotle and other philosophers after him been Japanese, European logic might not have traversed so many roundabout paths.

Expressions ending in nouns

Another notable aspect of the Japanese sentence is the occasional omission of the topic in the prescriptive sentences. This can be seen in the following sentences uttered in reply to the question, "What is that mountain?"

> *Fuji da!* (It's Mt. Fuji!) (a)
> *Fuji sa!* (It's Mt. Fuji!)
> *Fuji darō!* (It's perhaps Mt. Fuji!)

We can put *are wa* (that is) before all these sentences:

> *Are wa Fuji da!* (That is Mt. Fuji!)

In other words, the sentence *Fuji da!* of (a) is a part of a sentence of prescription. So far there is no problem. Difficulty arises from the fact that there is the same abbreviated form *Fuji da!* for narrative sentences. Suppose you travel on a train along the Tōkaidō line. You happen to see on your right the majestic view of Mt. Fuji and you involuntarily exclaim:

Fuji da! (b)

This *Fuji da* belongs to the narrative sentence group. This is not a sentence in which *are wa* (that is) is omitted at the beginning. If fully expressed it would be:

Fuji ga mieru! (Mt. Fuji can be seen!)

That is to say, the *Fuji da* of (b) is a compressed form of a narrative sentence and is sometimes simply expressed as *Fuji!* This sentence differs from the *Fuji da* uttered in response to the question, "What is that?"

Generally speaking, there are two kinds of Japanese sentences composed only of a noun or of a noun plus *da*: a part of a prescriptive evaluation sentence, and a compressed form of a narrative sentence. This discovery was made by Mio Isago, author of *Kokugohō Bunshōron* (The Japanese Diction).[7] Scholars before him had noticed the *Fuji da!* of (a) but had not noticed the *Fuji da!* of (b). The discovery of the *Fuji da!* of (b) is significant, since it can explain all the noun endings in *waka, haiku,* and forms similar to them. Sentences with the particle *kana* (which expresses strong feeling) attached to the nouns also belong to this class. The following are examples of this:

Aki kaze ni	The brightness
tanabiku kumo no	Of the moonlight,
taema yori	Emerging from between the
more-izuru tsuki no	clouds
kage no sayakesa.	That trail in the sky,
	Blown by the autumn wind.
	—FUJIWARA AKISUKE[8]

Tamagawa no	My sleeves
asaki nagare ni	Become dripping wet,
ishi nagete	As I throw stones
asobeba nururu	In the shallow Tama stream
waga tamoto kana.	In play.

—WAKAYAMA BOKUSUI[9]

Araumi ya	The rough sea—
Sado ni yokotō	The Milky Way lies spanning it,
ama-no-gawa.	To the isle of Sado.

—BASHŌ[10]

Hototogisu	I hear the cuckoo—
ichi ni no hashi no	As I crossed the first, second bridges,
yoake kana.	At dawn.

—KIKAKU[11]

Shigonin ni	The moon casts
tsuki ochikakaru	Its setting light
odori kana.	On four or five dancers.

—BUSON[12]

Yamada Yoshio called all these exclamatory sentences, considering them as expressions of emotion, and his classification has been esteemed by many scholars. If we stop to think, however, it is absurd that the above sentences have been considered expressions of emotions while sentences like the following have not:

Hito koishi	How I long for people!

hitomoshi goro o	The cherry blossoms fall,
sakura chiru.	At dusk when we light the candles.
	—SHIRAO[13]

The *waka* given above which begins with *Aki kaze ni* might just as well have used *kage zo sayakeki* (the moonlight is bright)—that is, subject and predicate. In the example here, however, the idea is expressed by the phrase *kage no sayakesa* (the brightness of the moonlight) in which the subject and predicate are one. When we compare *kage no sayakesa* with *kage zo sayakeki* (the moonlight is bright), it cannot be said that the former is stronger in emotion. If anything, the former expression has a tighter feeling for it sounds like a compressed version of the expression, *Kage no sayakesa naru kana!* (It's the brightness of the moonlight!).

In brief, among the sentences ending in nouns, there are sometimes compressed forms of descriptive sentences which belong to the same type as those ending in verbs and adjectives. This is a fifth characteristic of the Japanese sentence.

◆ 3. WORD AND PHRASE ARRANGEMENT

The principle governing word order

In principle a sentence is a group of words. Single-word sentences such as *Kaji!* (Fire!) exist, but sentences are usually composed of two or more words. Each language has its own rules governing word order. What are these rules in Japanese?

In the poet Hagiwara Sakutarō's article entitled "The Inconvenience of Japanese," he says that his late grandfather had a habit of saying:

> Japan is the only country in the world that walks on the path of righteousness. Consider—both Western and Chinese words are read upside down. Japanese is the only language that is rightside up and not on its head.

This statement is interesting as an expression of the state of mind of people who think that things which are familiar are generally right. The observation made by Hagiwara's grandfather, however, cannot simply be rejected as a childish point of view. Japanese word order is consistent and based on the ironclad rule: "If words and phrases called A are dependent on words and phrases called B, A always comes before B." Take, for example, *shiroi hana* (a white flower). In this case *shiroi* (white) is dependent on *hana* (flower), because *shiroi hana* is a kind of *hana* and not a kind of *shiroi*. There are all kinds of flowers—white, red, large, small—and a white flower belongs to one of these categories. Therefore, if the whole phrase *shiroi hana* (a white flower) is connected with another word in a sentence, it is done in the same way as when *hana* alone is used. We can say *hana ga* or *hana o* as well as *shiroi hana ga* or *shiroi hana o*.* In brief, *shiroi* is dependent on *hana*. The phrase *utsukushiku saku* (beautifully bloom) is similarly a kind of *saku* (to bloom) and not a kind of *utsukushiku* (beautifully). *Hana ga saku* (flowers bloom) and *niwa de saku* (bloom in the garden) are kinds of *saku,* and both *hana ga* (the flowers) and *niwa de* (in the garden) are dependent on *saku* (bloom). Thus all such dependent words like *utsukushiku, hana ga,* and *niwa de* are placed before *saku*.

Sometimes, however, when the first word is more important in meaning, the second word appears dependent on the first, as in the following examples: *saite iru* (is in bloom) and *saku tokoro da* (is about to bloom). Grammatically, however, *saite* (in bloom) is dependent on *iru* (is), and *saku* (bloom) is dependent on *tokoro da* (is about to). It is *iru,* and not *saite,* that determines to what words the phrase *saite iru* will be connected. *Iru* is used in phrases like *iru toki* (the time one is), *iru hazu da* (one ought to be or stay), *iru ka* (does one stay?). *Saite* is used in phrases like *saite shimau* (completely bloom), *saite wa inai* (is not in bloom). The whole phrase *saite iru* (is in bloom) is used in phrases like *saite iru toki* (when it is in bloom), *saite iru hazu da* (must be in bloom), *saite iru ka?* (is it in bloom?). In all cases it is used in exactly the same way as *iru* alone. In brief, *saite iru* is a form of *iru* and not a form of *saite*. Grammatically, *saite* is dependent on *iru*.

Ga indicates a subject; *o* indicates an object.

This ironclad rule that the dependent element comes first and the independent element comes last applies to everything in Japanese from large things like groups of words constituting sentences to small things like two-word phrases.

Take, for example, the following sentence:

Moshi ashita ame dattara / watashi wa yame ni shimasu.
If it rains tomorrow / I'll give up.

If this sentence is written in English, either the dependent clause or the independent clause can come first without giving the impression of inversion. In Japanese, however, the order is solidly fixed. It is not impossible to say, *Watashi wa yame ni shimasu, moshi ashita ame dattara,* but such a sentence would definitely give an appearance of having been inverted.

In combinations such as *hana ga* (the flower), which consists of a noun + a particle, and *saku darō* (will bloom), which consists of a verb + an auxiliary verb, the noun or the verb also comes first. But the particle *ga* and the auxiliary verb *darō* assume grammatical leadership and they decide what will follow them, as in the expressions *hana ga aru* (the flower exists), *hana ga saku* (the flower blooms), and *hana ga saku darō kara* (since the flower will bloom).

At any rate, the order of Japanese words and phrases is very consistent and for that reason we cannot simply laugh at Hagiwara's grandfather's statement. However, if we followed his statement to its logical conclusion, we could also say that Japanese is a topsy-turvy language and Japan a country which always takes the wrong road.

Languages with similar word order

The word order of Japanese is consistently governed by a single rule. Many languages in the world have a similar word order. In the Far East, such languages include Korean, Manchurian, modern Mongolian, and Ainu.

The Altaic languages, such as ancient Mongolian and Turkish, and the Ural languages like Hungarian are similar to Japanese, except that modifiers designating person come after the noun. Burmese, Tibetan, and Lepcha, a language widely discussed nowadays, also resemble Japanese except for their personal noun modifiers, which come after the nouns in principle. Verb modifiers, however, come before the verbs. Consequently, the verbs come at the end of the sentence and in this respect they look very much like Japanese. According to Kimura Ichirō, the word order of contemporary Hindustani is similar to Japanese.[1] According to Izui Hisanosuke, other languages of this type include the language of the Miao tribe in the mountains of inner Tonkin, India's Santali (which forms a branch of the South Asian languages), the Bantu languages of Africa, Avar in the Caucasian language groups, Basque in Europe, and many others.

Moreover, in Latin, a representative language in Europe, one could use a number of word orders, but its standard form placed verbs at the end as in Japanese.[2] It is said that even English had the same form in ancient times.[3] Consequently, we cannot say that the word order of Japanese is peculiar to it.

What, then, are the languages whose word orders differ the most from Japanese? It is often said that modern English is very different from Japanese, but the Celtic languages are even more unlike Japanese in that the verb comes first, and both the subject and object follow it.[4] This group of languages perhaps differs the most from Japanese. In English, modifiers of nouns frequently come before nouns, but in French they frequently come after nouns, which makes French quite dissimilar to Japanese. In the Far East, the word order of Thai and Vietnamese are most different from Japanese.

Freedom in Japanese word order

Is Japanese word order free or not? There are two answers to the question. Matsuo Sutejirō, an authority on classical grammar, takes the position that it is free and gives the following example:

> *Kono akatsuki | hototogisu | futakoe mikoe | kanashigeni | Heianjō o | tōnan yori | seihoku ni | sujikai ni | naki-suginu.*
> Early this morning, the cuckoo cried sadly two or three times as it flew diagonally across the Heian capital from southeast to northwest.[5]

He argues that since there are nine interchangeable elements in the above sentence, the number of sentences that can be made out of it by interchanging words would be:

$$1 \times 2 \times 3 \times 4 \times 5 \times 6 \times 7 \times 8 \times 9 = 362,880$$

This argument, however, takes the fact that a sentence can still be understood even if its elements are interchanged, while ignoring the effect on the sentence's feeling if elements have been interchanged.

Take, for example, the sentence *Neko ga nezumi o toraeru* (A cat catches a rat). While it is true that the meaning is not altered no matter how the three elements in this sentence are interchanged, *neko ga toraeru nezumi o* gives a definite feeling that words have been transposed. Similarly, in the previous example beginning with *kono akatsuki hototogisu,* if the phrase *naki-suginu* were placed in the middle of the sentence, all the words and phrases following it would seem dislocated. Thus, we cannot very well say that there is real freedom in the order of Japanese words.

The word order of Japanese truly does have more freedom than Chinese and English. The German and French word orders also seem to be more rigidly fixed than Japanese, but Latin was very fluid in this respect. According to Mario Pei, the word orders of the Spanish and Italian languages, belonging to the Latin tradition, are likewise very fluid, and when British and American students first learn Spanish—especially the literary language—they have a hard time finding the subject, which can be lurking anywhere, even at the very end of a long sentence.

It would be going too far, however, to call freedom of word order a characteristic of Japanese. Both Mario Pei[6] and Serge Elisseeff[7] place Japanese in a class of languages whose word orders are comparatively rigid.

Modifiers at the beginning

The word order of Japanese in which dependent elements come before the principal elements has greatly influenced

Japanese expressions. People frequently complain that when the modifiers are long, it is difficult to tell what the sentence is trying to say.

The popular charades television program is interesting in that it reflects the word order in Japanese. For example, when it is Mizunoe Takiko's turn in a contest between the red and the white teams and she is told to act out the phrase, *Eiga sutā ni mitorete inu no ashi o funzuketa otoko* (A man who stepped on a dog's foot, being fascinated by a movie star), does she begin her gestures from the beginning of the phrase *eiga sutā ni* (a movie star)? No. She first of all puts up her thumb to show that it is a man. After this she pantomimes *eiga sutā ni mitorete* (fascinated by a movie star), because this order will make it easier for her enthusiastic team members to guess the answer. When she finally has them give the phrase, they begin to say, *otoko ga eiga sutā ni mitorete* (a man is fascinated by a movie star), but that is not the real answer. Thus, she waves her hand to show that the order is wrong and makes gestures in sequence: "a movie star," "fascinated," "a dog," "a foot" "stepped on," "a man." This leads them to a perfect answer. If the topic is not just "a movie star" but "a movie star coming this way," Mizunoe will most likely pantomime "a movie star" first and then "coming this way." If the topic is "a sleeping dog," she will first indicate that it is a dog and then act out "sleeping." After that she will surely signal them to turn it around. Although this is a very roundabout method, it is necessary because all modified words come after the modifiers in Japanese.

In this sense, we Japanese suffer from a lack of ease in expressing quickly what we want to say, since all modifiers come before the essential word. Criticisms like the following by Nagano Masaru, a Japanese language scholar, arise from that fact.

> *Watanabe keiji wa   chimamire ni natte   nigedashita zoku o oikaketa.*
> In Japanese word order: Detective Watanabe, smeared with blood, the running-away thief, pursued.
> In other words we can interpret this sentence to mean either "The detective Watanabe, who was smeared with blood, pursued the thief running away," or "The detective Watanabe pursued the thief who was running away smeared with blood."[8]

In conversation, of course, modifiers can be put after the noun.

> *Kondo otonari e kita oyomesan mita? Iro no shiroi, se no takai.*
> Have you seen the new bride who recently moved in next door—the tall, fair-complexioned one?

> *Kinō mata ano otoko ga yattekimashita yo, konoaida hōhō no tei de nige-kaetta.*
> Yesterday that man came again—the one who beat a hasty retreat the other day.

Such a device, however, cannot be used freely, and while the novelist Akutagawa Ryūnosuke devised the following manner of writing, no one followed him.

> *Futari ga niwa kara kaette kuru to, Teruko wa otto no tsukue*

*no mae ni, bonyari dentō o nagamete ita, aoi yokobai ga tatta
hitotsu, kasa ni hatte iru dentō o.*

When the two came back from the garden, Teruko
was sitting before her husband's desk, absent-mindedly
gazing at the electric light—the light on whose shade
a single green leaf-hopper was crawling.[9]

Predicates at the end

In a Japanese sentence the predicate, which holds the
sentence together, comes at the very end. This is effective
in making the end of a sentence clear and definite, but we
often become irritated because we do not know the meaning till the end since the basic meaning of a sentence rests
in its verb. When we read

*Chiji wa subete no kyoku no subete no ka no subete no gyōmu no
shinkō jōtai o tsune ni shōchi shite inakereba naranai . . .*

The governor must always be aware of the state of
progress of all the projects of all the sections of all the
bureaus . . .

we first feel that governors must have a terrible time. The
sentence, however, continues, . . . *wake dewa nai . . .* (it is not
that), reversing its meaning. Similarly, when a person
says, *Kono hon o kimi ni age . . .* (I will give this book to you),
you think he will give it to you and you put out your hand.
Then he says, . . . *tara yorokobu darō to . . .* (if I do so you will
be pleased) and your expectation is reversed. "O my!" you
think, but suddenly he says, . . . *omou kara isso no koto age . . .*
(so I think, therefore, I would rather . . .) and you then

think he will give it to you after all. However, he goes on to say, . . . *yō ka to omou ga mā yosō* (. . . give it to you, but I won't), and you are thus rejected at the last moment. It is amusing to use such a technique in playing a trick on someone or making some kind of excuse. But it is often inconvenient when you want to express your thoughts clearly and precisely.

The preamble to the Japanese constitution is no exception. It begins,

> *Wareware wa, izure no kokka mo, jikoku no koto ni nomi sennen shite takoku o mushi shite wa naranai node atte . . .*
> We, no country should devote itself solely to affairs of its own, ignoring other countries . . .

and we are puzzled about the meaning of "we." When we look at the next part of the sentence,

> *seiji dōtoku no hōsoku wa, fuhenteki no mono de ari, kono hōsoku ni shitagau koto wa jikoku no shuken o iji shi . . .*
> the law of political morality is universal, and to follow this law (is) to maintain one's own country's sovereignty . . .

we still don't see the end. After reading further in the preamble we come to

> *takoku to taitō kankei ni tatō to suru kakkoku no gimu de aru to shinzuru.*
> is the duty of every country that desires to stand on equal footing with other countries, (we) believe.

Now we finally become aware that the predicate verb for the subject "we" is "believe," but it was a tantalizing experience to have been left hanging in midair for so long.

In old European rhetoric a sentence in which the predicate verb comes at the very end is called a periodic sentence (which Kadono Kiroku translates as *tōbi-bun*), and it keeps the reader in suspense till the very end. Such a sentence, however, should be used only when one aims at producing a special effect. When we try to write Japanese in a natural order, however, all the sentences become periodic, which is a burden on the reader. In English, the predicate verb comes right after the subject and such a sentence is called a loose sentence (Kadono calls it *sanretsu-bun*). Because its principal part comes first, it is quite lucid.

If the preamble to the constitution, discussed above, were written in English, it would begin, "We believe that . . ." The relation between the subject and predicate verb "we believe" is obvious. We are envious of English in this respect.

The Japanese have invented various forms of expression to overcome such difficulties. The following is an example of one of the most moderate.

> *Watashi wa omowazu iki o nonda. Sōshite setsuna ni issai o ryōkai shita. Komusume wa, osoraku wa korekara hōkō-saki e omomukō to shite iru komusume wa, sono futokoro ni zōshite ita ikutsuka no mikan o mado kara nagete, wazawaza fumi-kiri made miokuri ni kita otōto tachi no rō ni mukuita node aru.*

I held my breath involuntarily, and instantly understood everything. The girl—the girl who was probably on her way to a new master's house—threw out of the window some oranges she had placed in her pocket and rewarded her brothers who had come all the way to the railway crossing to see her off.[10]

If we follow this formula, the preamble to the constitution would be: *Wareware wa shinzuru. Izure no kokka mo . . . kakkoku no gimu de aru* (We believe: every country . . . is the duty of every country).

In the past, too, the Japanese invented other new forms of expressions. For example:

Negawakuwa	Would that
hana no moto nite	I could die
haru shinan	Under the cherry blossoms—
sono kisaragi no	In spring in the second month,
mochizuki no koro.	At the time of the full moon!

—SAIGYŌ

The device Saigyō uses here is the expression *negawakuwa* (Would that I . . .), which makes the sentence easier to understand than the ordinary *Hana no moto nite haru shinan . . . koto o negau* (To die under the cherry blossoms in spring—I wish). Similarly, *Hakarazariki, kyō futatabi kangun o min towa* (It was unexpected—that today I should see the imperial army again) is much easier to understand than *Kyō futatabi kangun o min towa hakarazariki* (That today I should see the imperial army again was unexpected). Other expressions such as *oshimurakuwa* (it is regrettable that), *iwaku* (one says that), *shirazu* (I did not know that) have all been invented out of necessity. The following song makes use of such a device:

> *Beniya de musume no iu koto nya*
> *haru no otsuki sama usugumori. . . .*
> What the young girl says at the rouge shop—
> "The spring moon is slightly veiled. . . ."

If we use this kind of device, the preamble to the constitution would take the following form: *Warera no shinzuru tokoro dewa* . . . (What we believe are . . .).

Furthermore, the Japanese experimented with changing the positions of words and phrases without changing the form. This can usually be seen in daily conversations as illustrated below:

> *Dōshita no? Me no ue no tokoro? Harete iru wa yo.* (What's the matter—*right above your eyes?* It's swollen.)
> *Ima chotto butsuketan da, hashira ni.* (I just bumped into— a pillar.)
> *Abunakatta wa ne. Chotto matte ne, okusuri o sagashite kuru kara.* (Wasn't that terrible? Wait a moment, *while I go and look for some medicine.*)

The parts underlined have been inverted, but they sound very natural. Such expressions are found in *Nihongo no Gendai Fūkei* (The Modern Landscape of Japanese),[11] which was compiled by Iwabuchi Etsutarō and is a collection of natural, present-day conversations, illustrating modes of the language.

Such expressions are also found in literary writings, such

as the following translated passages from Lafcadio Hearn:

Watakushi ga atsui cha no saigo no ippai o nonda toki ni,
watashi no me wa omowazu kami-dana no hō e ugoita. Soko
ni, chīsai tōmyō ga mada moete ita. Sono toki watashi wa,
daruma no mae nimo tōmyō no moete iru koto ni ki ga tsuita.
Hotondo dōji ni, daruma ga watashi no hō o massugu ni
miteiru koto o mitometa—futatsu no me de.

As I swallowed the final bowl of warm tea, my gaze
involuntarily wandered in the direction of the household gods, whose tiny lamps were still glowing. Then
I noticed that a light was burning also in front of
Daruma; and almost in the same instant I perceived
that Daruma was looking straight at me—with two
eyes![12]

Inversions like those illustrated above are so common in
poems that we hardly have the feeling that the word order
is reversed. For example,

Tsuki mireba	When I gaze at the moon,
chiji ni mono koso	I become
kanashikere	Variously sad—
<u>*wagami hitotsu no*</u>	*Though the autumn is not*
<u>*aki niwa aranedo.*</u>	*For myself alone.*
	—ŌE NO CHISATO[13]

Yawaraka ni	The banks
yanagi aomeru	Of the Kitakami river,
Kitakami no	Where the willow had turned

kishibe me ni miyu	Softly green,
nake to gotoku ni.	Came into view—
	As if telling me to cry.

—ISHIKAWA TAKUBOKU[14]

Totose henu	Ten years have passed;
onaji kokoro ni	You cry
kimi naku ya	With the same thought,
haha to naritemo.	*Though you are a mother now.*

—MIKI ROFŪ[15]

As already mentioned, Latin was a language in which it was possible to use all kinds of word order, but the standard form placed the verb at the very end as in Japanese. They say that in Old English, too, the predicate verb was commonly placed at the end or near the end of a sentence and apparently took a form like "I . . . believe." Ōkubo Tadatoshi urges us at every opportunity to change the word order of Japanese, putting the verb near the beginning of a sentence.[16] His deeply felt wish can be fulfilled if we only care to do so.

◆ 4. WORD AND PHRASE COMBINATION

The connection between one word and another is not clearly indicated in Japanese. What we now express by *Haru ga kuru* (Spring comes) was formerly expressed by *Haru tatsu*. *Haru* (spring) is said to be the subject of *tatsu* (comes), but neither has *haru* taken a subject form nor is there any indication that *tatsu* itself is the predicate of *haru*. Only when they are placed next to each other, as in *haru tatsu*, does *haru* become the subject of *tatsu* with regard to the meaning of the phrase. When you say "Spring comes" in English, "spring" is the same as the Japanese *haru*, as explained in V, Chapter 2 (p. 228). "Comes" denotes "the thing comes," and is joined to "spring." Unlike Japanese, it does have a connecting element. The old form in Japanese is similar to the Chinese word *li chun* 立春, a tendency which can be seen in Japanese expressions everywhere.

In the *Makura no Sōshi*, we find the following passage which illustrates a lack of connectives between words:

> *Tōkute chikaki mono, gokuraku, fune no michi, danjo no naka.*
> Things distant and yet near: the Buddhist paradise, the sea route, the relations between man and woman.

The relations between the words *gokuraku, fune no michi,* and *danjo no naka* are all left to the reader's imagination. So also is the relation between these three and *tōkute chikaki mono* (things distant and yet near). People dislike using case particles in *waka* and *haiku,* believing that they slacken the composition and make it conceptual. The following examples illustrate this and are therefore without particles.

Haru no sono	The spring garden—
kurenai niō	The peach blossoms
momo no hana	In glowing red;
shita-teru michi ni	A girl comes and stands under
ide-tatsu otome.	them,
	On the sunny path.
	—ŌTOMO YAKAMOCHI[1]

Me niwa aoba	To the eye, green leaves;
yama hototogisu	To the ear, the mountain
hatsu-gatsuo.	cuckoo;
	To the taste, the first bonito.
	—SODŌ[2]

Araumi ya	The rough sea—
Sado ni yokotō	The Milky Way lies spanning it,
ama-no-gawa.	To the isle of Sado.
	—BASHŌ

In present-day Japanese sentences, clarity of meaning is valued, and case particles are thus used to make the relations between words clear, which is an improvement in the Japanese language. In conversations, however, the frequent omission of particles is still preferred for the reason that it prevents speeches from becoming harsh as here, where the particles *wa* and *o* are omitted:

Atashi, komatchatta wa. (I'm at a loss about what to do.)*

*The nominative particle *wa* is omitted after *atashi*.

Anata, ano kata to no o-yakusoku, dō nasaru? (What are you going to do about your appointment with him?)*

Joining sentences

The relations between sentences as well as words tend to be obscured, and connectives are omitted as much as possible. In the following quotation from the *Tsurezure-gusa* there are no connectives:

Ari no gotoku atsumarite, tōzai ni isogi, namboku ni hashiru. Takaki ari, iyashiki ari, oitaru ari, wakaki ari, yuku tokoro ari, kaeru ie ari, yūbe ni inete ashita ni oku. Itonamu tokoro nanigoto zo ya. Sei o musabori, ri o motomete yamu toki nashi.
Getting together like ants; hurrying about east and west; running north and south. Some are high in rank, some are low, some are old, some are young. There are places to go; houses to return to. They sleep at night, get up in the morning. What are they engaged in? They covet life, seek profit without end.

Kobayashi Hideo, the linguist, names Ōoka Shōhei as a contemporary writer who does not use connectives.[3]

Sometimes in Japanese sentences there is no indication of even a complete change in context. Such sentences are difficult to understand unless one is used to them. In former times books had no quotation marks. In the chapter called "Kiō" in the *Heike Monogatari* (The Tale of the Heike

---

*Here also *wa* is omitted after *anata,* and the objective particle *o* is omitted after *o-yakusoku.*

Clan),[4] there is the following story. Watanabe Kiō, a samurai of the Minamoto clan, became a subject of Taira-no-Munemori through deceit. Munemori was very much pleased with him, and enjoyed calling out, "Kiō! Kiō!" morning and night even though he had no particular need of the services of the man. One day, however, an incident occurred:

> *Munemori no kyō isogi idete, Kiō wa aru ka sōrawazu to mōsu.*
> *Suwa kyatsu me o tenobi ni shite tabakararenuru wa. Are*
> *okkakete ute to notamae domo . . .*
>
> Lord Munemori hurried out and asked, "Is Kiō there?" "No, he isn't," they replied. "So then the fellow sought a chance and deceived us. There, run after him and kill him," said the lord, but . . .

On first reading this quotation, one might think that Lord Munemori came out in a hurry and said, *Kiō wa aru ka, sōrawazu* (Is Kiō there? . . . No, he isn't).* But actually this is not so. At present we would put the two sentences *Kiō wa aru ka* and *sōrawazu* within separate quotation marks, because *Kiō wa aru ka* is spoken by Munemori and *sōrawazu* by some attendant who was there but not named. The next part of the passage from *Suwa kyatsu me o* (So then that fellow . . .) as far as *okkakete ute* (chase and kill him) was also spoken by Munemori. This, too, we know only after we read as far as *notamae*† *domo* (he says, but . . .).

*In English, quotes must be added to designate the speaker. The Japanese original has no quotation marks; thus, it is not clear who the speaker is.

†An honorific expression for "say." This shows the speaker is Munemori.

Up to that point we might mistakenly think that the passage is a description of Munemori's mind.

This kind of sentence can also be found in modern writing. The following is a passage from *Botchan*[5] by Natsume Sōseki, where Botchan goes fishing, invited by "Red Shirt."

> *Kimi tsuri ni yukimasen ka to Akashatsu ga ore ni kiita . . .*
> *Ore wa sō desu nā to sukoshi susumanai henji o shitara, kimi*
> *tsuri o shita koto ga arimasu ka to shikkeina koto o kiku.*
> *Ammari nai ga, kodomo no toki, Komme no tsuribori de funa o*
> *san biki tsutta koto ga aru. Sorekara Kagurazaka no Bishamon*
> *no ennichi de hassun bakari no koi o hari de hikkakete, shimeta*
> *to omottara, pochari to otoshite shimatta ga, kore wa ima*
> *kangaetemo oshii to ittara, Akashatsu wa ago o mae no hō e*
> *tsukidashite ho-ho-ho-ho to waratta.*

Red Shirt asked me, "Don't you want to go fishing?" ... When I said a little reluctantly, "Well," he asked me rudely, "Have you ever fished?" "Not much, but when I was a child I once caught three crucian carps in an angling pond at Komme. And once on a fete day at the Bishamon temple at Kagurazaka, I hooked up an eight-inch carp, but when I thought I had it, the carp fell into the water with a splash. Even now I think it was a shame," I said to Red Shirt. Thereupon Red Shirt stuck out his chin and laughed, "Ho-ho-ho-ho."

In this writing Botchan is the speaker from *Ammari nai ga* (not much but) as far as *ima kangaetemo oshii* (even now it was a shame). However, as we continue to read the passage from "*shikkeina koto o kiku. Ammari nai ga kodomo no toki . . .* (he asked rudely. Not much, but when I was a child . . .)," we cannot help having the feeling that the passage from *ammari nai ga* on is an expression of Botchan's thoughts. When we see the words *to ittara* (when I said) after *ima kangaetemo oshii*, however, we realize for the first time that they were Botchan's words. Mōri Yasotarō, the translator of *Botchan* into English, has made it very clear that the passage from *ammari nai ga* on is uttered by Botchan: "I told him not much, that I once caught three gibels when I was a boy. . . ." Although the Japanese sentences are not very explicit in this respect, the writer himself probably does not care if the reader takes the passage as a portrayal of Botchan's mind. This may be an interesting way to write in a literary work, but it cannot be considered the proper way of writing.

In the chapter "Kiritsubo" in the *Genji Monogatari* (The Tale of Genji), there is the following passage: *Miya wa ootonogomorinikeri* (The prince has retired). It is not clear whether this is a descriptive sentence or a part of conversation, and different opinions exist on the subject. Shimazu Hisamoto, one of the foremost critics of the *Genji Monogatari*, is unable to decide and suggests that the person concerned may have uttered it partly to himself.[6] Such ambiguity surely cannot be to the credit of the author.

Such being the sequence of words and phrases in Japanese, the boundary between what is actually seen and the content of one's imagination is also not readily distinguishable. The following quotation from Futabatei illustrates such ambiguity.

Mazu dokoka no kaiinu ga en no shita de ko o unda to suru.
Chippokena mukumuku shita no ga kasanariatte, kubi o
motagete mii mii to chibusa o sagashite iru tokoro e oyainu ga
yoso kara kaette kite, sono soba e dosari to yoko ni nari,
katappashi kara kakaekonde peropero nameru to, chīsai kara
shita no saki de taai mo naku korokoro to korogasareru.
Korogasarete wa ōsawagi shite mata yochiyochi to hatte . . .

Let's say, someone's dog bore puppies under the ve-
randa. The tiny plump things lie one on top of another
and pop up their heads, whining and searching for
their mother's teats. Just then she comes back and
heavily throws herself down by their side. She hugs
and licks them one after another and the pups, being
tiny, are easily rolled over by the tip of her tongue.
Every time the pups roll over, they are thrown into
great confusion and begin crawling about tottering-
ly. . . .[7]

Although we cannot discern whether the passage beginning
with *Chippokena* (The tiny . . .) in the above quotation is an
actual description or just the writer's imagination, most
readers take it to be the latter.

Linking participial adjectives

In his essay entitled "The Merits of Japanese," Yoshikawa Kōjirō says that very few languages can link words
together as freely as Japanese and points to the following
waka poem which expresses a very complex idea in a single
sentence:

Sode hijite	Will the wind of today,
musubishi mizu no	The first day of spring,
kōreru o	Melt the frozen water—
haru tatsu kyō no	The water I used to scoop with
kaze ya tokuran.	my hands,
	Wetting my sleeves?

—KI NO TSURAYUKI[8]

The author says that if one were to express this idea in a Chinese poem, which is known for its brevity, it would require four sentences:

記曾沾雙袖　臨流濺濺弄

今日春又回　東風乃解凍[9]

In the Japanese poem above, the simple connection of *sode hijite musubishi* (to scoop with my hands, wetting my sleeves) with *mizu* (water), and *haru tatsu* (spring begins) with *kyō* (today) are worthy of note.

Generally speaking, the *rentai-shūshokugo*, or participial adjectives, in Japanese can be readily linked with nouns, as shown in the following examples:

Waga koto to	The parsley roots—
dojō no nigeshi	Where the loach swam away,
nezeri kana.	Thinking someone's after him.*

—JŌSŌ[10]

---

*Someone came to pick the parsley growing in the swampy water, when a loach suddenly moved away, thinking the person came to catch him. The noun modifier is *nigeshi* (that swam away), which modifies *nezeri* (parsley), so literally it might read: "The loach-escaping parsley."

Zetchō no	The reliable-looking castle
shiro tanomoshiki	On the top of the hill—
wakaba kana.	The young leaves.*

—BUSON

Umasō ni	The shelter from rain—
naniyara nieru	Something is being cooked
amayadori.	Deliciously.†

(Senryū)

Mari mochite	The children without balls
asobu kodomo o	Gaze admiringly
mari motanu	At the children playing with
kodomo mihoruru	balls—
yamazakura bana.	The mountain cherry blossoms.‡

—KITAHARA HAKUSHŪ

The particle *no* has the function of producing modifiers for nouns and sometimes connects them with extraordinary things. For example:

---

*The words *shiro tanomoshiki* (the castle reliable-looking) modifies *wakaba* (young leaves), so literally it means: "The-castle-on-the-hilltop-reliable-looking young leaves."

†In this poem *nieru* (being cooked) modifies *amayadori* (sheltering from rain), so literally it means: "Something-deliciously-being-cooked rain shelter."

‡Grammatically, *mihoruru* (look admiringly at), together with the whole phrase before it, modifies *yamazakura* (mountain cherry blossoms). Actually, some children are playing with balls under the blossoms, and those without balls are looking enviously at those with balls, not at the blossoms.

Yama wa kure	Night fell in the mountains;
no wa tasogare no	The fields are pampas grasses
susuki kana.	In the evening twilight.*

—BUSON

Bakesōna	The wintry shower at the temple
kasa kasu tera no	That lent me
shigure kana.	A ghostly-looking umbrella.†

—BUSON

"Wasureji" no	Since my future,
yukusue made wa	Of which you pledged, "I will
katakereba . . .	not forget you,"
	Is difficult to trust . . .‡

Kimi no wakarazuya ni mo hotohoto kanshin suru yo.
I'm really amazed at your being such a simpleton.§

Expressions like the above are also used in daily conversation, and they are sometimes the cause of misunderstandings. A fastidious-looking gentleman ordered lunch in a restaurant. They took pains to serve him the best food but as they

---

*In this poem the particle *no* unites *tasogare* (evening twilight) with *susuki* (pampas grass), so literally it means: "The pampas grasses of the evening twilight."

†*Bakesōna* refers to something that looks as if it could become ghostly. The oil-paper umbrella must have been broken and eerie looking. Here *no* unites *tera* (the temple) with *shigure* (wintry shower).

‡In this poem *wasureji* (I will not forget you) modifies *yukusue made* (one's future, or forever); therefore it literally means: "my future of your 'I will not forget you.' "

§*Wakarazuya* means a stupid person, and the particle *no* unites this word with *kimi* (you); therefore, the literal meaning is: "I'm really amazed at the stupid person of yours."

had feared, the gentleman refused to eat, saying, *Kuu mono ga nai* (There is nothing to eat). The head cook, quite abashed, rushed to the table and asked, "What food would you like . . .?" The man ill-humoredly replied, *Naifu to fuōku ga nai* (There is no knife and fork).* In English such ambiguity of expression would probably not occur, since prepositions and relative pronouns could also be used, such as "with which."

Wa, the particle designating the topic in Japanese, sometimes unites the topic with the predicate in a most unusual way.

> *Wagahai wa neko de aru.*[12]
> I am a cat.

The usage of *wa* in the above sentence is a common one and the case particle *ga* could be substituted for it. A completely different usage of *wa,* however, can be seen in the following examples of Mikami Akira:

> *Mikan wa mi o tabe, kinkan wa kawa o taberu.*
> As regards the tangerine, we eat the fruit; as regards the kumquat, we eat the skin.

> *Kantō wa Edo ni gozansu.*
> It is Edo of Kantō.

> *Genta-kun wa kinō ojisan ga nakunattan desu.*
> As regards Genta, his uncle died yesterday.[11]

*****Kuu mono* can mean "a thing to eat" or "a thing with which to eat," like *kaku mono* which means either "a thing to write on" or "a thing to write with."

In these sentences, the connections between words cannot be shown by the simple insertion of some case particle. The above examples are contractions of sentences that should be written as follows:

Mikan wa (doko o taberu ka to iu to) mi o tabe, kinkan wa (doko o taberu ka to iu to) kawa o taberu.
(If we ask what we eat in tangerines,) we eat the meat in tangerines, and (if we ask what we eat in kumquats,) we eat the skin in kumquats.

Kantō wa (sono uchi no doko ka to iu to) Edo ni gozansu.
(If we ask what part of Kanto it is,) it is Edo of Kantō.

Genta-kun wa (kyō dōshite yasunda ka to iu to) kinō ojisan ga nakunattan desu.
(If we ask why Genta was absent today, it is because) Genta's uncle died yesterday.

Flexibility of noun phrases

There is the following type of expression in Japanese: *Boku wa unagi da.* (For my part, I'll eat eel.) Literally, it means, "I am eel." This is an expression you use, for instance, when you go into a restaurant and are asked, "What would you like to eat?" It is a peculiar expression, however, when you stop to think about it. Natsume Sōseki, the novelist, said, "I am a cat," but here the person is not saying that he is an eel in imitation of Sōseki. He means: *Boku wa unagi o taberu* (I will eat eel). The verbal element, its so-called predicative nature according to the grammarian Hashimoto Shinkichi, has been eliminated from the above sentence and the auxiliary verb *da* has been added, forming the expression: *Boku wa unagi da.*

Among the popular themes in the comic dialogue called *manzai* which is performed on stage, there is one called *Bakagai-ya gokko* (Playing the *baka*-clam seller).* "A" becomes a *baka* seller and pretends to carry the clams on a pole, saying, *"Bakā, bakā."* "B," acting as a buyer, holds a bamboo basket and calls, *Oi, bakā!* (Hey, *baka* clams! *or* Hey, you fool!). "A" then says, *O, baka wa dotchi da?* (Where are you who wants *baka* clams? *or* Where are you, fool?). "B" answers, *O, kotchi da* (It's me). The *baka* in the expression *Baka wa dotchi da? O, kotchi da* is a condensation of "the person who buys *baka*," and the humor stems from this.

The auxiliary verb *da* after a noun is sometimes omitted, as in the following examples:

> *Haru wa akebono (ga ii).*
> Spring is (best) at daybreak.

> *Hana wa sakuragi (ga saijō da).*
> Among flowers, the *sakura* (is the best).

In brief, a noun in the center of a long phrase is sometimes made to represent the whole phrase.

Similar expressions are frequently found in proverbs, *haiku,* and *waka,* as illustrated below. When we say *nomi to ieba* (if one says a chisel), we naturally expect a verb phrase to follow. However, a noun can be placed here instead and

---

Bakagai is a round clam, but literally it means "a fool clam," *baka* being "a fool."

not be considered ungrammatical. This is an example of an arbitrary way of combining words and phrases in Japanese.

Nomi to ieba *tsuchi.*	When one says a chisel, Then a hammer (is needed). (Proverb)

Ureitsutsu *oka ni noboreba* *hana-ibara.*	When I climbed a hill, Worryingly— A thorny wild rose! —BUSON

Osaereba susuki *hanaseba kirigirisu.*	When I press it—a pampas grass; When I let it go—a cricket! *(Senryū)*

Shikishima no *Yamato-gokoro o* *hito towaba* *asahi ni niō* *yamazakura-bana.*	When someone asks, "What is the Japanese spirit Of the land of Shikishima?" The mountain cherry blossoms, Glowing in the morning sun.* —MOTO-ORI NORINAGA

Expressions like the following also belong to the same type:

Kiite gokuraku *mite jigoku.*	When heard—a paradise; When seen—a hell. (Proverb)

*Shikishima is another name for Japan.

Asagao ni	The well bucket,
tsurube torarete	Taken by the morning glory—
morai mizu.	A gift water.

—KAGA CHIYOJO[13]

The sentences ending in nouns or nouns plus *kana,* given above, are contractions of the *juttei* (declarative) sentences in V, Chapter 2 (p. 223), dealing with the classification of sentences. Therefore, there is no conflict if this type of sentence is placed next to ordinary sentences ending in verbs, as in the following poems:

Haru no tani	In a spring valley,
akaruki ame no	In the midst of a bright rain,
naka ni shite	A nightingale sang—
uguisu nakeri	The quietness
yama no shizukesa.	Of the mountains.

—ONOE SAISHŪ[14]

Botan-bana wa	The peony is quiet,
saki-sadamarite	Having completely
shizuka nari	Bloomed—
hana no shimetaru	The firmness
ichi no tashikasa.	Of the flower's position.

—KINOSHITA RIGEN[15]

Yamazato wa	In the mountain hamlet,
manzai ososhi	The New Year *manzai* dancers
ume no hana.	are late—
	The plum blossoms.

—BASHŌ

Monzen ni	Before my gate,
fune tsunagikeri	Someone has tied a boat—
tade no hana.	A jointweed flower.

—SHIKI

Many poems of this type end in the particle *kana,* as in the following examples:

Oharame no	Five Oharame women,
gonin sorōte	All alike
awase kana.	In lined kimono.*

—BUSON

Kakure sunde	Living in seclusion,
hana ni Sanada no	Sanada chants *utai,*
utai kana.	Viewing the cherry blossoms.†

—BUSON

Sushi-oke o	When I wash
araeba chikaki	The wooden *sushi* bowl,
yūgyo kana.	O, the fishes swimming nearby!‡

—BUSON

*They come to Kyōto from the village of Ōhara, carrying on their heads a basket of sticks or flowers to sell.
†Sanada Yukimura (1567–1615) is the name of a celebrated warlord. *Utai* means "chanting of a Nō text." A townsman might have chanted folk songs when viewing the cherry blossoms, but Sanada, being a warrior, probably chanted a Nō text.
‡*Sushi-oke* is a large wooden bowl in which *sushi* (seasoned rice or seasoned rice cakes) is made. In olden times it was customary to wash kitchen utensils in nearby streams.

Uchihatasu   A *boro*-samurai walks with one
boro tsuredachite   He's about to fight an avenging
natsu-no kana.   duel—
                       The summer field.*

—BUSON

Word modulation

We often see sentences in Japanese whose beginnings and endings are not consistent. Ōkubo Tadatoshi calls them *watakushi-no-yukuefumei-gata* (the lost-I type) sentences.[16] For example:

> *Watakushi wa, Yoshida Shushō wa, Nihon no hoantai wa, guntai dewa nai to itte oru node arimashite, guntai de aru mono o, guntai de nai to itte oru.*
> I (think that what) Prime Minister Yoshida says (is absurd. He says) that the Japanese National Security Forces are not an army; he says that which is an army is not an army.

The predicate verb for the *watakushi* (I) in the beginning of the sentence does not appear later in the sentence at all. It is natural for such sentences to often occur in the spoken language where they cannot be reworded, but they appear in writing, too. Nakahira Satoru, a scholar in French language studies, once collected such sentences and wrote an article about them in the magazine *Gengo Seikatsu.*

---

*Boro or *komusō* is a flute-carrying mendicant samurai-monk in a face-concealing rattle-hat. This poem is a poetic rendering of a story that appears in the *Tsurezure-gusa,* Section 115.

This problem arises from the fact that in Japanese the predicate verb for the subject is placed at the very end of the sentence. Therefore, we can marvel at the good memory of the compiler of the preamble to the Constitution, already mentioned, who kept in mind the predicate verb for the opening *Wareware wa* (We . . .) until the very end of the sentence.

Formerly such incongruity between the beginning and the ending of a sentence was apparently not considered a bad thing. Saeki Umetomo, a Japanese scholar of classic literature, has collected examples of such sentences in his *Fude no Sore* (Deviations in Writings), and one of these examples is the following passage appearing in the chapter called "The Last Moments of Sanemori" in the *Heike Monogatari:*

> *Ana yasashi. Ikanaru hito nite watarase-tamaeba, mikata no on-zei wa mina ochiyuki-sōrō ni, tada ikki nokorase-tamaitaru koso, yū ni oboe-sōrae, nanorase-tamae.*
>
> Alas! May I ask who you are? While all our soldiers have taken flight, you alone have remained on horseback—this made me admire you. Please give your name.

When the writer first began by saying, *Ikanaru hito nite . . .* (Who are you . . .) he was perhaps intending to say immediately afterwards, *tada ikki nokorase-tamaitaru zo* (that have solely remained on horseback?). The writer, however, changed his mind after having written *nokorase*, and instead wrote *taru koso yū ni oboe-sōrae* (that you have remained on horseback made me admire). Thereupon the phrase at the beginning, namely, *ikanaru hito nite watarase-tamaeba,* became unnecessary.

We can find a similar passage in Chapter Nineteen of the famous *Tsurezure-gusa:*

> *Ii-tsuzukureba, mina Genji Monogatari, Makura no Sōshi nado ni kotofurinitaredo, onaji koto mata imasarani iwaji to ni mo arazu. Oboshiki koto iwanu wa hara fukururu waza nareba, fude ni makasetsutsu, ajikinaki susabi nite, kaiyari sutsubeki mono nareba, hito no mirubeki ni mo arazu.*

> As I continue thus, I see that all this has been said in the *Genji Monogatari* and *Makura no Sōshi.* However, there is no reason why I should not repeat it now. Since it is unpleasant not to say what I think, (I continue) to write at random—an insignificant pastime, something which should be torn and thrown away as I write, and therefore, it should not be seen by others.

In the above passage, there should be some verb between the phrases *fude ni makasetsutsu* (at random) and *ajikinaki susabi nite* (it is an insignificant pastime) in order to make sense. Perhaps the writer at first intended to put some verb after *ajikinaki susabi,* but he did not, and made the phrase *ajikinaki susabi nite,* taking the form of noun+*nari* (is), which consequently disassociated the first half from the second half of the passage.

Japanese figures of speech include the *iikake* (pun). This also is a kind of "sentence in which the beginning and the end are inconsistent." The following are examples of this:

Ikanaru hito nite . . . nokorase-tamaitaru
What person . . .   has remained

nokorase tamaitaru koso yū ni oboe-sōrae
that you remained, I admire

Tachiwakare inaba
After I depart and go away

Inaba
no yama no mine ni ōru matsu
the pines that grow on the top of the
Inaba mountains

matsu to shi kikaba
If I hear that you are waiting*

In music, this would be something like "modulation."
The *waka* poem beginning with *Tachiwakare* has gone
through modulations twice and has come back to the
original melody—a splendid technique.

---

*Inaba, "if one leaves," is also the name of a province. *Matsu,* "pine
tree," as a verb means "to wait." Another verse follows *kikaba: Ima kaeri
kon* (I will come back immediately). The whole poem means: "After I
depart and leave *(inaba)*, I will come back immediately if I hear that
you are waiting *(matsu)*, like the name of the trees called *matsu* that
grow on the top of the Inaba mountains."

◆ 5. TERSE EXPRESSIONS

Omission of subjects and modifiers

The Japanese language is said to contain many abbreviations. The grammarian Matsuo Sutejirō considered the large number of honorifics, freedom of word order, and the existence of numerous abbreviations in Japanese as its three distinguishing characteristics. I am not in total agreement with him regarding his selection of these three but it is true that Japanese contains many terse expressions which do not fully express things clearly stated in other languages.

People frequently refer to "the omission of the subject" but this is not accurate. The truth is that Japanese utilizes a way of "expression in which the subject is not present."

(1) *O-atataka ni narimashita nē.* ([It] has become warm, hasn't it?)

(2) *Hontō desu nē.* ([It] is true.)

In the above expressions we do not have the feeling that something is missing, for the subject was deliberately left out in the first place. Logically speaking, it can be said that *kion ga* (the temperature) is omitted in (1) but actually we hardly ever say, *Kion ga atataka ni narimashita nē* (The temperature has become warm). "It has become warm" in its entirety is equal to *O-atataka ni narimashita.* Similarly, it cannot also be said that the subject *anata no yū koto wa* (what you say) has been omitted before *Hontō desu nē.* In this case the whole expression *O-atataka ni narimashita* corresponds to *Hontō desu nē.*

Aren't there any examples then in which the subject has been omitted? Such expressions cannot be said to be totally nonexistent. The following can be considered an abbreviation of the subject, if not an omission: *Nani mo gozaimasen ga dōzo meshiagatte kudasai* (There is nothing—that is, it's not much of a dinner—but please eat it). In this sentence the subject, *meshiagatte itadaku yō na mono* (things that we wish you to eat), has been omitted.

Hamao Arata, the distinguished former president of Tōkyō University, was well-known for his natural and faultless personality. Once he invited a great many foreigners to a garden party and said in English, "Although there is nothing, please eat the next room," which startled his guests. "Eat the next room" was an incredible thing to say, and none of them understood what he meant by "there is nothing to eat."

With the exception of words for the subject, complements for the verb *aru* (to be) have frequently been omitted since ancient times. The following is an example from the *Heike Monogatari* in which some phrase like *rippa ni* (in glory) has been omitted before the verb *arishi* (was).

> *Ware yo ni arishi toki wa, musume domo o nyōgo kisaki to koso omoishi ka.*
> In the days when I was (in glory), I thought my daughters were court ladies and imperial consorts.

Similarly, in this passage from the *Tsurezure-gusa,* the phrase *jissai ni* (in reality) is omitted before *aru:*

> *Aru nimo sugite hito wa mono o iinasu ni . . .*

People speak about things, going beyond what (actually) exists.

The sentence *Takusan aru* (There is plenty) can also be expressed by simply *Aru* (There is). In the *kyōgen* (a comic interlude in the Nō drama) called *Neongyoku,* Tarōkaja, the Daimyō's chief servant, has had the Daimyō fill his cup with sakè and says: *Arimasu, arimasu* (There is, there is). He does not mean "There is some more left." He means "There is plenty in the cup."

Among the adjectives, *yoi* (good) and *nai* (not) are frequently used without complements. *Konna ureshii koto wa metta ni nai* (There seldom is such a delightful thing) is often shortened to *Konna ureshii koto wa nai* (There isn't any such delightful thing). This expression often startles Westerners. In the sentence, *Ureshii to ittara nai* (Speaking of delightfulness, there isn't any), the *nai* refers to the implied expressions *Hoka ni nai* (There isn't any elsewhere) and *Konna ureshii koto wa nai* (There isn't such a delightful thing).

The omission of a complement can be seen in the following case involving *yoi* or *ii* (good, or all right):

A: *Motte yarō ka?* (Shall I carry it for you?)
B: *Ii wa.* (That's all right.)

In the example *ii wa* the expression *motte kurenakutemo* (even if you don't carry it for me) is omitted. Sometimes *takusan* (plenty; enough) is also used to express the same thing. Such expressions are commonly known to be troublesome for foreigners. When the word *takusan* is used, it is certainly natural to literally interpret the sentence to mean "Please carry many things for me" although it actually means just the opposite.

Ellipsis in the predicate

The practice of stating only the subject, complements, modifiers, and the like without expressing their accompanying verbs can frequently be found in other languages as well as in Japanese. It is especially noticeable in the latter, however, because predicate verbs come last in Japanese and thus can be guessed. Moreover, Japanese people try to avoid using verbs as they have a decisive tone. For example:

O-nori wa o-hayaku.
(Please be) quick in getting on.*

Mitsugo no tamashii hyaku made.
A three-year-old child's spirit (is unchangeable) till he is a hundred.†

(Proverb)

Ellipses can also be seen in the following lines:

Haru wa basha ni notte.
Spring (will come) on a carriage.‡
　　　　—YOKOMITSU RIICHI[1]

---

*Some verb like *negaimasu* (please do . . .) is omitted after *o-hayaku*.
†Some verb like *kawaranai* (is unchangeable) is omitted after *hyaku made*.
‡Some verb like *yatte kuru* (will come) is omitted at the end.

Omocha wa no ni mo yama ni mo.
(There are) toys in the fields and in the mountains.*
—SHIMAZAKI TŌSON[2]

Words of this kind are frequently omitted by women. In the novel *Konjiki Yasha,* there is a scene at Atami beach in which O-miya says to Kan'ichi: *Kan'ichi-san, sore jā ammari da wa* (That's too much, Kan'ichi). Her omission of what is too much is a characteristically Japanese one. In his English translation, Lloyd specifically uses the word "cruel": "How cruel you are, Kwanichi!"

Abbreviated expressions like the above have existed in Japan from the time of the *Genji Monogatari* (The Tale of Genji). The difficulty experienced in reading the *Genji Monogatari* lies partly in its omission of specific adjectives in such situations, leaving the reader to draw his own inference. Origuchi Shinobu, a scholar of Japanese literature, has interpreted the expression *aware ni obosu* (to feel that something is charming), which frequently appears in classical narratives, to be a contraction of *aware ni nani nani ni obosu* (to feel that something is charmingly such and such) in which the adjective "such and such" has been omitted. He has also interpreted the expression *ito asamashi* (very shocking) to be a contraction of *ito asamashiku nani nani* (very shockingly such and such) in which the adjective "such and such" is omitted.

Generally speaking, in ancient writings people frequently left some words unsaid which people would now state clearly. Therefore, one must pay attention when reading

*Some verb like *aru* (there are) is omitted at the end.

classical literature. Take the following passage which appears in the *Genji Monogatari* as an example:

> *Omoi-agareru keshiki ni kiki-oki tamaeru* [. . .] *musume nareba yukashikute.* . . .
>
> As she is a daughter [of a person] who listens in a self-conceited attitude, she has intrigued me. . . .
>
> —from "Hahakigi"

Kitayama Keita, who has been annotating the *Genji Monogatari* for a number of years, says that in the space within the brackets, the words *hito no* (of a person) should be inserted.[3] If one does not know this, he will misunderstand and think that the person who looks conceited is the young lady. Similarly, in the famous opening passage of the same novel, namely, *izure no ontoki ni ka* (in which reign), the phrase *mikado no* (emperor's) has been omitted after *izure no* (which). It is said that because of this omission the honorific *ontoki* (an emperor's reign)* has been used. Such sentences are very difficult to interpret.

---

*The honorific prefix *on* attached to the noun *toki* (time). *Ontoki* is used only in reference to an emperor.

◆ POSTSCRIPT

In this book I intended to examine the Japanese language from all angles, clarifying its nature. Due to the limitations of time and space, however, I have had to lay down my pen with regret in the middle of my schedule.

It is almost senseless to discuss the characteristics of Japanese without making reference to the morphological aspect of the language. I had therefore definitely wanted to touch upon such problems as the analytical expressions in Japanese nouns and, in contrast to this, the synthetic expressions in verbs, the special characteristics of the particles *ga* and *wa*, the special characteristics of the auxiliary verbs *da* and *noda*, and the tense and voice of verbs. Considering that many books have been written on such subjects, however, I have decided to leave them out altogether. To those who are interested in these problems, I recommend Mikami Akira's *Gendaigohō Josetsu* (An Introduction to Modern Japanese Syntax) and *Gendaigohō Shinsetsu* (A New Theory of Modern Japanese Syntax)[1] in particular. In addition, there are larger works by Matsushita Daizaburō[2] and Sakuma Kanae.[3] I myself have written an article entitled "Grammar" in the chapter called "The Japanese Language" in the *Sekai Gengo Gaisetsu* (An Outline of World Languages), Volume II, edited by Ichikawa and Hattori.[4] I have also written a short article on this problem entitled "The Characteristics of Japanese as a Language," which appeared in the *Bunshō Kōza* (Lectures on Writing), Volume II, published by Kawade Shobō.[5]

In the chapter "Vocabulary" I should have written about the formation of the Japanese vocabulary, but it would have required a longer chapter. I especially wanted to discuss the characteristic way in which numerals and personal names are formed.

Likewise, I should have emphasized one aspect in which the Japanese language differs most from others—its complicated arrangement of letters. The mixed usage of *katakana, hiragana, kanji,* roman letters, and Arabic figures, as the following example illustrates, is something which cannot be found in other languages.

Ｙシャツ見切り品 ￥200 より
Wai-shatsu mikiri-hin nihyaku-en yori
A bargain sale of white shirts from ￥200 up

Mario Pei calls the complexity of spelling one of the great characteristics of the English letter structure, but fails to take note of the fact that English uses roman letters, a practice he must have taken as a matter of course. If that is the case, the general use of written symbols other than roman letters in the Japanese language—especially the use of ideographs—must be considered a characteristic in itself.

Moreover, the usage of Chinese characters for their meaning to represent words which originated in Japan (i.e., the Yamato words) is an unparalleled accomplishment, and gave rise to the practice of using the characters to inscribe sounds which have no connection whatever with the characters themselves. For example, the character 下 (down) represents the following different sounds: *shita, shimo, saga, sa, kuda, o, oro, ka, ge*. Such a mode of expression is not found anywhere else except among the ancient Egyptians and the pre-sixteenth century Mexicans. The usage of phonetic symbols like *furigana* (*kana* written at the side of Chinese characters to show their readings) and *okurigana* (*kana* added to a Chinese character to show the Japanese declension) is also unique. To those who wish to consult additional literature on the nature of the Japanese character system, I recommend: the article entitled "Characters" in the chapter called "The Japanese Language" by Hayashi Ōki in the aforementioned *Sekai Gengo Gaisetsu*, Volume II; Matsuzaka Tadanori's article entitled "The Characteristics of the Japanese Language Viewed from Its Characters" published in the *Bunshō Kōza*, Volume III; and also Ikegami Teizō's articles in the magazines *Kokugogaku*,[6] *Kokugo Kokubun*,[7] and *Gengo Seikatsu*.

We create Japanese

How should we evaluate the Japanese language when thus viewed in all its aspects? Japanese does have various defects, but it is also true that we can say and write whatever we think in Japanese. Fortunately, we can use it to write scientific theses and business papers, and it would be neither possible nor advisable to abandon this language.

The great complexity of the Japanese language is said to be its weakest point. This is especially true of its written characters. There is no use grieving over it, however, for in its very confusion lie both good and bad elements from which we can pick only the beneficial ones. Therefore, we can take this confusion as an opportunity for the future development of the Japanese language. What is required of us at this juncture is the serene wisdom to select what truly should be selected.

On the one hand, a language is a natural development, but, on the other, something created. Even German, which is said to be a model of systematic languages, is a creation of the German people over a period of several generations. We who are living at the present time cannot help feeling a heavy responsibility for the future of the Japanese language.

◆ SUPPLEMENTARY NOTES

INTRODUCTION

[1]Shiga Naoya (1883–1971), an outstanding novelist of present-day Japan. *Kaizō* is one of the first-rate general magazines in Japan, started in 1919, published by Kaizō-sha. This article appeared in the April number, 1946, pp. 94–97.

[2]Meillet, Antoine, and Cohen, Marcel, eds., *Les Langues du monde* (Centre National de la Recherche Scientifique, Paris, 1952). Japanese translation, *Sekai no Gengo*, ed. Izui Hisanosuke (Asahi Shimbun, 1954), p. 1091.

[3]*Kokugo Bunka Kōza* [Japanese culture courses] (Asahi Shimbun, July 1941–January 1942), IV, pp. 195–6.

[4]McGovern, William Montgomery, *Colloquial Japanese* (London: Kegan Paul, 1920), p. 2.

[5]*Kokugo Bunka Kōza*, IV, p. 11.

[6]*Kokugo Bunka Kōza*, VI, p. 23.

[7]Jespersen, Otto, *Language* (New York: Norton & Co., 1964), p. 427.

[8]Ishiguro Yoshimi, *Nihonjin no Kokugo Seikatsu* [The function of speech in Japanese daily life] (Tōkyō University Press, 1951), p. 6.

[9]*Gengo Seikatsu* [The function of speech in daily life] (Chikuma Shobō, 1955), No. 45, p. 14.

[10]Fukuzawa Yukichi (1834–1901), educator and pioneer in the

world of thought in the early Meiji period, and also the founder of Keiō School.

[11]Novelist and dramatist (1887–1974).

[12]Kōbunsha, 1956.

[13]Sugiura Ken'ichi, *Jinruigaku* [Anthropology] (Dōbunkan, 1954), p. 208.

PART I

CHAPTER 1: AN ISOLATED LANGUAGE

[1]Emeritus professor of linguistics at Tōkyō University.

[2](1876–1967), former professor of Japanese at Kyōto University and editor of the Japanese dictionary *Kōjien*.

[3]Sanseidō, Tōkyō, 1947, pp. 55–56.

[4]*Kōza Nihongo* [The Japanese language courses] (Ōtsuki Shoten, 1955), III, p. 143.

[5]*Kotoba no Kenkyūshitsu* [A research room for language], ed. NHK (Kōdansha, 1955), V, pp. 224–34.

CHAPTER 2: CONTACT WITH OTHER LANGUAGES

[1]*Kotoba no Kenkyūshitsu* [A research room for language], ed. NHK (Kōdansha, 1954), IV, p. 14.

[2]Pei, Mario, *The World's Chief Languages* (London: George Allen & Unwin Ltd., 1949), p. 86.

[3]*Kokugo Bunka Kōza* [Japanese culture courses] (Asahi Shimbun, July 1941–January 1942), VI, p. 136.

[4]*Gengo Seikatsu* [The function of speech in daily life] (Chikuma Shobō, 1955), No. 45, p. 10.

[5]Four volumes, Fuzambō, 1915.

[6]*Kōza Nihongo* [The Japanese language courses] (Ōtsuki Shoten, 1955), II, p. 114.

[7]One of the most valuable dictionaries of ancient times. Author unknown, but probably written in the late Heian period. It divides Chinese characters into 120 parts, giving their Japanese readings, mostly using *katakana*. It also shows the accents of Japanese words used at that time.

[8]*Kotoba to Seikatsu* [Language and life], ed. Nishio Minoru (Mainichi Library, 1955), p. 12.

[9]Kikuchi Kan, *Ren'aibyō Kanja* [A love patient], *The Complete Works of Kikuchi Kan*, Vol. 3 (Heibonsha, 1927), p. 368. Kikuchi Kan (1888–1948) was a prominent novelist and dramatist.

[10]Hakusuisha, 1954, p. 116.

[11]Literary critic and emeritus professor of French literature at Kyōto University.

[12]*The Outline of History* (New York: Garden City Publishing Co., 1920), p. 991.

[13]Kindaichi Kyōsuke, *Gengo Kenkyū* [A study of language] (Kawade Shobō, 1933), pp. 217–21.

[14]Iwanami Shoten, 1944, pp. 584–89.

[15]*Kokugo Bunka Kōza*, VI, p. 305.

[16]*Nihongo no Junketsu no tame ni* [For the purity of the Japanese language] (Awaji Shobō, 1956), p. 65.

PART II

CHAPTER 1: REGIONAL DIFFERENCES

[1]Meillet, Antoine, and Cohen, Marcel, eds., *Les Langues du monde.* Japanese translation, *Sekai no Gengo,* ed. Izui Hisanosuke (Asahi Shimbun, 1954), p. 260.

[2]Pei, Mario, *The Story of Language* (New York: New American Library, 1964), p. 331.

[3]Jespersen, Otto, *Mankind, Nation and Individual from a Linguistic Point of View* (Bloomington: Indiana University Press, 1964), p. 34.

[4]Jespersen, *Mankind,* p. 34.

CHAPTER 2: OCCUPATIONAL DIFFERENCES

[1]Senkusha, pp. 58–61.

[2]*Kokugo Undō* [The Japanese language movement] (Kokugo Kyōkai, 1937–45), Vol. II, No. 8, p. 21.

[3]*Kotoba no Kōza* [Lectures on language] (Sōgensha, 1956), Vol. I, pp. 190–91.

[4]"The Inconvenience of the Japanese Language," Asahi Newspapers, March 12, 1955, p. 5.

[5]*Gengo Seikatsu* [The function of speech in daily life] (Chikuma Shobō, 1954), No. 38, p. 5.

[6]*Kokugo Bunka Kōza* [Japanese culture courses] (Asahi Shimbun, July 1941–January 1942), V, p. 66.

[7]*Kotoba to Seikatsu* [Language and life], ed. Nishio Minoru (Mainichi Library, 1955), p. 57.

[8]A romantic poet (1885–1942).

[9]Hokuryūkan, 1925.

[10]The book contains 250 lines of poetry, each line having four characters. No character in the whole book is repeated.

[11]*Kokugo Bunka Kōza*, V, pp. 152–53.

CHAPTER 3: DIFFERENCES BY STATUS AND SEX

[1]Jespersen, Otto, *Mankind, Nation and Individual from a Linguistic Point of View* (Bloomington: Indiana University Press, 1964), p. 127.

[2]Miyatake Masamichi, *Nan'yō no Gengo to Bungaku* [The languages and literatures of the South Sea Islands] (Yukawa Kōbunsha, 1943), p. 114.

[3]A comic novel written by Jippensha Ikku (1765–1831).

[4]Izui Hisanosuke, *Gengo no Kenkyū* [A study of language] (Yū-shindō, 1956), p. 221.

[5]Originally a novel by Tokutomi Roka (1868–1927). Shioya Sakae and E. F. Edgett, trans., *Namiko* (Yūrakusha, 1905), pp. 18–19.

[6]Iwanami Shoten, 1938, p. 199.

[7]A poet and writer (1903–74) of children's songs and folk songs.

[8]Jespersen, Otto, *Language* (New York: Norton & Co., 1964), p. 250.

[9]Jespersen, *Language*, p. 237.

[10]Boas, Franz, *Handbook of the American Indian Languages* (Washington: Smithsonian Institution, 1911), Part I, p. 79.

[11]A court novel of the Heian period written by Lady Murasaki Shikibu (c. 978–1016), a court lady; one of the masterpieces in Japanese literature.

[12]The oldest collection of poems in Japan, containing about 4,500. Its compilation began in the early Nara period and ended by 806 A.D.

[13]Omodaka Hisataka, *Man'yōshū Shinshaku* [A new interpretation of the *Man'yōshū*] (Kyōto: Hoshino Shoten, 1931), Vol. 2, pp. 269–70.

[14]In forty-eight volumes, an epic-like narrative of war between the Taira and the Minamoto clans, written sometime during the 15th or 16th century. Author unknown.

[15]A celebrated general of the period of war between the Taira and the Minamoto clans in the late 12th century.

[16]A familiar character in the Nō drama and *jōruri*, together with Naozane.

[17]Shunkan (1142–78) was a high priest who supported the ex-emperor Goshirakawa's attempt to overthrow Kiyomori, the head of the Taira clan; he was captured and exiled to Kikai-gashima island, where he died.

[18]p. 28.

[19]Gendai Kanazukai is the standard of the use of *kana* in the colloquial form of modern Japanese, based on modern pronunciation. It was officially established in November 1946.

CHAPTER 4: DIFFERENCES BY SITUATION

[1]An anthology of poems collected by imperial command in 905.

[2]The literal meaning of this name is "One poem from a hundred poets." This game is based on the book *Hyakunin Isshu,* which is said to have been compiled by the famous poet Fujiwara Teika (1162–1241). The game consists of picking up the right cards as the reader reads the poems.

[3]Jespersen, Otto, *Mankind, Nation and Individual from a Linguistic Point of View* (Bloomington: Indiana University Press, 1964), p. 45.

[4]A literary critic, 1871–1902.

[5]One of the greatest tanka poets of modern Japan, 1882–1951.

[6]Novelist, 1864–1909.

[7]Novelist and poet, 1868–1910.

[8]Novelist, 1867–1903.

[9]"How Foreigners Look at the Japanese Language," *Gengo Sei-katsu* [The function of speech in daily life] (Chikuma Shobō, 1955), No. 49, p. 9.

[10]Meiseisha, 1916.

[11]*Gengo Seikatsu*, No. 21, p. 39.

[12]Bally, Charles, *Le Langue et la vie* (Zurich: Max Niehans, 1935). Japanese translation by Kobayashi Hideo (Iwanami Shoten, 1941), p. 96.

[13]*Gendai Zuisō Zenshū* [A complete collection of modern essays] (Sōgensha, 1954), Vol. 17, pp. 132–34, under the title: "Polite and Impolite Words" by Miyagi Otoya.

PART III

CHAPTER 1: THE SYLLABLE

[1]Sanseidō, 1947, pp. 105–6.

[2]A poet of the early Nara period (8th century), noted for his long poems on legendary subjects in the *Man'yōshū*.

[3]Pei, Mario, *The Story of Language* (New York: New American Library, 1964), p. 93.

CHAPTER 2: THE PHONEMES

[1]A scholar of Japanese classical literature, famous for his studies on the special usage of *kana* in ancient Japanese as well as for his studies on ancient phonology.

[2]*Kokugo to Kokubungaku* [Japanese and Japanese literature] (Tōkyō University Press, June 1953), pp. 55–56.

[3]Meillet, Antoine, and Cohen, Marcel, eds., *Les Langues du monde*. Japanese translation, *Sekai no Gengo*, ed. Izui Hisanosuke (Asahi Shimbun, 1954), p. 655.

[4]Sakuma Kanae, *Nihon Onseigaku* [Japanese phonetics] (Kazama Shobō, 1963), p. 111.

[5]*Sekai no Gengo*, p. 237.

[6]1795–1859, a pupil of Moto-ori Norinaga.

[7]*Sekai no Gengo*, p. 91.

[8]Pei, Mario, *The Story of Language* (New York: New American Library, 1964), p. 326.

[9]1823–1900, British philologist.

[10]Jespersen, Otto, *The Growth and Structure of the English Language* (New York: Doubleday & Co., 1955), p. 3.

[11]Pei, *Story of Language*, p. 158.

[12]Evening edition, *Tōkyō Mainichi*, November 15, 1952, p. 3.

[13]Jespersen, *Growth and Structure*, p. 3.

CHAPTER 3: THE SOUND SYSTEM

[1]Fujioka Katsuji (1872–1935) was a linguist famous for his advocacy of the similarity of Japanese and the Ural-Altaic languages. This was at the end of the Meiji period, when there was much speculation about the origin of the Japanese language.

[2]Ma Hsuch-liang, *A Study of the Sani Language*, ed. Chinese Academy of Science (Shanghai: Shan-wu Publishing Co., 1951), pp. 3–16.

[3]Founder of the Tendai sect of Buddhism in Japan on Mount Hiei.

[4]1867–1902, poet and critic of the Meiji period.

[5]*Tezukayama Gakuin Tanki Daigaku Kenkyū Nempō* [Tezukayama

Gakuin Junior College research annual] (1954), No. 2, p. 50.

⁶A great scholar and statesman of the mid-Edo period. *Tōga* is an etymological study of Japanese.

⁷*Nihon no Shingakki* [A new school term in Japan] (Yomiuri Shimbun, 1955), p. 185.

CHAPTER 4: FROM SYLLABLES TO WORDS

¹Meillet, Antoine, and Cohen, Marcel, eds., *Les Langues du monde.* Japanese translation, *Sekai no Gengo,* ed. Izui Hisanosuke (Asahi Shimbun, 1954), p. 727.

²Arisaka Hideyo, *Kokugo On'in-Shi no Kenkyū* [A study of the history of Japanese phonology] (Sanseidō, 1944), p. 681. Arisaka Hideyo (1908–52) was a linguist famous for his researches in Japanese phonology.

³Meillet and Cohen, *Sekai no Gengo,* p. 613.

⁴Jones, Daniel, *The Phoneme* (Cambridge: Heffer and Sons, 1950), p. 152.

⁵Pike, Kenneth L., *Tone Languages* (Ann Arbor: University of Michigan Press, 1948), pp. 79, 95.

⁶Koizumi Yakumo is the Japanese name of Lafcadio Hearn, a man of letters who wrote about Japan and introduced her to the world. Originally English, he was born in Greece, lived in the United States, came to Japan in 1890, and became naturalized.

⁷Pike, *Tone Languages,* footnotes on pp. 5 and 6.

⁸Ward, I. C., *An Introduction to the Ibo Language* (Cambridge: Heffer and Sons, 1936), pp. 38–41.

⁹Pike, *Tone Languages,* p. 23.

¹⁰Pike, *Tone Languages,* p. 36.

¹¹Tanigawa Tetsuzō, *Nihonjin no Kokoro* [The mind of the Japanese] (Iwanami Shoten, 1938), pp. 178–79.

PART IV

CHAPTER 1: SIZE AND CONSTRUCTION

¹Tanizaki Jun'ichirō, *Bunshō Tokuhon* [A reader on writing] (Chūōkōron-sha, 1942), p. 51.

²Okamoto Chimataro, *Nihongo no Hihanteki Kōsatsu* [A critical study of Japanese] (Hakusuisha, 1954), p. 116.

³Quoted from R. Taylor, *Te Ika a Maui,* pp. 328–29, in Lucien Levy-Bruhl, *How Natives Think* [English translation of Levy-Bruhl's *Les Fonctions mentales dans les sociétés inférieures* by Lillian

A. Clare] (New York: Washington Square Press, 1966), p. 151.

[4]Levy-Bruhl, *How Natives Think*, p. 136.

[5]*Shingo-ron* [On new words] in *The Complete Works of Yanagida Kunio* (Chikuma Shobō, 1963), Vol. 18, p. 453.

[6]Levy-Bruhl, *How Natives Think*, p. 148.

[7]"The Characteristics of the Japanese Language" in Watsuji Tetsurō, *Zoku Nihon Seishin-shi Kenkyū* [Continued studies in Japanese spiritual history] (Iwanami Shoten, 1935), p. 417.

[8]Sanseidō, 1943, pp. 148–49.

[9]*Kokugo Undō* [The Japanese language movement] (Kokugo Kyōkai, 1937–45), Vol. V, No. 8, p. 46.

[10]Pei, Mario, *The Story of English* (New York: Fawcett Publications, 1962), p. 240.

[11]Pei, *Story of English*, pp. 239–40.

[12]Matsuzaka Tadanori, *Kokugo Mondai no Honshitsu* [The essence of Japanese language problems] (Kōbundō Shobō, 1942), p. 55.

CHAPTER 2: CHARACTERISTICS OF WORDS

[1]Nihon Gengo Gakkai, 1950, pp. 1–23.

[2]Wang Li, *Shina Gengogaku Gairon* [An introduction to Chinese linguistics] (Sanseidō, 1941), p. 1.

[3]Jespersen, Otto, *The Growth and Structure of the English Language* (New York: Doubleday & Co., 1955), p. 6.

[4]Yoshioka Shūichirō, *Sū no Yūmoa* [The humor of numerals] (Gakuseisha, 1956), p. 95.

[5]*Gengo Seikatsu* [The function of speech in daily life] (Chikuma Shobō, 1953), No. 21, p. 14.

[6]Jespersen, Otto, *Language* (New York: Norton & Co., 1964), pp. 330–31.

[7]Ueda Bin was a professor of English at Kyōto University and an introducer of European literature to Japan.

[8]The magazine *Nō Plays* (Nōgaku Kyōkai, 1951), Vol. V, No. 11, p. 30.

[9]*Kōza Nihongo* [Japanese language courses] (Ōtsuki Shoten, 1955), II, p. 118.

[10]Vandryes, Joseph, *Language*. Japanese translation by Fujioka Katsuji (Tōkō Shoin, 1942), p. 182.

[11]Miyatake Masamichi, *Nanyō no Gengo to Bungaku* [The languages and literatures of the South Sea Islands] (Yukawa Kōbunsha, 1943), p. 70.

[12]Vandryes, Joseph, *Language,* pp. 200–202.

CHAPTER 3: THE CULTURAL INDEX
[1]Tachibana Shōichi, "The Dialects on Cattle" in the magazine *Hōgen* [Dialects], Vol. 3, No. 10 (October 1933), pp. 31–38.

[2]Shibuzawa Keizō, *Nihon Gyomei no Kenkyū* [A study of the names of Japanese fish] (Kadokawa Shoten, 1959), pp. 15–16.

[3]*Kokugo Undō* [The Japanese language movement] (Kokugo Kyōkai, 1937–45), Vol. II, No. 5, p. 22.

[4]Sasaki Tatsu, *Gogaku Shiron-shū* [Preliminary essays on linguistics] (Kenkyūsha, 1950), p. 303.

[5]*The Collected Works of Fukuda Tsuneari* (Shinchōsha, 1957), Vol. 7, pp. 9–10.

CHAPTER 4: NATURE
[1]*Bungei Shunjū,* December, 1935, p. 238. *Bungei Shunjū* is a general magazine on literary arts, started in 1923 by Bungei Shunjū-sha, with Kikuchi Kan as editor.

[2]*Terada Torahiko Zenshū* [The complete works of Terada Torahiko] (Iwanami Shoten, 1950), Vol. V, p. 575.

[3]Compiled by Kokugakuin University, 1935.

[4]Levy-Bruhl, Lucien, *How Natives Think* (New York: Washington Square Press, 1966), p. 150.

[5]Po Chu-i (772–846) was a famous Chinese poet of the Tang dynasty whose works greatly influenced the literature of Japan's Heian period.

[6]A *haiku* book or *saijiki* written by Kigen in 1713. Kokusho Kankōkai reprinted it in 1917.

[7]A book of essays by Yoshida Kenkō (1283–1350), a well-known poet of his time. He was formerly a court official, but later became a monk and lived at Narabigaoka, Kyōto.

[8]The novel *Nowaki* (1908).

[9]Kaizōsha, 1924.

[10]Kokinshoin, 1936, p. 126.

[11]Levy-Bruhl, *How Natives Think,* p. 149.

[12]*Fūdo to Bungaku* [Natural features and literature] in *Terada Torahiko Zenshū* [The complete works of Terada Torahiko], rev. ed., (Iwanami Shoten, 1950), Vol. V, p. 596.

[13]*Nihonjin no Kokoro* [The mind of the Japanese] (Iwanami Shoten, 1938), p. 291.

[14]Palmer, L. R., *An Introduction to Modern Linguistics* (London: Macmillan Co., 1936), footnote 1, p. 177.

[15]Levy-Bruhl, *How Natives Think*, p. 151.

[16]Vandryes, Joseph, *Language*. Japanese translation by Fujioka Katsuji (Tōkō Shoin, 1942), p. 353.

[17]Hattori Shirō, *Mōko to sono Gengo* [Mongolia and its language] (Yukawa Kōbunsha, 1943), p. 163.

[18]Shibuzawa Keizō, *Nihon Gyomei Shūran* [A collection of names of Japanese fish] (Kadokawa Shoten, 1958), Vol. II, pp. 203–32.

[19]Its literal meaning is "Grass Skylark," an insect like a cricket. The essay is in the Koizumi Edition, *Writings of Lafcadio Hearn* (Boston: Houghton Mifflin Co., 1923), Vol. X, pp. 380–91.

CHAPTER 5: HUMAN BIOLOGY AND EMOTIONS

[1]Fukushima Masao, "Shōkō no Atama" [A military officer's head] in the magazine *Shisō no Kagaku* [The science of thought], Vol. V, No. 1 (January 1949), pp. 26–38.

[2]Levy-Bruhl, Lucien, *How Natives Think* (Washington Square Press, 1966), p. 149.

[3]Nihon Jōmin Bunka Kenkyūsho, 1954.

[4]*Gengo Seikatsu* [The function of speech in daily life] (Chikuma Shobō, 1955), No. 45, p. 11.

[5]*Gengo Kenkyū* [A study of language] (Nihon Gengo Gakkai, 1950), combined Nos. 26 and 27, p. 36.

[6]Levy-Bruhl, *How Natives Think*, p. 135.

[7]Haga Yaichi, *Nihonjin* [The Japanese people] (Fuzambō, 1939), p. 158.

[8]Candau, Sauveur Antoine, *Basuku no Hoshi* [The stars of Basque] (Tōhō Shobō, 1956), p. 29. Father Candau (1897–1955) was a French missionary and teacher.

[9]Minami Hiroshi, *Nihonjin no Shinri* [The psychology of the Japanese] (Iwanami Shoten, 1954), p. 59.

[10](Boston: Houghton Mifflin Co., 1946), pp. 222–27.

[11]Ichikawa Sanki, *Konchū, Gengo, Kokuminsei* [Insects, language, national traits] (Kenkyūsha, 1939), p. 252.

[12]Ikejima Shimpei, *Henshūsha no Hatsugen* [An editor's proposal] (Kurashi-no-techō-sha, 1955), p. 115.

[13](Boston: Houghton Mifflin Co., 1946), p. 43.

[14]Takagi Masataka, *Nihonjin no Seikatsu Shinri* [The Japanese psychology of living] (Sōgensha, 1954), p. 115.

[15]Watanabe Shin'ichirō, *Ren'ai Sahō* [The etiquette of love] (Shikisha, 1955), p. 109.

[16]Shimmura Izuru, *Kokugo no Kijun* [The standard of the Japanese language] (Kenbunkan, 1943), p. 168.

[17]Minami Hiroshi, *Nihonjin no Shinri* [The psychology of the Japanese] (Iwanami Shoten, 1954), pp. 60–66.

[18]Saitō Kiyoe, *Kokubungaku no Honshitsu* [The essence of Japanese literature] (Meiji Shoin, 1924), pp. 6–7, 22–33.

[19]First published in 1907 by Ōkura Shoten. This anecdote is found in *The Complete Works of Natsume Sōseki* (Sōseki Zenshū Kankōkai, 1936), Vol. X, p. 348.

CHAPTER 6: FAMILY AND SOCIETY

[1]Hattori Shirō, *Mōko to sono Gengo* [Mongolia and its language] (Yukawa Kōbunsha, 1943), pp. 164–65.

[2]Seijisha, 1942, pp. 214–17.

[3]Nihon Hyōron Shinsha, 1952, p. 21.

[4]*Nihonjin* [The Japanese people], compiled by Yanagida Kunio (Tōkyō Mainichi Newspapers, 1955), p. 178.

[5]*Gengo Seikatsu* [The Function of Speech in Daily Life] (Chikuma Shobō, 1953), No. 26, p. 14.

[6]Sekai-no-Nippon-sha, 1948, pp. 140–44.

[7]*Gengo Seikatsu,* No. 34, p. 14. The speaker is Nakamura Shigeru.

[8]*Nihon Shakai no Kazokuteki Kōsei* [The family-like formation of Japanese society] (Nihon Hyōron Shinsha, 1952), p. 21.

[9]Kishida Kunio, *Nihonjin towa* [What are the Japanese?] (Kadokawa Shoten, 1954), p. 84.

[10]*Nihonjin,* p. 59.

[11]Candau, Sauveur Antoine, *Eien no Kessaku* [The eternal masterpiece] (Tōhō Shobō, 1955), p. 81.

[12]Benedict, Ruth, *The Chrysanthemum and the Sword* (Boston: Houghton Mifflin Co., 1946), p. 133.

[13]Wakamori Tarō, *Nihonjin no Kōsai* [The social relations of the Japanese] (Kōbundō, 1953), p. 15.

CHAPTER 7: ABSTRACT IDEAS

[1]Miyauchi Hideo, *Eigo no Kangaekata* [The way of thinking in English] (Kokusai Shuppansha, 1951), p. 93.

[2]*Kokugo Undō* [Japanese language movement] (Kokugo Kyōkai, 1937–45), Vol. V, No. 9, p. 16.

[3]One of the annual events of the court held on the 7th day of the first month, when *aouma* horses from the two offices (the Right and Left) in charge of horses were submitted to the inspection of the emperor, after which a banquet was held.

[4]Satake Akihiro, *Kodai Nihongo ni okeru Shikimei no Seikaku* [The nature of the names of colors in ancient Japanese] in the magazine *Kokugo Kokubun* (Kyōto University Press, June, 1955), Vol. 24, No. 6, pp. 13–16.

[5]A verse of a popular song.

[6]The 30th night of the lunar calendar when there is no moon, meaning something improbable.

[7]1826–97, a Dutch scholar and philosopher in the last days of the Tokugawa shogunate and the early Meiji period. He went to Holland to study Dutch, and became one of the first translators of Western philosophical terms.

[8]*Kotoba no Oitachi* [The growth of language] (ed. and pub. NHK, 1956), p. 125.

[9]*Kotoba to Seikatsu* [Language and life], ed. Nishio Minoru (Mainichi Library, 1955), p. 65.

[10]Mikami Akira, *Gendai Gohō Josetsu* [An introduction to modern syntax] (Tōkō Shoin, 1953), pp. 2, 73.

PART V

CHAPTER 1: FORM AND LENGTH

[1]An outstanding short-story writer (1892–1927).

[2]A poet-priest (1119–90) of the late Heian period.

[3]This passage appears in Section 19 of the Essays.

[4]A *tanka* poetess and critic (1878–1942).

[5]A collection of essays by Sei Shōnagon, a court lady of the mid-Heian period. It is one of the masterpieces in Heian literature.

[6]Poet and writer (1896–1933) of juvenile stories.

[7]*Kōza Nihongo* [Japanese language courses] (Ōtsuki Shoten, 1955), IV, p. 138.

[8]A judicial case (1950–57) concerning Itō Sei's Japanese translation of D. H. Lawrence's *Lady Chatterley's Lover*, which was charged with public indecency.

[9] A mass murder at Teigin Bank (Teikoku Ginkō) in 1948.

[10]Ōkubo Tadatoshi, *Kotoba no Majutsu to Shikō* [The magic of language and thought] (Shunjūsha, 1956), p. 70.

[11]One of the eighteen famous pieces of the Kabuki plays.

[12]One of the plays of the Kabuki, composed by Kawatake Mokuami (1816–93), in which each of the five thieves makes a long speech.

[13]A Chinese pastoral poet (365–427) of the Eastern Tsin dynasty.

CHAPTER 2: SENTENCE TYPES

[1]Kenkyūsha, 1954, p. 1.

[2]Shūbunkan, 1940, pp. 224–25.

[3]Tōkō Shoin, 1953, p. 155.

[4]Sakuma Kanae, *Nihongo no Gengo Rironteki Kenkyū* [The theoretical study of the Japanese language] (Sanseidō, 1943), p. 144.

[5]Vandryes, Joseph, *Language.* Japanese translation by Fujioka Katsuji (Tōkō Shoin, 1942), p. 185.

[6]Sakuma Kanae, *Nihongo no Gengo Rironteki Kenkyū,* p. 147.

[7]Mio Isago, *Kokugohō Bunshōron* [The Japanese diction] (Sanseidō, 1948), pp. 71–75.

[8]A poet (1090–1155) of the late Heian period.

[9]A romantic poet (1885–1928) of the Meiji-Taishō period.

[10]Matsuo Bashō (1644–94), a great *haiku* poet of the early Edo period.

[11]Enomoto Kikaku (1661–1707), a *haiku* poet, pupil of Bashō.

[12]Yosano Buson (1716–83), a *haiku* poet and artist of the mid-Edo period.

[13]Kaya Shirao (c. 1738–91), a *haiku* poet of the late Edo period, formerly a retainer of the Ueda clan.

CHAPTER 3: WORD AND PHRASE ARRANGEMENT

[1]Kimura Ichirō, *Indogo Yonshūkan* [The Indian language in four weeks] (Daigaku Shorin, 1943), p. 10.

[2]*Kotoba no Kōza* [Lectures on language] (Sōgensha, 1956), Vol. I, pp. 83–84.

[3]Izui Hisanosuke, *Gengo no Kenkyū* [A study of language] (Yūshindō, 1956), p. 28.

[4]Vandryes, Joseph, *Language.* Japanese translation by Fujioka Katsuji (Tōkō Shoin, 1942), p. 220.

[5]Matsuo Sutejirō, *Kokugo to Nihon Seishin* [The Japanese language and the Japanese spirit] (Hakusuisha, 1939), p. 33.

[6]Pei, Mario, *The Story of Language,* (New York: New American Library, 1964), p. 327.

[7] *Les Langues du monde.* Japanese translation *Sekai no Gengo,* ed. Izui Hisanosuke (Asahi Shimbun, 1954), p. 369.

[8]*Kotoba no Kenkyūshitsu* [A research room for language], ed. NHK (Kōdansha, 1954), IV, p. 181.

[9]From the short story *Aki* [Autumn].

[10]Quoted from the short story *Mikan* [Oranges] by Akutagawa Ryūnosuke.

[11]Chikuma Shobō, 1955.

[12]Lafcadio Hearn, "Otokichi's Daruma," in *The Writings of Lafcadio Hearn* (Boston: Houghton Mifflin Co., 1923), Vol. X, p. 391. This is from the original; its Japanese translation, quoted here, is by Tanabe Ryūji.

[13]A poet of the late 9th century.

[14]A romantic poet (1886–1912).

[15]This is the third stanza of a poem called "Furusato" [A native town] by Miki Rofū (1889–1964), a symbolist poet.

[16]*Hyakumannin no Gengogaku* [The linguistics for a million people] (Shinkōsha, 1947), pp. 143–47.

CHAPTER 4:   WORD AND PHRASE COMBINATION

[1]Poem No. 4139 in the *Man'yōshū.* Ōtomo Yakamochi (718–85) was one of the compilers of the anthology and a son of Tabito, also a poet.

[2]Yamaguchi Sodō (1642–1716), a *haiku* poet of the early Edo period.

[3]*Kōza Nihongo* [Japanese language courses] (Ōtsuki Shoten, 1955), VI, pp. 68–69.

[4]A war chronicle in the form of a long epic poem in twelve books, describing the rise and fall of the Heike clan. It is said to have been written by Shinano no Zenji Yukihira sometime before 1220.

[5]Natsume Sōseki's novel, first published in the magazine *Hototogisu* in 1906.

[6]Shimazu Hisamoto, *Genji Monogatari Kōwa* [Lectures on the *Genji Monogatari*] (Chūkōkan, 1930–36), Vol I, pp. 68–70.

[7]Futabatei Shimei, *Heibon* [Mediocrity] (Iwanami Bunko, 1940), p. 28. It was first published in the *Asahi* newspapers in 1907.

[8]Ki no Tsurayuki (?–945) was a famous poet and compiler of the *Kokinshū* anthology. This poem appears in the anthology.

[9]*Gendai Zuisō Zenshū* [A complete collection of modern essays] (Sōgensha, 1954), Vol. 21, pp. 187–88.

[10]Naitō Jōsō (1661–1704), a *haiku* poet, was a priest and a disciple of Bashō.

[11]Mikami Akira, *Gendai Gohō Josetsu* [An introduction to modern syntax] (Tōkō Shoin, 1953), pp. 128–30.

[12]This is the title of one of Natsume Sōseki's novels.

[13]Kaga Chiyojo (1703–75), a *haiku* poetess.

[14]Onoe Saishū (1876–1957), a *waka* poet.

[15]Kinoshita Rigen (1881–1925), a *waka* poet.

[16]*Kotoba no Kenkyūshitsu* [A research room for language], ed. NHK (Kōdansha, 1954), I, pp. 170–71.

CHAPTER 5: TERSE EXPRESSIONS

[1]Novelist (1898–1947).

[2]Poet and novelist (1872–1943).

[3]Kitayama Keita, *Genji Monogatari no Gohō* [The syntax of the *Genji Monogatari*] (Tōkō Shoin, 1951), p. 96.

POSTSCRIPT

[1]Tōkō Shoin, 1955.

[2]i.e., *Hyōjun Nihon Bumpō* [A standard Japanese grammar] (Chūbunkan Shoten, 1928).

[3]Such as *Nihongo no Gengo Rironteki Kenkyū* [The theoretical study of the Japanese language] (Sanseidō, 1943).

[4]Kenkyūsha, 1955.

[5]1954.

[6]Published by Kokugo Gakkai, Tōkyō University, since 1948.

[7]Published by Kokubun Gakkai, Kyōto University, since 1931.